■ The Montana State Constitution

**The Oxford Commentaries on the State Constitutions of the United States**
*G. Alan Tarr, Series Editor*

*Professor G. Alan Tarr,* Director of the Center on State Constitutional Studies at Rutgers University, serves as General Editor for this important new series which in its entirety will cover each of the 50 states. Each volume of The Oxford Commentaries on the State Constitutions of the United States contains a historical overview of the state's constitutional development, plus a section-by-section analysis of the state's current constitution. Other features included in the volumes are the text of the state's constitution, a bibliographic essay, table of cases, and index. This series provides essential reference tools for those investigating state constitutional development and constitutional law.

# The Montana State Constitution

Larry M. Elison
and
Fritz Snyder

*Foreword by Governor Marc Racicot*

THE OXFORD COMMENTARIES ON THE STATE CONSTITUTIONS OF THE UNITED STATES
*G. Alan Tarr, Series Editor*

OXFORD
UNIVERSITY PRESS

OXFORD
UNIVERSITY PRESS

*Oxford University Press, Inc., publishes works that further Oxford University's objective of excellence in research, scholarship, and education.*

Oxford New York
Auckland Cape Town Dar es Salaam Hong Kong Karachi Kuala Lumpur Madrid Melbourne Mexico City Nairobi New Delhi Shanghai Taipei Toronto

With offices in
Argentina Austria Brazil Chile Czech Republic France Greece Guatemala Hungary Italy Japan Poland Portugal Singapore South Korea Switzerland Thailand Turkey Ukraine Vietnam



Previously published in 2000 by Greenwood Press

Published by Oxford University Press, Inc.
198 Madison Avenue, New York, New York 10016

Oxford is a registered trademark of Oxford University Press
Oxford University Press is a registered trademark of Oxford University Press, Inc.



---

Library of Congress Cataloging-in-Publication Data

Elison, Larry M.
The Montana state constitution / Larry M. Elison and Fritz Snyder ; foreword by Marc Racicot.
p. cm. — (The Oxford commentaries on the state constitutions of the United States)
Includes bibliographical references and index.
ISBN 978-0-19-977881-2 (hardback)
1. Constitutions—Montana. 2. Constitutional history—Montana. I. Snyder, Fritz.
II. Montana. Constitution (1972) III. Title. IV. Series.
KFM94011972.A6 E435 2011
342.78602—dc22 2011001553

**Note to Readers**
This publication is designed to provide accurate and authoritative information in regard to the subject matter covered. It is based upon sources believed to be accurate and reliable and is intended to be current as of the time it was written. It is sold with the understanding that the publisher is not engaged in rendering legal, accounting, or other professional services. If legal advice or other expert assistance is required, the services of a competent professional person should be sought. Also, to confirm that the information has not been affected or changed by recent developments, traditional legal research techniques should be used, including checking primary sources where appropriate.

*(Based on the Declaration of Principles jointly adopted by a Committee of the American Bar Association and a Committee of Publishers and Associations.)*

# CONTENTS

## ■ SERIES FOREWORD

In 1776, following the declaration of independence from England, the former colonies began to draft their own constitutions. Their handiwork attracted widespread interest, and draft constitutions circulated up and down the Atlantic seaboard, as constitution-makers sought to benefit from the insights of their counterparts in sister states. In Europe, the new constitutions found a ready audience seeking enlightenment from the American experiments in self- government. Even the delegates to the Constitutional Convention of 1787, de- spite their reservations about the course of political developments in the states during the decade after independence, found much that was useful in the newly adopted constitutions. And when James Madison, fulfilling a pledge given during the ratification debates, drafted the federal Bill of Rights, he found his model in the famous Declaration of Rights of the Virginia Constitution.

By the 1900s, however, few people would have looked to state constitutions for enlightenment. Instead, a familiar litany of complaints was heard whenever state constitutions were mentioned. State constitutions were too long and too detailed, combining basic principles with policy prescriptions and prohibitions that had no place in the fundamental law of a state. By including such provisions, it was argued, state constitutions deprived state governments of the flexibility they needed to respond effectively in changing circumstances. This—among other factors—encouraged political reformers to look to the federal government, which was not plagued by such constitutional constraints, thereby shifting the locus of political initiative away from the states. Meanwhile, civil libertarians concluded that state bills of rights, at least as interpreted by state courts, did not adequately protect rights and therefore looked to the federal courts and the federal Bill of Rights for redress. As power and responsibility shifted from the states to Washington, so too did the attention of scholars, the legal community, and the general public.

During the early 1970s, however, state constitutions were "rediscovered". The immediate impetus for this rediscovery was former President Richard Nixon's appointment of Warren Burger to succeed Earl Warren as Chief Justice of the United States Supreme Court. To civil libertarians, this appointment seemed to signal a decisive shift in the Supreme Court's jurisprudence, because Burger was expected to lead the Court away from the liberal activism that had characterized the Warren Court. They therefore sought ways to safeguard the gains they had achieved for defendants, racial minorities, and the poor during Warren's tenure from erosion by the Burger Court. In particular, they began to look to state bills of rights to secure the rights of defendants and to support other civil-liberties claims that they advanced in state courts.

The "new judicial federalism," as it came to be called, quite quickly advanced beyond its initial concern to evade the mandates of the Burger Court. Indeed, less than two decades after it originated, it became a nationwide phenomenon. For when judges and scholars turned their attention to state constitutions, they discovered an unsuspected richness. They found not only provisions that paralleled the federal Bill of Rights, but also constitutional guarantees of the right to privacy and of gender equality, for example, that had no analogue in the U.S. Constitution. Careful examination of the text and history of state guarantees revealed important differences between even those provisions that most resembled federal guarantees and their federal counterparts. Looking beyond state declarations of rights, jurists and scholars discovered affirmative constitutional mandates to state governments to address such important policy concerns as education and housing. Taken altogether, these discoveries underlined the importance for the legal community of developing a better understanding of state constitutions.

Yet the renewed interest in state constitutions has not been limited to judges and lawyers. State constitutional reformers have renewed their efforts with noable success: since 1960, ten states have adopted new constitutions and several others have undertaken major constitutional revisions. These changes have usually resulted in more streamlined constitutions and more effective state governments. Also, in recent years political activists on both the left and the right have pursued their goals through state constitutional amendments, often enacted through the initiative process, under which policy proposals can be placed directly on the ballot for voters to endorse or reject. Scholars too have begun to rediscover how state constitutional history can illuminate changes in political thought and practice, providing a basis for theories about the dynamics of political change in America.

Larry M. Elison and Fritz Snyder's excellent study of the Montana Constitution is the latest volume in the series, The Oxford Commentaries on the State Constitutions of the United States, which reflects this renewed interest in state constitutions and will contribute to our knowledge about them. Because the constitutional tradition of each state is distinctive, the volume begins with the history and development of the Montana Constitution. It then provides the complete text of Montana's current constitution, with each section accompanied by commentary that explains the provision and traces its origins and its interpretation by the courts and by other governmental bodies. Finally, the book concludes with a table of cases cited in the history and the constitutional commentary, as well as a subject index.

*G. Alan Tarr*

# FOREWORD

In a specially called election held on June 6, 1972, Montanans approved their new state constitution by a margin of only 2,532 votes. The document, hailed by many as a model state constitution, continues today to reflect the special character of this immense landscape, sparsely populated by people whose ancestors were adaptable, ruggedly individualistic, and who, above all, believed in the virtues of the common people. Consider the constitution's opening words:

> We the people of Montana grateful to God for the quiet beauty of our state, the grandeur of our mountains, the vastness of our rolling plains, and desiring to improve the quality of life, equality of opportunity and to secure the blessings of liberty for this and future generations do ordain and establish this constitution.

To me, those words are chock-full of hope and pride and love of land—so much so that they should be considered not just a formal preamble to a legal document, but a constant reminder of the meaning of the remaining provisions of the document a sort of moral and spiritual mooring for the constitution.

Some very progressive ideas are given life in the Montana Constitution. From my own perspective, I would have to rank the public's right to participate in the operations of government and the right to observe its deliberations and documents as having the most "modernizing" effect on the way state and local governments operate. The requirement of a balanced budget also seems an especially farsighted addition, but was actually a part of our 1889 Constitution. The sections that address protection and improvement of the environment touch upon why so many of us remain or re-locate in this remarkable place. Also, the guarantee of equal educational opportunity and a basic system of free, quality public education ensures balanced spending on behalf of all public school stu-dents, proving to be a powerful factor in education policy debates and school spending decisions. Finally, I am certain the initiative and referendum provisions, while they have in some form or other existed since the time of the 1889 Constitution, will play a greater role in the future, as the constant struggle to hold government accountable to its owners—the public—continues.

The 1972 Montana Constitution has made quite a difference in the relationship that Montanans have with their government. One need only read the court decisions involving the public's right to participate in and observe government business to appreciate that, and the fact that the constitution creates opportunities for the balancing of competing interests results in a flexibility that will serve us well into the twenty-first century.

In this day and age there is much discussion of a perceived lack of trust in all levels of government. But if Montanans studied their state constitution, I think they would come away with the belief that the protections it affords, as well as the opportunities for participation in governmental processes that it provides, are meant to build trust rather than destroy it.

This book is a much-needed history and analysis of the 1972 Montana Constitution. It is comprehensive in scope, with summaries and sometimes contrasting interpretations by Montana courts, attorneys general, and of course the constitutional convention delegates themselves. I am sure that *The Montana State Constitution* will prove to be a valuable resource to those who are interested in our state's laws, in its history, and in how government impacts all of us.

*Marc Racicot, Governor*

# ■ PREFACE

A unique group of Montanans, selected from all walks of life, imbued with a healthy sense of empowerment and an unusual commitment to principle not often encountered in political bodies, created and secured ratification of one of the more innovative state constitutions of the twentieth century. Direct amendment and judicial interpretation of the original document have modified the 1972 Montana Constitution to reflect a more traditional vision of government. But the body of the constitution is still largely intact and only marginally tested.

The early interpretation of the 1972 Constitution, roughly the first fifteen years, reflects an erratic but generally conservative political posture. Jurisprudentially, the early interpretation was eclectic and more conservatively activist than textualist or progressive, impelled by the court's desire to reach subjectively "fair" but often ad hoc decisions. Finally, political implications of the case often dictated the results.

The Montana Supreme Court of the 1990s was composed of a majority of justices who were intellectually astute, legally knowledgeable, and who had some sense of vision relative to the Montana Constitution. That has not always been the case. The Montana Supreme Court has generally claimed one or more outstanding jurists among its number, but rarely a majority. The majority in the 1990s was inclined to be less activist, although more progressive. Since the document is relatively progressive, it is understandable that the justices would pay more attention to the language and spirit of the constitution. The most recent cases have been decreasingly result-oriented and sometimes politically unpopular (see *Gryczan v. State,* 1997).

Several factors have contributed to the court's quarter-century pattern of inconsistent interpretations. First, and most important, the membership of the court had changed dramatically over the course of 25 years. Second, the members of the court are elected and required to run for re-election every eight years, whether opposed or not. Electing a judiciary necessarily influences who will become judges and what decisions will be rendered. Proof that an appellate court, or an individual justice on the court, pursues a different judicial philosophy or decides a case differently because elected rather than appointed is generally lacking, although California Supreme Court Justice Rose Bird's position on capital punishment led to her removal from office. The impact of an elected judiciary can only be inferred. Third, philosophical differences have divided the court, resulting in compromises that are not useful in developing a theory of constitutional interpretation. Fourth, biases of the individual jurists, largely based on prior experience, have been more likely to influence opinions than jurisprudential ideas related to state constitutional interpretation. Fifth, the court is very busy, usually handing out over 400 decisions a year (there is no intermediate court of appeals in Montana). The obvious difficulty of responding, in some consistent fashion, to the many dimensions of state constitutional interpretation may overwhelm all other considerations.

In the 1990s the court exhibited a growing awareness of the need to develop a more consistent philosophy of constitutional interpretation, and among a majority of the justices there was an increasing respect for each other, regardless of personal differences relative to a case before the court and regardless of recognized differences in jurisprudential position. This augurs well for the future of the Montana Constitution.

Part I is a brief history of the 1972 Montana Constitution.

Part II is an analysis of the 1972 Montana Constitution, outlining each provision: the source; the political, economic, and other concerns that led to adoption; subsequent court interpretations; and changes, if any, in the provision since 1972. There have been a number of changes, mostly reversions to earlier positions. Two dramatic examples are the reinstatement of governmental immunity and the elimination of mandated welfare obligations. The authors intend the discussion of each section to be a thorough explanation of the section based on the language of the section, the history, the politics surrounding the development of the section, and the legal interpretations, including appellate decisions and attorney general opinions. Montana Attorney General Opinions in this book are abbreviated "Op. Att'y Gen.," with the volume number preceding the abbreviation and the page number in the volume where the opinion appears following the abbreviation.

The proceedings of the 1971–1972 Constitutional Convention are in *Montana Constitutional Convention: 1971–1972,* published by the Montana legislature in cooperation with the Montana Legislative Council and the Constitutional Convention Editing and Publishing Committee (Helena, MT, 1979) in eight volumes Volumes I and II contain the convention committee reports, noted in the two volumes as "comments"; volumes III through VII contain the convention debate with transcripts of all comments and speeches by individual delegates; volume VIII is the index to the first seven volumes by article and section, by topic, and by individual names. Volumes I through VII are consecutively paginated. The analysis of the 1972 Constitution as referenced herein cites committee reports in volumes I and II as "MCC Rep. [page]" and delegate comments in volumes III through VII as "MCC Tr. [page]." No volume number is given because of the consecutive pagination.

# PART ONE
# The History of the Montana Constitution

Montana's constitutional development traces primarily to two periods: the 1880s, which culminated in the Constitution of 1889, under which Montana was admitted to statehood; and the 1960s and early 1970s, which culminated in Montana's Constitution of 1972. Each constitution reflects the period in which it was framed; even though largely patterned after existing state constitutions, each had roots in Montana's own political, economic, and social experience.

In the territorial period (1864–1889), the primary constitutional goal was to achieve statehood and gain freedom from the restraints of federal territorial administration. Fundamental law for the Territory of Montana was the 1864 Organic Act, amended in 1867 and modified by subsequent federal law. The principal features included: congressional authority over the composition, length, and frequency of sessions of the territorial legislative assembly and the power of annulment over territorial enactments; presidential appointment of the territorial governor and secretary, which was overwhelmingly partisan and usually a reward for service outside of Montana; presidential appointment of the territorial chief justice and two associate justices; and an elected, non-voting delegate to the House of Representatives.

Despite the specter of congressional annulment and limited restrictions on the power to tax and spend, the territorial legislature levied taxes, organized and regulated local governments, adopted civil and criminal codes, established lower courts and an educational system, provided for roads and other public services, and passed mining, water, and range law.

Throughout the period both houses of the bicameral legislature were elected on the basis of population. A seven-member council and a 13-member assembly formed the legislature until 1878, when federal requirements for all territories were revised to provide for 12 members in the upper house and 24 members in the lower house. Federal law providing that the legislature meet in annual sessions from 1864 to 1869 was changed to provide for biennial sessions for the remainder of the territorial period. Sessions were limited to 40 days until 1880 and to 60 days thereafter.

For a territory to be admitted into the union as a state, the people of the territory had to first adopt and ratify a constitution. The drive for statehood commenced with an irregular and ill-fated constitutional convention convened in April 1866 by Acting Governor Thomas F. Meagher. The legislative assembly was in its second session; the territory's settlers numbered fewer than 20,000, still largely clustered in the mining centers of southwestern Montana. Fifty-five delegates met in Helena for six days and produced a constitutional document. The delegates borrowed from the proposed Colorado Constitution of 1865, which relied upon the Kansas Constitution of 1859. The document was never printed or submitted to the electorate. The only copy of the document was lost, and what details are known are derived from press reports. This early convention did little more than give notice of a serious commitment to seek statehood.

From 1883 on, pressures for statehood mounted in Montana as its population increased, its economy became more diverse, its communities grew and dispersed, and railroad lines provided new east/3-west and north/3-south links to the rest of the nation.

In 1883 the Montana territorial legislative assembly passed a House Joint Resolution providing for a constitutional convention. Territorial voters elected 45 delegates at a special election on November 6, 1883. Thirty-nine of the delegates were apportioned among 13 counties, and six were elected at-large. Three of the delegates had served in the earlier constitutional convention. The convention assembled in Helena on January 14, 1884, with instructions to adopt rules and draft a constitution which would be submitted to Montana voters at the 1884 general election.

The delegates brought experience in territorial government in Montana and elsewhere to the convention. Lawyers predominated, joined by delegates with mining, stock raising, farming, and other experience. Democrats outnumbered Republicans. The majority had been in Montana since the early 1860s and many had moved from mining to other occupations. William A. Clark, prominent as a mine owner and banker, was elected chairman.

The rules provided for 22 committees, 6 for administrative and editing tasks and 16 standing committees to frame separate constitutional articles. Basic to committee deliberations were appropriate sections drawn from other state constitutions and pertinent resolutions and petitions presented to the convention. The committees reported to the full convention, which debated the recommendations as a committee of the whole, and adopted each accepted article in formal convention. The proposed constitution was approved by a vote of 15,506 to 4,266.

The principal features of the proposed constitution included: a bicameral legislature restricted to biennial sessions of 40 days; a Senate composed of 21 members and a House composed of 45 members; representation for both houses to be based on population, except that each county was guaranteed one senator; seven elected executive officers, including a governor, the executive officers charged with administering such matters as school lands, prison management, and tax equalization; and an elected judiciary, consisting of a supreme court, district courts, county courts, justices of the peace, and such municipal courts as the legislature might provide.

Despite cautions during committee and full convention debates about the need to limit the constitution to fundamental law, the 1884 Constitution contained detailed procedures for each branch of government; detailed proscriptions for the exercise of legislative power; and extensively detailed substantive provisions dealing with revenue and finance, public indebtedness, corporations, and railroads.

A first reading of Montana's 1884 Constitution suggests special attention directed toward what would appear to be uniquely Montana (e.g., the tax exemption for mining claims, the right to cross private property for reservoirs and ditches, and the treatment of public land grants). Further study reveals that the Colorado Constitution had similar provisions derived from other constitutions. Colorado's models had been the recent constitutions of Illinois and Pennsylvania, documents written in 1870 and 1873. The Illinois and Pennsylvania constitutions were responsive to abuses characterized by legislative favors to developing industries and by hundreds of private bills and special local laws. The Montana Constitution of 1884 and the succeeding statehood Constitution of 1889 descended from and took on the character of most late-nineteenth-century state constitutions, hallmarks of which were procedural and substantive restrictions on the legislature, a fragmented executive, and emphasis on prescriptive detail rather than fundamental law.

Territorial Delegate Joseph K. Toole presented the ratified 1884 Constitution to both sessions of the forty-ninth Congress (1885–1887), but Montana statehood remained mired in the broader politics of the admission of western states and the unresolved question of whether the Dakota Territory would be admitted as one or two states. By 1884 the Montana Territory had a population of about 135,000, which was adequate to support statehood, but the more significant issue was political. Other territories, including Dakota, Wyoming, Idaho, Washington, New Mexico, Arizona, and Utah, were also contesting for statehood. All faced delays based partly on specific local circumstances, but chiefly on partisan congressional considerations stemming from Democratic and Republican concern about preserving existing balances of political power. At that time Democrats controlled the Montana Territory. From 1884 through 1888 on the national level, the Republican Senate regularly blocked admittance of Democratic-controlled territories, while the Democratic House prevented the admission of Republican-controlled territories. The impasse ended with the party conventions of 1888, when the Democrats adopted a plank for statehood for Montana, Dakota, Washington, and New Mexico, and the Republicans added Wyoming, Idaho, and Arizona. The long-awaited congressional action came early the following year. On February 22, 1889, President Cleveland signed an Omnibus Bill, authorizing Montana, Washington, North Dakota, and South Dakota to call constitutional conventions and submit ratified constitutions to Congress.

Montana responded quickly to congressional authorization. On July 4, 1889, 75 delegates convened in Helena to draft a constitution. Thirty-nine of the delegates were Democrats, 36 were Republicans, and of the total number, 22 were lawyers. Mining, banking, and stock raising interests were zealously represented with 16 of the delegates holding mining interests. Deliberation continued for six weeks. The lines of continuity to the 1884 convention and constitution were numerous. William A. Clark again was elected president of the convention, and six veterans of 1884 returned and headed standing committees. The 1884 Constitution was the primary basis of committee and convention deliberations. Although each provision was debated, nearly 90 percent of the text of the 1884 Constitution was re-adopted. Many of the changes were in the details. For example, legislative sessions were increased from 40 to 60 days; there were to be 16 members of the Senate, one senator from each county; and 55 members of the House. Executive terms were extended from two to four years, and additional procedures to protect state funds were mandated. County courts were eliminated and their probate responsibilities were assigned to the district courts. Eight instead of four judicial districts were established, with the legislature authorized to increase that number.

Other changes reflected attitudes about representative democracy and organizational concerns (e.g., legislative proposals to amend the constitution or call a constitutional convention required a two-thirds vote, instead of a majority vote, and only three amendments could be considered at a general election). An elected Board of Regents was replaced by a Board of Education to supervise the university and other educational institutions. Membership of the Board included the governor, state superintendent of public instruction, the attorney general, and eight members appointed by the governor. A constitutionally established Bureau of Industrial Resources with an elected commissioner gave way to provision for creation of a Bureau of Agriculture, Labor and Industry with an appointed commissioner.

The 1889 Constitution was enacted more as a tool to achieve statehood than to provide a well-thought-out structure of governance for the new state.

The delegates, not surprisingly, were driven by self-interest and concerns about government abuse of power. Typical of state constitutions of its time, it minimized the powers of the executive branch and maximized the powers of the legislature. It forced the governor to work with myriad boards and commissions, particularly a powerful Board of Examiners consisting of the governor, the secretary of state, and the attorney general. The Board of Examiners had the powers now entrusted to the Department of Administration, which included the power to examine, and approve or reject claims against the state.

The delegates vigorously argued a number of issues. For example, after contentious debate, the delegates voted to include the right to a grand jury and the right of foreigners to own mines. The inclusion of a provision prohibiting bringing armed men into the state to preserve the peace pitted unions against mine owners. Representation in the legislature divided populous, more urban counties and rural counties. Ultimately, the delegates decided that every county in the state, regardless of population, was entitled to one senator, although counties were of little significance in terms of independent political control.

The delegates voted down the requirement that voters be able to read and write and defeated woman suffrage by a vote of 34 to 29. The vote was remarkably close, considering that this was 30 years before ratification of the Nineteenth Amendment to the U.S. Constitution, which guaranteed women the right to vote. In 1914 a constitutional amendment to give Montana women the right to vote passed by a vote of 41,302 to 36,788.

Indicative of the strength of the mining industry was the constitutional exemption from taxation of minerals in place; only surface improvements and annual net proceeds were subject to tax. In 1889 most western states followed this approach in taxing mines.

The Enabling Act conditioned statehood on a number of provisos, many dealing with the title, management, and sale of public lands. For example, Montana was required to disclaim right and title to Indian lands and to recognize that Indian lands were to remain under the absolute jurisdiction and control of Congress. In accepting grants of land included in the Enabling Act, Montana was required to disclaim right and title to the unappropriated federal public lands within the boundaries of the state. Apart from arrangements affecting public lands, Montana was required to assume the debts and liabilities of the Territory of Montana, to secure "perfect toleration of religious sentiment," and to establish and maintain non-sectarian public schools open to all children of the state.

Montanans ratified the 1889 Constitution by an overwhelming 91.6 percent vote, 24,676 to 2,274. The document contained approximately 28,000 words. President Benjamin Harrison proclaimed Montana the Union's forty-first state on November 8, 1889. The election for state legislators was far more contentious, and Montana commenced statehood with both houses evenly divided between Democrats and Republicans. The Montana Senate ultimately sent four senators to Washington, D.C., where the Republican majority promptly seated the two Republicans, Senators Wilbur Fisk Sanders and T.C. Power. The two Democrats returned to Montana.

The 1889 Constitution provided two methods for change, both originating in legislative action and both requiring a two-thirds vote of the members of each house. The legislature could (1) submit to the voters the question of calling a convention to revise, alter, or amend the constitution or (2) submit up to three proposed amendments at each general election. The Montana Constitutional Convention Memorandum notes that between 1889 and 1972 more than 500 amendments were introduced in the legislature, and of that number 61 were approved by the legislature for submission to the voters. (One amendment in 1904 was divided into two amendments when the secretary of state placed it on the ballot, increasing the number of amendments to 62.) Of the 62 approved, one was vetoed by the governor and four more were invalidated by the supreme court prior to the election in which they would have been considered. Of the 58 amendments submitted for voter approval, 18 were rejected and 40 were approved, of which three were annulled by the supreme court for procedural irregularities, leaving 37 amendments approved and in effect.

Some of the more significant rejections included increasing the biennial legislative session from 60 to 80 days (in 1968); eliminating the constitutional status of justice of the peace, police, and municipal courts (in 1962); creating a separate appointive Board of Education and Board of Regents (in 1969); and increasing the number of permissible amendments to be voted on at a general election from three to six (in 1968). Of the many important amendments approved, some of the more notable include provision for initiatives and referenda for new laws excluding constitutional amendments, thereby increasing voter participation in the political process (in 1905); labor reforms, including prohibiting employment of children in underground mines (in 1904); limiting to the eight-hour day work in mines, smelters, and government employment (in 1905) and in all other employment except farming and stock raising (in 1936). The most numerous amendments dealt with finance, such as the state mill levy on property that increased from 1.5 mills to 2.5 mills in 1911, graduated and progressive personal and corporate income taxes in 1933; debt limit for cities, towns, and school districts (in 1950), and an "antidiversion amendment" earmarking as exclusively for highways all revenues from fees and taxes on motor vehicles and fuels (in 1956). The legislature was authorized to provide, by general or special law, for any form of local government (in 1922).

Although the proposal to increase the number of permissible amendments to be voted on at a general election from three to six had been defeated in 1968, in 1970 a similar amendment, restricted to executive reorganization scheduled for the 1972, 1974, and 1976 general elections, was approved. A related constitutional amendment was proposed mandating that all administrative boards, commissions, and agencies be allocated within no more than 20 departments by July 1, 1973. While no proposal for a constitutional convention was submitted prior to

1970, the work on executive reorganization and the above special amendments was closely associated with the calling of a constitutional convention.

Of the 20 articles in the 1889 Constitution, nine remained unchanged by amendments during the period prior to the 1972 Constitutional Convention, including Article 1, Declaration of Rights; Article V, State Institutions and Public Buildings; Article XV, Corporations; and Article XVII, Public Lands. The 157 sections of the 1889 Constitution were increased to 181 through amendments.

In Montana, as elsewhere in the nation, the early years of the twentieth century produced increased demands for government services and programs. By 1920, the original 20 executive offices, commissions, and boards had grown to 104. Montana followed a national move toward administrative reorganization by the legislative creation of a State Efficiency and Trade Commission in 1919. Its report noted constitutional obstacles to reorganization, primarily in the boards manned by ex-officio executive officers. Two decades later, the 1941 legislature established a Select Committee on State Governmental Organization. Again, its conclusions noted that constitutional limitations stood in the way of complete reorganization. After World War II, Montana was one of many states to establish a "Little Hoover Commission" to consider problems of state government. While the Commission on the Reorganization of State Government avoided recommendations for constitutional change, it again emphasized the obstacles created by the assignment of executive officers to head administrative boards. One of the Commission's recommendations led to the establishment in 1957 of the Legislative Council to serve as an interim research arm of the legislature. Its third study, in 1960, dealt with the organization and administration of state government, and once again, Montana's long ballot and government by boards and commissions were strongly criticized.

Veteran politicians, as well as newcomers to the political process, realized that structural changes were necessary. For example, under the 1889 Constitution, Montana limped along with a restrictive constitutional limit on property taxes that resulted in exceedingly disparate per-student educational expenditures. Montana provided limited state aid for special services, such as highways and public welfare, and was one of only four states providing no general local government aid. Only three states provided less per capita state aid to counties and municipalities (Constitutional Convention Study No. 15: *Taxation and Finance*, p. 307).

By the time of the 1960 census, Montana's population was classified as more urban than rural, with just over half of its 700,000 people living in communities or suburban clusters of over 2,500. Many of the state's eastern counties had lost population in the previous decade. Meanwhile, the total number of 56 counties had not been altered since 1925, and under the 1889 apportionment plan, each county was represented in the legislature by one senator and at least one representative. As rural Montana gradually lost population to the slowly expanding urban or near-urban areas, rural voters had an increasingly disproportionate quantum of political power.

In 1962 the U.S. Supreme Court found reapportionment cases to be justiciable as based on the equal protection clause of the Fourteenth Amendment to the U.S. Constitution (*Baker v. Carr*, 1962), and two years later in 1964 it announced the one person, one vote principle (*Reynolds v. Sims*, 1964), requiring seats in both houses of bicameral state legislatures to be based on population. When the 1965 Montana legislature failed to accomplish reapportionment, a citizen suit in federal district court in Montana resulted in the court's devising an apportionment plan for the 1966 election. The plan established a Senate of 55 members and a House of 104 members. Populous counties were to elect from two to six senators and as many as twelve representatives. Counties of small population were joined to create Senate and Representative districts of two to four counties, for election of one or two legislators. The 1967 legislature carried forward this apportionment plan by statutory enactment.

In the shift of representation brought about by reapportionment, western timber and mining counties gained six senators and seven representatives at the expense of 26 rangeland counties in south central and southeastern Montana. There was a shift in representation from rural to urban counties in each of the state's regions. Reapportionment diminished the representation of ranchers and farmers in the legislature, increased the representation of the professions, and left traditionally conservative rural areas increasingly opposed to any change. At the same time, the Anaconda Company had declined in power, and news coverage became more objective after the Anaconda Company sold its newspapers in 1959. A new activism surfaced in Montana.[1] Despite these changes, the Senate elected in 1966 included many senators with considerable legislative experience, and seasoned rural as well as urban legislators joined forces to accomplish the next step toward constitutional revision: the assignment to the Legislative Council by the 1967 legislature of a study of the Montana Constitution, to determine if it was adequately serving the current needs of the people. Three senators and five representatives were members of the council subcommittee, and they reviewed each article of the constitution and compared the articles with similar provisions in six constitutions, selected because of their recent adoption or their evaluation as excellent state constitutions.

The Legislative Council's 1968 report concluded that there was a need for substantial revision of the Montana Constitution and that changes should be aimed at providing for active, dynamic government. Of the 262 sections in the 20 substantive articles of the constitution, 124 sections (48 percent) were deemed to be adequate as presently written, although most could be improved.

---

[1] Michael P. Malone et al., *Montana: A History of Two Centuries*, rev. ed. (Seattle: University of Washington Press, 1991), p. 368.

Fifty-three sections (20 percent) should be revised and 85 sections (32 percent) should be repealed. The next step recommended by the Council was creation of a Constitutional Revision Commission by the 1969 legislature. The Council charged it to complete a detailed study of the Montana Constitution and to make recommendations for improvements. If the Commission were to determine that a constitutional convention would be the most feasible method of constitutional improvement, it should draft a proposed constitution.

The 1969 legislature moved Montana toward constitutional revision by establishing a Constitution Revision Commission composed of four senators, four representatives, four members appointed by the governor, and four members appointed by the state supreme court. The Commission was to study the constitution and make recommendations for change and for the most feasible way to bring about constitutional revision. The Commission was also charged with disseminating information on the constitution. In important anticipatory action, the legislature approved and the governor signed a referendum to be submitted to the voters in the 1970 general election on the question of whether Montana should call a constitutional convention.

The Constitution Revision Commission first organized subcommittees to work separately on legislative and executive articles, a judicial article, a taxation and finance article, and a local government article. Their reports were presented to the full Commission in December 1969 which unanimously endorsed a convention as the best method of constitutional change. Thereafter, in addition to deliberations on enabling legislation and convention procedures, the Commission concentrated its efforts on a public education program to provide information on the 1889 Constitution, proposals for change, and the forthcoming vote on calling a convention.

The Commission's work occurred simultaneously with the activities of the Montana Commission on Executive Reorganization, and the coalescing movement toward constitutional reform also drew support from the Montana League of Cities and Towns and the Montana Association of County Commissioners. Among the aims of these organizations were a greater measure of home rule for localities and modification of the intricate pattern of legislative control over local government.

Beyond governmental circles, citizen groups with specific programs for improved state and local government reached independent conclusions that the Montana Constitution needed modernization. The list included the Montana Citizens Committee on the State Legislature, Montana Citizens for Court Improvement, the Judicial Reform Committee of the Montana Bar Association, and the Montana League of Women Voters, whose studies of executive reorganization and state-local relations had preceded the comprehensive study of the state constitution carried out in 1969–1970. During the spring and summer of 1970, state organizations spanning business, labor, farm, and professional interests endorsed the calling of a convention, and most newspapers in the state added their support. A bipartisan Montana Constitutional Convention Committee campaigned for the proposed constitutional referendum.

Much of the Montana political climate of the early 1970s reflected the national mood: the new environmental movement, the rising fortunes of the Democrats as the administration of Richard Nixon collapsed, and a general distrust of government growing out of the Watergate hearings, coupled with the malaise of the never-ending conflict in Viet Nam.

In November 1970, the referendum on calling a convention passed by a vote of 133,482 to 71,643. Statewide, the majority of voters in all but five rural counties gave their approval to the measure. The 1971 legislature enacted enabling legislation for the election of convention delegates and established a Constitutional Convention Commission to prepare for the convention, undertake studies and research, and assemble essential information for the delegates, without making recommendations. The legislature appropriated $500,000 for the convention, $149,000 for the Commission, and $41,000 for the expenses of the election on ratification.

Montana voters elected 100 delegates to the convention on November 2, 1971: 58 Democrats, 36 Republicans and 6 Independents. The delegates to the convention assembled for a preliminary session on December 1, 1971. Working sessions commenced January 17 and continued until March 24, 1972.

Two key factors influenced the selection of the 100 convention delegates: (1) the cumulative impact of reapportionment was "a massive shift of political power and voting strength from rural areas to urban, from farms to cities, from cows to people"; and (2) a recent vote on a sales tax referendum, opposed by 70 percent of the voters, which redounded against its Republican and corporate sponsors. "The combined impact helps explain the fifty-eight Democrats and six Independents elected to the Constitutional Convention, the nineteen women, the twenty-four lawyers, the forty-one professionals, including thirteen educators. There were just twenty farmers and ranchers."[2]

During the legislative session which authorized the convention, the issue arose as to whether legislators could be delegates. Article V, section 7 of the 1889 Constitution said: "No senator or representative shall, during the term for which he shall have been elected, be appointed to any civil office under the state." The Montana Supreme Court interpreted this section to prohibit members of the legislature in 1971 from serving as delegates to the 1972 Constitutional Convention (*Legislative Assembly v. Lennon*, 1971). The decision discouraged most long-term members of the state legislature from seeking to become convention delegates. Although 18 former legislators were among the 100 delegates, the newcomers clearly had the upper hand. Few of the delegates were indebted

---

[2] Harry W. Fritz, "The 1972 Montana Constitution in a Contemporary Context," *Montana Law Review* 51 (1990): 270.

to special interests or to other delegates. Also, there was little history of antagonism among the delegates.

Ineligibility of nearly all prominent state politicians, a significant factor in who was selected to serve as delegates, proved to be serendipitous. Convention president Leo Graybill later noted:

> The delegates brought none of the acrimony and bitterness to the Convention that sometimes develops between seasoned politicians with preconceived positions on major state issues. Thus the delegates were able to approach the principal issues . . . in an objective manner, and they also avoided a good deal of the pressures to which legislators are subjected.[3]

It was suggested that what all the delegates had in common "was virtually complete ignorance of the art of constitution writing and a somewhat unfounded self-assurance" ("Montana: Fresh Chance Gulch," 1972, p. 18). By contrast the Missoula newspaper (*Missoulian*) commented: "Person for person the delegates are more capable people than legislators. But as a group they are more fragmented." None of the delegates to the 1972 Constitutional convention had experience writing a constitution, but it is rare that anyone is privileged to participate in the drafting of more than a single constitution. Many of the delegates had studied both the federal and Montana constitutions prior to the date of the convention. Others had experience in the interpretation of constitutional provisions. A review of the Constitutional Transcripts indicates that the delegates relied on their own experience coupled with 2,300 pages of carefully researched reports prepared by a group of dedicated researchers, many of whom were recent college graduates. The reports covered most of the topics addressed in the constitution, including human rights, welfare, education, taxation, legislative government, and the environment. Other information came from some 1,500 unsolicited letters offering suggestions.

The delegates included three professors, 24 attorneys, a beekeeper, a retired FBI agent, and a Methodist minister who preached, "Praise the Lord and pass the Constitution." One delegate, Robert Kelleher, fought in vain to establish a parliamentary system of government and to legalize homosexuality and prostitution. Delegate Daphne Bugbee, an architect from Missoula, said: "We want our government to serve us, to be where we can look at it, feel it, touch it, and know it." Delegates to the convention brought a large measure of creative energy and independence. The constitution, as ratified, indicates the populist inclination of the delegates in its consistent enhancement of the powers of the voters and the encouragement of direct participation in governmental decision making; for example, relaxing the requirements necessary to place initiatives and referenda

---

[3] Leo Graybill, Jr., "Foreword," in *Montana Constitutional Convention: 1971–1972* (Helena: Montana Legislative Council and Constitutional Convention Editing and Publishing Committee, 1979), p. i.

on the ballot; requiring that the question of whether to hold a constitutional convention be submitted to the voters at least every 20 years; requiring local governments to periodically review the structure of local government; and providing the public a right to participate in the operation of government agencies.

Almost all delegates received their first choice of committee assignment with no delegate assigned to more than one substantive committee. The voters elected delegates on a partisan basis, but the sentiment in the convention was to organize it in a bipartisan fashion. Thus seating was alphabetical rather than by party. The president of the convention appointed both Democrats and Republicans to chair committees, and he appointed a delegate from the opposite party to be a co-chairperson of each committee.

The purpose of carefully weighing the committee membership was to force the conflict of ideas into the committees where significant debate took place. Since the second strongest faction of most committees submitted a minority report, the convention debate was a true contest between principal contenders on any given point[4]; for example, some members of the legislative committee were committed to a unicameral legislature and some favored a bicameral legislature. In the judiciary committee there was vigorous disagreement between those delegates dedicated to removing the judiciary from the electoral process and others equally committed to retaining an elected judiciary.

There were ten substantive committees:

Bill of Rights
Legislative
Executive
Judiciary
Local Goverment
Education and Public Lands
Revenue and Finance
Public Health, Welfare, Labor, and Industry
Natural Resources and Agriculture
General Government and Constitution Amendment

There were four procedural committees:

Administration
Public Information
Rules and Resolutions
Style, Drafting, Transition, and Submission

[4] Leo Graybill, Jr., "Foreword," in *Montana Constitutional Convention: 1971–1972* (Helena: Montana Legislative Council and Constitutional Convention Editing and Publishing Committee, 1979), p. ii–iii.

The rules required each committee to conduct one final public hearing at a time when no other public hearings were being held so that delegates from other committees could attend. Thereafter, a committee report was filed with the convention, and debate occurred in the committee-of-the-whole. After adoption by the committee-of-the-whole, each article was assigned to the Style and Drafting Committee and again reported to the convention before final passage. All the convention's votes, deliberations, and committee meetings were open to the press and public. There was no issue on which debate was limited; the delegates discussed fully all motions, amendments, and viewpoints.

The 16-member Montana Constitutional Commission had been appointed to hire a staff to study the issues and make arrangements. The commission was forbidden to make recommendations about a new constitution. As a result, the 100 delegates started from scratch with no recommendations, but with stacks of research material. Delegates looked to the hired research analysts for expert advice instead of to the lobbyists roaming the Capitol halls.

Since the convention was organized in a unicameral format, things tended to be fluid and votes could change quickly; for example, the convention approved a measure to have the state finance campaigns of supreme court candidates so they would not have to seek financial support from special interests. Delegates killed the proposal later the same day. It was subsequently revived and passed only to be permanently killed later.

The delegates decided that all convention proceedings should be open to the public and, to maximize public participation, passed a rule requiring three days' advance notice for committee hearings so that interested parties, including the press, could attend. Montanans appreciated the openness, and perhaps the sense of inclusion with which the convention was carried forth helped secure a favorable vote.

Late in the convention, a backlash against the press developed over the right-to-know proposal. This proposal, which became Article II, section 9, stated that persons should not be denied the right to inspect documents or attend meetings of public agencies "except in cases in which the demand for individual privacy clearly exceeds the merits of public disclosure." Newspapers criticized the exception, calling it the "right to conceal." The *Billings Gazette* did so in a rare front-page editorial. However, the delegates were not intimidated and overwhelmingly voted to retain the right-to-know section as it was proposed.

There were many contentious issues. Delegates retained the strict ban against providing state funds for non-public education, but added a provision protecting non-public education from losing federal aid because of the state restriction (Article X, section 6). By a 53–40 vote, delegates approved the sentence allowing the state to distribute federal funds "provided to the state for the express purpose of distribution to non-public education." Delegates voted 52–43 against adding an amendment to the right-to-bear-arms section (Article II, section 12) that would have outlawed the registration and licensing of firearms.

Delegates initially voted 59–31 to remove any age limit for those seeking the state's highest elective offices, but more than one-fourth of the delegates changed their positions less than a day later and voted for the 25-year age requirement. The convention's Legislative Committee's recommendation for an ombudsman as a troubleshooter for public complaints was voted down.

The section dealing with the protection and improvement of the environment (Article IX, section 1) proved to be particularly controversial. The delegates rejected, by a 51–43 vote, the proposal that would have allowed suits against individuals or government agencies, subject to legislative limitations. A delegate also tried to insert a public trust statement, which would have set the state's environment up as a trust, held for the citizens by the state. His attempt failed 58–34. Objections were raised, saying it would infringe on private property rights. "If you want socialism to step in the door, just vote for this proposal," said one delegate. By a 44–40 vote the adjectives "clean" and "healthful" were removed from section 1. Delegates argued that the words could not be defined and would be subject to court interpretation that could dilute the intent of the section. However, the words were restored later that same day. The Natural Resources Committee also rejected another plea from environmental groups that citizens be allowed to go to court against polluters without proving monetary damages. The Committee rejected the idea, fearing "frivolous" lawsuits.

Democrats, Republicans, and Independents lined up against other Democrats, Republicans, and Independents on many issues. However, partisanship was not absent from the convention. Democratic delegates to the convention generally opted for reform, while a large number of Republicans opposed most changes. The State Press Bureau analyzed the votes of the 100 delegates on nine key issues. Taken as a whole, delegates cast their votes for the reform position 47 percent of the time. Democrats voted for reform 57 percent of the time, Republicans 32 percent, and Independents 42 percent. The analysis showed a striking difference between votes of urban and non-urban delegates. The 50 delegates who lived in the seven most populous cities voted for reform 58 percent of the time. The 50 delegates living in towns and in rural areas voted for reform 36 percent of the time.

Debates on a unicameral versus a bicameral legislature, on retention of the death penalty, and on legalization of gambling were particularly vigorous and difficult. The delegates eventually concluded that convention resolution and inclusion of any of the three issues as an inseparable part of the proposed constitution would defeat the entire constitution, and they agreed to submit the three issues for separate ballot consideration. The convention made a further decision to submit the constitution to the voters at a special election to be held June 6, 1972. The special election included the three separate issues on unicameral versus bicameral legislature, retention of the death penalty, and legalization of gambling.

The 1889 Constitution only hinted at non-discrimination, but the 1972 Constitution is very specific in its dignity section (Article II, section 4).

Discrimination by individuals, firms, and government is barred on the basis of race, color, sex, culture, social origin or condition, or political or religious ideas. This protection does not extend to Indian reservations located within the boundaries of the state of Montana. Every citizen now has the right to participate in governmental decision making (Article II, section 8). For the first time, children under the age of 18 have the protection of the Declaration of Rights, except where precluded by laws which enhance their protection. There remain disagreements as to whether laws purporting to enhance the protection of children while denying them adult rights are beneficial for the child (Article II, section 15). The 1889 Constitution did not have a section or an article on the environment. Now the preamble of the 1972 Constitution alludes to the environment ("the quiet beauty of our state"); section 3 of the Declaration of Rights makes the "right to a clean and healthful environment" an inalienable right, and Article IX is entirely devoted to the environment and natural resources.

The Montana Supreme Court enjoined the expenditure of $45,000 in convention funds appropriated for "voter education," to be disbursed in the interim between adjournment of the convention (March 24) and the vote by the people (June 6). Denied public funds, delegates, in their individual capacity, mounted an energetic campaign and were enthusiastically joined by the Montana League of Women Voters and numerous organizations of labor, educators, environmentalists, public employees, and some business groups. A private organization, "Citizens for Constitutional Improvement," spent roughly $10,000 to promote ratification. Much of the opposition focused on the taxation article (Article VIII). The Farm Bureau Federation, the Taxpayers Association, and many independent farmers, ranchers, and political conservatives feared the implications of shifting the administration of property taxes from county government to state government (now section 3). Many of these same groups and persons opposed removal of the two-mill limit on property tax levies and were convinced that taxes would increase if the constitution passed. These same people voiced concern about the uncertain import of the new water rights section (Article IX, section 3). The highway lobby, composed of contractors, tracking firms, oil companies, and car dealers objected to modification of the constitutional section (now Article VIII, section 6, subsection (2)) which had earmarked fuel and vehicle tax funds exclusively for highway construction. The new subsection permitted the legislature, by a three-fifths vote of the members of each house, to appropriate fuel and vehicle tax funds for purposes other than highway construction. Charles S. Johnson, in an article in the *Montana Journalism Review*, after noting the above, commented: "A voter's reaction to a proposal usually can be measured by how much he thinks it will cost him." Supporters of the constitution who thought the right-to-bear-arms section should have included language prohibiting state registration and licensing of firearms, argued that the constitution would be in jeopardy if the anti-registration clause were not included. One delegate said: "There are 15,000 to 20,000 people who are pretty emotional about this." A newly formed right-wing organization, "Citizens for Constitutional Government," spent over $20,000 to oppose virtually every provision representing change. Among the major daily newspapers, the *Great Falls Tribune* and the *Missoulian* endorsed ratification while the *Billings Gazette* and the *Butte Standard* took no position.

To educate the voters, the constitutional convention sent to each one a 24-page guide titled, "Proposed 1972 Constitution for the State of Montana: Official Text with Explanation." This gave an explanation of most sections. Since the voters presumably relied on these explanations for their understanding of various sections, these explanations might be useful in helping to determine the meaning of disputed or unclear sections (noted in this book as *Montana Constitutional Convention Explanation*).

Montana voters narrowly approved ratification of the new constitution by a vote of 116,415 to 113,883. The bicameral legislature was selected over a unicameral legislature, the death penalty was retained by a vote of 3 to 1, and gambling was legalized. In this regard voters from the city of Butte provided a curiosity. The side issue of gambling would only take effect if the people voted both in favor of the new constitution and also in favor of the gambling provision. While 73 percent of Butte voters favored the gambling provision, only 47 percent voted in favor of the constitution itself.[5]

Controversy over the election quickly culminated in a lawsuit brought by the Farm Bureau Federation. Notwithstanding the controversy, Governor Forest Anderson proclaimed ratification on June 20, 1972. The Farm Bureau Federation lawsuit claimed that the total number of votes cast in favor of the constitution was less than 50 percent. A substantial number of persons voted on one or more of the separate issues but failed to vote for or against the constitution. The suit contended that if the total number of votes cast at the election were considered, ratification had been approved by only 49 percent of voters, not the required majority. On August 18, 1972, in a 3–2 decision, the Montana Supreme Court ruled that the constitution had been approved. A federal district court in Montana reached a similar decision in a related lawsuit on July 11, 1973, and the U.S. Supreme Court affirmed that decision on December 3, 1973.

Neither political party expressed a formal position on the new constitution, but most major Democratic candidates and office holders and a few prominent Republicans supported ratification. Exit polls showed that Democrats favored it more than Republicans, urban voters more than rural voters, younger voters more than older voters, and men more than women.[6]

---

[5] Ellis Waldron & Paul B. Wilson, *Atlas of Montana Elections, 1889–1976* (Missoula: University of Montana Publications, 1978), pp. 262–263.

[6] Thomas Payne & Elizabeth Eastman, "The Montana Voter and the 1972 Constitutional Election," *Montana Public Affairs Report*, no. 13 (December 1972) (Missoula: University of Montana, Bureau of Government Research) [unpaginated 4-page report].

Only 12 states revised their constitutions from 1901 to 1997, and seven of these were between 1965 and 1974. In that same ten-year period, voters rejected six constitutions proposed by conventions and three others submitted by state legislatures. Of the 50 state constitutions, only Georgia's (1983) and Louisiana's (1975) are newer than Montana's. The length of the Montana Constitution is about 13,200 words, the seventh shortest of all state constitutions, and about half the length of Georgia's and about one-quarter the length of Louisiana's.

As previously noted, the 1972 Constitution mandates that the question of whether to hold a new constitutional convention be submitted to the voters at least every 20 years. In 1990 the question of calling a constitutional convention was submitted to the voters and 84 percent of the voters said no. Perhaps the fierce opposition to the 1972 Constitution dissipated over the course of nearly 20 years; or perhaps the conservative opponents mistrust whoever might be selected as delegates and dislike risking more changes, while the more liberal supporters are satisfied with the 1972 Constitution and fear the specter of revisionist delegates in control of a new constitutional convention. The other constitutionally required periodic review is voter review of local government (Article XI, section 9). The constitution requires that, every ten years, voters in each local government must vote on whether to undertake local government review. A yes vote on local government review requires the election of a local government study commission. In 1994, voters authorized study commissions in 33 of the 56 counties, and in 79 of the 126 municipalities.

Montana's Constitution has been amended 21 times since 1972, the least of the three most recent state constitutions. Of all 50 state constitutions, Montana's Constitution has been amended the second fewest number of times. The more significant of the amendments include the following:

C-1 in 1974 established a resource indemnity trust fund of $100 million to insure restoration of land after the removal of natural resources and to be funded by taxes on the extraction of natural resources.

C-2 in 1974 revived sovereign immunity to the extent specific enactments passed by two-thirds vote of each house of the legislature provided governmental immunity. Prior to this amendment the Montana Supreme Court had modified the original language of Article II, section 18, that had purported to eliminate sovereign immunity absolutely and completely.

C1-1 in 1974 provided for 90-day biennial legislative sessions. This passed for perceived budgetary reasons coupled with a general distrust of legislative political action, the theory being that the less time the legislature is in session the less damage they can do. Montana is one of only a few states in which the legislature meets every other year except for occasional special sessions called by the governor.

C-3 in 1976 created a coal tax trust fund to be funded by taxation on the extraction of coal. The fund accumulated over $600 million in the first 20 years of its existence, spawned a great deal of political bickering and one noteworthy U.S. Supreme Court case.

C-6 in 1978 provided optional, rather than mandatory, local government review.

C-18 in 1988 changed public assistance from a non-fundamental constitutional right to a legislative prerogative. If the legislature decides to provide public assistance, it has the additional power to determine, within the limits of equal protection and due process, eligibility, duration, level of assistance, and procedures termination. As originally ratified in the 1972 Constitution, public assistance or welfare was mandatory, although not included in Article II, the Declaration of Rights. The Montana Supreme Court had interpreted the original language of this section as subject to Montana's middle-tier analysis, saying that to meet constitutional demands any classification of welfare recipients must first demonstrate that the classification is reasonable and then must demonstrate that the state's interest in the classification is more important than the people's interest in obtaining welfare benefits, *Butte Community Union v. Lewis* (1986).

## ■ CONCLUSION

Themes in Montana Constitutional Development and Prospects for the Current Constitution-Is It an Adequate Basis for Government in the Twenty-First Century and Beyond?

The 1972 Montana Constitution embodies a sense of liberty, idealism, and pragmatism. It is a grand document but not perfect. Mistakes were made,[7] compromises were necessary,[8] and responses to past political grievances were

[7] There appears to have been a failure to think through and fully understand all of the ramifications of the equal protection provision of Article II, section 4. For example, Article II, section 4 provides that "no person shall be denied the equal protection of the laws. Neither the state nor any person, firm, corporation, or institution shall discriminate against any person in the exercise of his civil or political rights on account of race, color, sex, culture, social origin or condition, or political or religious ideas." The provision is obviously intended to reach private discrimination directed against any person in the exercise of "civil or political" rights. The convention delegates did not suggest what would be encompassed by "civil or political rights," nor has any Montana court given a precise definition for these terms. It appears that the delegates intended to limit the protection against private discriminatory actions to "civil or political rights"; that is, personal rights would not be protected against private discriminatory actions. However, the language could be interpreted to limit protection against discrimination by state action. Such an interpretation could exclude personal rights of disclosure and autonomy protected by Article II, section 10, the privacy section, from protection against state discriminatory actions. Other terms found in Article II, section 4 may ultimately pose some difficulty: for example, the meaning of "human dignity," and the meaning and application of "social origin or condition" and "political ideas." The right to privacy provision was apparently intended to encompass private as well as state action. The provision does not so state and the court has interpreted the provision otherwise. See, for example, *State v. Long* (1985).

[8] The judicial article was vigorously debated resulting in compromises that satisfied no one.

incorporated.[9] Mistakes, compromises, and political grievances were minimal. Grand ideas and powerful, if not always precise, language dominate the document.[10]

The structure of government continued by the 1972 Montana Constitution, while largely patterned after the United States Constitution, is decidedly different. Like the United States Constitution, the structure divides power among three branches of government. Unlike the United States Constitution, which purports to limit government to the exercise of delegated and enumerated powers, the Montana constitutional grant of power from the people is general and nonspecific.[11] The Montana Constitution allocates legislative power to a legislature,[12] executive power to a governor,[13] and judicial power to the courts,[14] with few specific directives or limitations.[15] With a traditional pragmatic, modern western government structure in place, the recognized need for limits on governmental police power beyond balance and separation as found in the structure produced a Declaration of Rights. An overview of Article II, "The Declaration of Rights," presents the best picture of the intended relation between Montana government and the people of Montana.

The Declaration of Rights emphasizes the privacy of the individual within government. The privacy of the individual is divided between the freedom from government intrusion, encompassing such rights as the following:

1. section 11, freedom from unreasonable searches and seizures of persons, papers, homes, and effect
2. section 23, freedom from imprisonment to secure testimony and section 27, freedom from imprisonment for debt
3. section 25, freedom from self-incrimination
4. section 29, freedom from governmental taking of property without just compensation;

---

[9] See Article II, section 16.

[10] Montana constitutional provisions incorporating grand ideas include the "right to know," the "right of participation," the "right of privacy," the "dignity of the human being," and the "right to a clean and healthful environment." See Article II, sections 3, 8, 9, 10.

[11] Article II, section 1 states that "[a]ll government of rights originates with the people . . . and is instituted solely for the good of the whole."

[12] See Article V of the Montana Constitution.

[13] See Article VI, section 4 of the Montana Constitution.

[14] See Article VII, section 1 of the Montana Constitution.

[15] See, for example, "The state shall appraise . . . " Article VIII, section 3; and "The state and each person shall maintain and improve a clean and healthful environment . . . " Article IX, section 1. As to specific directives, see generally Articles VIII, IX, X, XI, XII, and XIII of the Montana Constitution.

and the freedom to choose, encompassing such rights as the following:

1. section 5, freedom of religion
2. section 7, freedom of expression
3. section 12, freedom to bear arms
4. section 31, freedom of contracts
5. section 3, freedom to pursue life's basic necessities; to enjoy and defend one's life and liberties; to acquire, possess and protect one's property; and to seek safety, health and happiness in all lawful ways and
6. section 34, freedom to make other personal choices not specifically enumerated. (These could include choices ranging from how one dresses, what one eats, and where one works to freedom of conscience and freedom of association, rights not specifically mentioned in Montana's Constitution, but necessarily implied.)

The Declaration of Rights also emphasizes the public rights of the individual. The public rights of the individual are divided between the right to know what government is doing, encompassing the single right found in:

section 9, the right to know;

and the right to participate in government, encompassing such rights as:

1. section 13, right to vote
2. section 6, freedom of assembly
3. section 7, freedom of expression
4. section 8, right of participation
5. The right of political association as implied from the rights of assembly and freedom of expression.
6. Article IV, section 4, eligibility for public office. (Other sections of the Montana Constitution list qualifications for certain offices.) 16
7. Article III, sections 4 and 5, the right to propose laws by initiative or to reject laws passed by the legislature by referendum; and Article XIV, sections 2 and 9, the right by initiative to call a constitutional convention or to amend the constitution.

Theories of equal protection and due process complete the overview of the limits on government and the relation between Montana government and the people of Montana.

---

[16] See Article V, section 4, qualifications for a candidate for the legislature; Article VI, section 3, qualifications for office of governor, lieutenant governor, secretary of state, attorney general, superintendent of public instruction, and auditor; and Article VII, section 9, qualifications for judges.

## A. Equal Protection

1. section 3, equality in the sense that "all persons" have certain inalienable rights
2. section 4, individual dignity and equal protection regardless of race, color, sex, culture, social origin or condition, or political or religious ideas
3. sections 14 and 15, adult rights and rights of persons not adults
4. section 28, rights of the convicted
5. section 31, no irrevocable grant of special privileges or immunities

## B. Due Process

1. section 11, searches and seizures
2. section 16, the administration of justice including access to courts and full legal redress
3. section 17, due process of law
4. section 18, state subject to suit
5. section 19, habeas corpus
6. section 20, initiation of (criminal) proceedings
7. section 21, bail
8. section 22, excessive sanctions
9. section 24, rights of the accused
10. section 25, self-incrimination and double jeopardy
11. section 26, trial by jury
12. section 29, eminent domain
13. section 31, no ex post facto laws

Together the delineated structure of government and the declared rights of the Montana Constitution provide an excellent foundation for government and a commendable explanation of the relation between government and the individual.

The structure of government and the declared rights provide the foundation and the foresight to serve the people of the state in the twenty-first century and beyond. The structure is traditional and well tested. The liberties and rights include most of the best of what society has determined, through centuries of struggle and refinement, as essential to the well-being of humankind. Additions in this constitution have pushed beyond the known boundaries, demanding protection for "human dignity"; expanding ideas of individual privacy and citizen participation; and providing the basis for reinventing government without redrafting the constitution.

A state constitution should provide a bulwark for the protection of the people from government and it should provide a structure to insure fair and effective government operation. Both objectives were largely achieved. Also, "the constitution may provide a statement of goals which a government should strive to achieve."[17] Throughout the Montana Constitution are echoes of high-plains populism. Recognizing that government exists for the benefit of the people, a number of specific provisions provide the means to achieve responsiveness and accountability.[18]

The Declaration of Rights contained four new rights that emphasized the central role of the individual in government. Every person was afforded the right to participate in governmental decision making, the right to examine government documents and observe government deliberations, the right of individual privacy, and the unlimited right to sue government entities and their agents.[19]

Ronald K. L. Collins has noted seventeen provisions of Montana's Declaration of Rights (Article II, sections 1–35 of the Montana Constitution) that have no parallel in the Bill of Rights of the U.S. Constitution:[20]

Section 4 (equality and private discrimination)
Section 8 (right of participation)
Section 9 (right to know)
Section 10 (privacy)
Section 14 (adult rights)
Section 15 (rights of persons not adults)
Section 16 (administration)
Section 18 (state subject to suit)
Section 20 (initiation of criminal proceedings)
Section 23 (criminal detention)
Section 27 (imprisonment for debt)
Section 28 (rights of the convicted)
Section 29 (award of attorney fees in eminent domain)
Section 30 (treason and descent of estates)
Section 32 (civilian control of the military)
Section 33 (importation of armed persons)
Section 35 (special consideration for servicemen, servicewomen, and veterans)

[17] James H. Goetz, "Interpretations of the Montana Constitution: Sometimes Socratic, Sometimes Erratic," *Montana Law Review*, 51 (1990): 291.

[18] Ellis Waldron, "The Constitutional Tradition and Political Culture of Montana," in James C. Lopach (ed.), *We the People of Montana: The Workings of a Popular Government* (Missoula, MT: Mountain Press Publishing Co., 1983), 10.

[19] Ellis Waldron, "The Constitutional Tradition and Political Culture of Montana," in James C. Lopach (ed.), *We the People of Montana: The Workings of a Popular Government* (Missoula, MT: Mountain Press Publishing Co., 1983), 11. Note that the right of individual privacy existed prior to the 1972 Constitution but was not explicitly stated in the prior constitution. The unlimited right to bring suit against the government was subsequently amended and thereby drained of much of its significance.

[20] Ronald K.L. Collins, "Reliance on State Constitutions—The Montana Disaster," *Texas Law Review*, 63 (1985): 1122.

The convention continued the power of the governor to line-item veto and provided him or her with the amendatory veto. The amendatory veto allows the governor to amend or revise proposed legislation and return the proposed legislation to the assembly for further consideration. By contrast, judicial reform made little headway. The convention failed to establish a unified state court structure, failed to adopt a merit system for selecting judges, failed to provide public financing for judicial elections, and failed to abolish the constitutional status of justice-of-the-peace courts.

On the other hand, Article XI provided local government with many new options, including so-called home rule via the creation of local self-government charters. It required the legislature to provide procedures for adopting optional alternative forms of local government and it authorized the legislature to extend legislative powers to counties.

Environmental concerns of the 1889 and 1972 Constitutional Conventions reflect an enormous change in attitudes. 1889 convention president William A. Clark, a mining millionaire, offered the delegates the following explanation of the value of mining-generated, smoky Butte air:

> I must say that the ladies are very fond of this smoky city, as . . . [Butte] is sometimes called, because there is just enough arsenic there to give them a beautiful complexion, and that is the reason the ladies of Butte are renowned wherever they go for their beautiful complexions. . . . I say it would be a great deal better for other cities in the territory if they had more smoke and less diphtheria and other diseases. It has been believed by all the physicians of Butte that the smoke that sometimes prevails there is a disinfectant, and destroys the microbes that constitute the germs of disease . . . it would be a great advantage for other cities, to have a little more smoke and business activity and less disease.[21]

By contrast, leading Montana historian K. Ross Toole, writing in 1972, observed: "Missoula was often hidden from view by the stinking, yellowish-gray smog of a pulp plant, the effluent from an aluminum plant in Columbia Falls had yellowed every pine tree for miles around, and the stink of oil refineries in Billings stretched all the way to the town of Laurel."[22] The 1972 Constitution was touted as establishing the strongest environmental protections of any state constitution. The Declaration of Rights, Article II, states that all persons have an inalienable right to a clean and healthful environment. It added an entire article dedicated to the environment and natural resources. The environmental provisions fall into two broad categories: those addressing a standard of quality for the natural environment and those addressing particular issues of

---

[21] Quoted in Michael P. Malone, Richard B. Roeder, & William L. Lang, *Montana: A History of Two Centuries*, rev. ed. (Seattle: University of Washington Press, 1991), p. 150.

[22] K. Ross Toole, *Twentieth-Century Montana: A State of Extremes* (Norman: University of Oklahoma Press, 1972), pp. 287–288.

environmental management.[23] The environmental quality provisions deal with maintaining and improving a clean and healthy environment, protecting against environmental degradation, preventing unreasonable depletion of natural resources, and reclaiming lands disturbed by the extraction of natural resources. The constitution mandates the legislature to provide for administration of the standards and to provide adequate remedies for the enforcement of the standards.[24]

The convention made progressive efforts to reform permanently the state bureaucracy: (1) it established a uniform investment program; (2) it limited bureaucratic growth to 20 executive departments; (3) it placed the executive branch firmly under the governor's control; and (4) it assured public participation in executive decision making.[25] The constitution made it easier for voters to utilize initiatives and referendums, and they have become an increasingly important part of lawmaking in Montana.

One commentator noted that the 1972 Constitution was a monument to a new, urban Montana:

> Its ratification was approved in only twelve counties, but collectively they contained fifty-five percent of the state's total population, provided sixty-five percent of the favorable vote, and housed eight of Montana's ten largest cities. The three largest counties in eastern Montana . . . all favored the constitution.[26]

In the waning moments of the convention, delegate James C. Garlington expressed the sentiments of many delegates, in terms both eloquent and poignant:

> [A]s we prepare to close the journal of this Convention, I think we should pause a moment to reflect upon what has happened. . . . In one sense, we have finished our labors, but in a larger sense we have just begun. Ahead, I see not only the imminent task of ratification, but beyond that the more important task of leading our fellow Montanans into the reality of better government for a better society. Consider the Convention: conceived and born in partisan political strife, it has matured into thoughtful and objective concern for the rightness of things. Composed of people from every walk of life, amateurs one and all in basic constitutional doctrine, it has become soundly expert in applying proper principles with perceptive judgment. We, as individuals, have been transformed from willing volunteers to dedicated and competent students of government on a statewide basis. The endless hours of study, research, and mutual consultation, culminating in these weeks of exacting debate and

---

[23] John L. Horwich, "Montana's Constitutional Environmental Quality Provisions: Self-Execution or Self-Delusion?" *Montana Law Review*, 57 (1996): 332.

[24] Article IX, section 1, subsections (2) & (3).

[25] Wendy A. Fitzgerald, "Montana's Constitutionally Established Investment Program: A State Investing Against Itself," *Montana Law Review*, 51 (1990): 382.

[26] Fritz, "The 1972 Montana Constitution," 270.

decision, have developed in us all a new value which I am concerned that we neither lose nor underrate. In fact, I think it has fastened upon us a new commitment to go the next mile and make sure that our labors bear fruit. This has not come easily. This Convention bears the unmistakable imprint of expert and committed leadership, utterly devoted to the successful achievement of its goals. Where we were partisan, we are nonpartisan. Where we were inflexible, we are flexible. Where we were hesitant, we are confident. Where we were skeptical of each other, we enjoy mutual respect and confidence. Our debates and discussions have never been marred by angry exchange or sarcastic derision. For these good fortunes, we owe a debt of great gratitude to our President, whose constant daily example in the performance of his most difficult and uncharted tasks has led us this far . . .

I thought a Constitution should assure the citizen his personal freedoms. We have clearly done this by a Bill of Rights which not only has all the freedoms of the last 80 years but includes a broad band of additional rights that will serve well in our ever more complex society. A Constitution, I thought, should assure the citizen his political freedom, his right to vote, to be a candidate, to express his opinions, and to know what his government is doing to him and with him. Our personal example of totally public proceedings and our consistent opening of all the doors and desks of government to the eyes and ears of the governed, makes this a reality in Montana. If it has been done, it can be done again, and only good can flow from that process. As a cross check I have searched our document for a provision that sets one person or interest above another, and I find none. A good Constitution has only those fundamental structures and guidelines within which all the competing interests and pressures of society may freely move, winning or losing as their merits are tested. Our document meets this high standard. It grants no special privilege to anyone, neither does it impose any special burden. Suspicious of none, it expects the best of us all. Finally, I thought a Constitution should assure a person's future freedoms, meaning his right to try a new system, expel a bad system, devise a new solution to a new problem, and explore constantly the way to live better with government. This we have achieved. We have unshackled and energized our Legislature. We have coupled authority with responsibility in our Executive. We have set the stage for equality in the burden of taxation. We have launched a strong citizen force charged with finding better solutions to the almost infinite problems of education. We have provided maximum opportunity for the varied communities of Montana to govern themselves in their own way.

The press has described our work as middle-of-the-road, which I suppose is to imply shortsighted timidity in our judgments. This is a vague value judgment. The truth is that most of the people are in the middle of the road, and the Constitution has to be for most of the people. It therefore should be where they are, and that it appears to be so is a sign to me that it has been well done. . . . Derived as it is from the imperfect workings of imperfect people, it certainly has its faults. . . . [But] I think our Constitution is the finest gift to the young people of Montana that it is within our power to give. We are giving them the gift of participation in their present and the management of their future on a ship of state that is far more manageable and sensitive than the old one.

# PART TWO

# The Montana Constitution and Commentary

## PREAMBLE

> We the people of Montana grateful to God for the quiet beauty of our state, the grandeur of our mountains, the vastness of our rolling plains, and desiring to improve the quality of life, equality of opportunity and to secure the blessings of liberty for this and future generations do ordain and establish this constitution.

The preamble states four of humanity's most uplifting aspirations: an attachment to the land; a guarantee of freedom (a recognition of the need to protect individuals from the tyranny of government); a commitment to continue striving toward an improved quality of life; and the promise of equality of opportunity. It is original except for the introductory words "We, the people of Montana, grateful to [Almighty] God . . . " which were also the introductory words of the preamble to the 1889 Montana Constitution.

Constitutions rarely provide an interpretive guide and this document is no exception.[1] Constitutional interpretation is usually guided by the plain meaning of the text, by adherence to the intent of the framers, or by reliance on the

[1] Statutes often include an interpretive guide. For example, Montana Code Annotated, Section 45-1-102 (2) states: "[The provisions] are to be construed according to the fair import of their terms with a view to effect its object and to promote justice."

political and moral philosophies which give the document coherence and force. The preamble acts only as a general guide. Such an interpretive guide would help the people and their representatives keep an eye on constitutional goals. Courts tend to lose sight of constitutional goals in the compromises and responses necessary to decide contested cases, as well as the minutiae and details of managing the court's business. Legislative and executive branches are likely to be even less sensitive, less principled, and less oriented to the long-term goals of a constitution. Montana's Constitution presents a vision of good government, and a coherent set of political and moral ideals. The preamble sets the course in words that are both lofty and instructional.[2]

> The values and history of Montanans inextricably form the framework for the central references to the environment in the Montana Constitution. The first statement affirming Montanans' commitment occurs in the preamble to the constitution. . . . [T]he preamble demonstrates the preeminent concern for the environment, as represented by statements concerning the quality of life. . . . [The preamble] emphasizes these goals even over such fundamentals as liberty and equality of opportunity.[3]

Several cases have referenced the preamble but it has had minimal impact. One case places some importance on the language of the preamble, holding that the phrase "We the people of Montana . . . desiring . . . to secure the blessings of liberty . . . do ordain and establish this constitution," read in conjunction with sections 3, 4, and 17 of Article II, means that "physical liberty [is] a fundamental right, without which other constitutionally guaranteed rights would have little meaning" (*In re C.H.*, 1984, which upheld the incarceration of a juvenile for a status offense).

---

[2] Dan Himmelfarb, "The Preamble in Constitutional Interpretation," *Seton Hall Constitutional Law Journal*, 2 (1991): 204.

[3] Deborah Beaumont Schmidt & Robert J. Thompson, "The Montana Constitution and the Right to a Clean and Healthful Environment," *Montana Law Review*, 51 (1990): 412–413.

# Article I

## *Compact with the United States*

All provisions of the enabling act of Congress (approved February 22,1889, 25 Stat. 676), as amended and of Ordinance No. 1, appended to the Constitution of the state of Montana and approved February 22, 1889, including the agreement and declaration that all lands owned or held by any Indian or Indian tribes shall remain under the absolute jurisdiction and control of the congress of the United States, continue in full force and effect until revoked by the consent of the United States and the people of Montana.

Article I makes it clear that the new (1972) Constitution does not affect any agreements made with the United States government when Montana first became a state. The Montana Supreme Court said that federal law precluded an attempt by state courts to adjudicate rights in Indian trust land for the purpose of money damages (*Krause v. Neuman,* 1997). A state district court committed error by sustaining jurisdiction when a tribal court had previously assumed jurisdiction over the parties and subject matter by issuing a temporary restraining order against plaintiff. The supreme court exercised abstention, as a matter of comity, in holding that the tribal court retained jurisdiction (*Agri West v. Koyama Farms,* 1997).

# Article II

## *Declaration of Rights*

The "declaration of rights of the people of the State of Montana" of the 1972 Constitution incorporates the substance of the U.S. Constitutional "Bill of Rights" including the first nine amendments except number three. In addition, it includes some provisions found in the text of the federal constitution andfederal constitutional amendments other than the "Bill of Rights," such as theprohibition against ex post facto laws and laws impairing the obligation of contract, the guarantee of the privilege of the writ of habeas corpus, and the rightto vote. While most of the protections included in the 1972 "Declaration of Rights" are derived from the 1889 Montana Constitution, many of the specificprotections have been rewritten and important new protections have been added. The following discussion of Article II lists, explains, and interprets each of therights. Note that some of the rights are stated affirmatively; for example, ArticleII, section 2: "The people have the exclusive right of governing themselves asa free, sovereign, and independent state." Other rights are direct prohibitionsagainst government exercise of power; for example, Article II, section 7: "Nolaw shall be passed impairing the freedom of speech or expression." Some sectionsnecessarily require legislative action, such as section 35, which declares:"veterans may be given special considerations determined by the legislature."Other sections would seem to be both mandatory and self-executing, such assection 21, which states: "[a]ll persons shall be bailable by sufficient sureties."

## SECTION 1

**Popular Sovereignty**. All political power is vested in and derived from thepeople. All government of right originates with the people, is founded upontheir will only, and is instituted solely for the good of the whole.

The provision expresses the philosophy that government is founded on the will of the people (MCC Rep. 626) and is for the benefit of the people. Except for minor changes in punctuation, this section is derived from and identical to Article III, section 1 of the 1889 Montana Constitution. The practical value of the provision is minimal, although it does state the source of power or authority for the constitution. It is a foundational assumption of Lochean representational democracy, but the generality of the provision diminishes its value in deciding specific issues. Some cases have referred to it, but only in a hortatory sense and not as a specific, determinative requirement of state constitutional law. Cases have rarely cited Article II, section 1, and never determinatively (*Cox v. Lee Enterprises, Inc.*, 1986; and *Schuman v. Study Comm'n of Yellowstone County*, 1978). The value of the provision in case opinions is primarily supportive. Cases have cited the predecessor provision in the 1889 Montana Constitution to sustain challenged government procedures (nominating candidates and transferring gubernatorial power), holding that the processes were compatible with the generalized concept of representational democracy (*State ex rel. Lamey v. Mitchell*, 1934; *State ex rel. Mills v. Stewart*, 1922;*State ex rel. Metcalf v. Wileman*, 1914; and *State ex rel. Scharnikow v. Hogan*, 1900).

## SECTION 2

**Self-Government**. The people have the exclusive right of governing themselves as a free, sovereign, and independent state. They may alter or abolish the constitution and form of government whenever they deem it necessary.

The section purports to guarantee Montanans the right to govern themselves and to determine their form of government (MCC Rep. 626), emphasizing that the state of Montana is a sovereign and independent state, subject only to the will of the people of the state of Montana. This section is similar to Article III, section 2 of the 1889 Montana Constitution, but eliminates the meaningless language justifying change by the people only when deemed necessary "to their safety and happiness," and that "such change [must] be not repugnant to the Constitution of the United States."

To the extent the provision purports to mean what it says, it is in error. Montana is neither a sovereign state nor an independent state. It is a state equal to the other states within the "federal system" and is subject to the limitations of the U.S. Constitution and the power and control that is vested in the federal government, which power is derived from the people of the several states.

The value of the provision is minimal. Insofar as the provision states the general power of the people for self-government, it is a restatement of Article II, section 1. Insofar as it purports to create a sovereign and independent state, it fails. The 1995 legislature, dominated by a conservative majority, proposed several resolutions emphasizing state sovereignty and attempting to overrule decades of U.S. Supreme Court interpretations of the commerce clause of the U.S. Constitution. The 1995 legislature also seemed committed to overruling the supremacy clause of Article VI of the U.S. Constitution. It failed in both endeavors.

The fundamental right to alter or abolish the constitution is given specific content and accorded procedural direction in other sections. Article XIV, section 3 requires a periodic vote by the people on the issue of whether to hold a constitutional convention. Article XIV, sections 1 and 2 provide that the legislature may call an unlimited constitutional convention by two-thirds vote and the people, by initiative, may call for an unlimited constitutional convention.

The one significant case citing this provision held that an initiative which purported to amend the constitution was, in form, a constitutional amendment, but in substance, a legislative resolution (*State ex rel. Harper v. Waltermire*, 1984). The proposed amendment would have required the 1985 legislature to adopt a resolution requesting Congress to call a constitutional convention for the sole purpose of adopting a balanced budget amendment and would have required that, if the resolution was not adopted within 90 legislative days, the legislature would remain in session without pay until the resolution was adopted. In evaluating this peculiar, purported constitutional amendment, the court concluded that the initiative power does not include the power to enact a legislative resolution. By defining the purported constitutional amendment to be a legislative resolution (it did require a legislative resolution), the court indirectly limited the apparently unlimited language of the constitutional provision, changing "the people may alter . . . the constitution . . . whenever they deem it necessary" to "the people may alter . . . the constitution whenever they deem it necessary and . . . whenever the substance of the modification is appropriate" (p. 828).

## SECTION 3

**Inalienable Rights.** All persons are born free and have certain inalienable rights. They include the right to a clean and healthful environment and the rights of pursuing life's basic necessities, enjoying and defending their lives and liberties, acquiring, possessing and protecting property, and seeking their safety, health and happiness in all lawful ways. In enjoying these rights, all persons recognize corresponding responsibilities.

The section is a generalized statement of the inalienable rights of persons. Specifically, it guarantees only a "right to a clean and healthful environment."

All other phrases in the section alluding to "inalienable" rights are temporizing; that is, the right to pursue, to enjoy, and to seek. None of the other rights are possessed or guaranteed. The gist of the listed inalienable rights is in the nature of individual autonomy, often subsumed under the heading of privacy. If these phrases were to be given their apparent meaning as generalized limitations upon the exercise of police power, they would prevent government control of a variety of ordinary, as well as more idiosyncratic, human actions. However, the concluding phrase "in all lawful ways" compromises all the listed rights of autonomy, meaning that government is not constitutionally prohibited in placing unspecified limits on individual autonomy in "pursuing life's basic necessities, enjoying and defending life and liberty, acquiring, possessing and protecting property, and seeking safety, health and happiness." Finally, section 3 states that persons enjoying these rights recognize corresponding responsibilities. The nature of the corresponding responsibilities is unknown.

While there is a superficial similarity between this section and Article III, section 3, of the 1889 Montana Constitution, and some of the language is obviously derived from Article III, section 3, of the 1889 Montana Constitution, the 1972 provision expresses important new concepts relative to the environment, basic necessities, and health. Also, the last sentence of the section mentioning "corresponding responsibilities" is new. The court held that a provision of the 1889 Constitution, somewhat similar to Article II, section 3, inhibits police power (*Garden Spot Market, Inc. v. Byrne*, 1963). Article III, section, 3 of the 1889 Constitution protected and vested inalienable rights, to the extent they were identified. For example, *State ex rel. Schultz-Lindsay Construction Co. v. State Bd. of Equalization* (1965) held a non-resident contractor's license fee unconstitutional, and *Garden Spot Market, Inc. v. Byrne* (1963) held a tax on trading stamps to be unreasonably discriminatory in violation of Article III, sections 3 and 27 of the 1889 Montana Constitution.

Some of the language of the 1972 provision is similar to the language of the 1889 provision, but the focus of the two provisions is quite different. The 1889 provision, considered in its historical context, was primarily intended to protect vested rights, particularly vested property rights (*Hinds v. Wilcox*, 1898; and *Iverson v. Dilno*, 1911). By contrast, the 1972 Constitution focuses less on vested rights than on the creation of new rights such as environmental and basic human necessities, coupled with the obligations of citizenship. A secondary purpose of the 1889 provision was to guarantee "equality of persons" as to inalienable rights. Article II, section 4 of the 1972 Constitution covers the concept of "equal protection."

Are inalienable rights different from fundamental rights or different from other rights listed in the declaration of rights? Probably not. To some degree section 3 may be perceived as primarily hortatory, directional, and aspirational rather than as a statement of rights to be guaranteed by government either as protection from government or protection from other persons. Certainly, the generalized statement of inalienable rights has not been an effective protection for individual rights claimed in opposition to the exercise of state police power.

Rights not specifically mentioned elsewhere in the Declaration of Rights might be derived from this section, such as the right to travel. The court has suggested that the right to travel, a fundamental right under federal law, does not encompass the right to drive on public roads free from government regulation and the right to drive on public roads is not a fundamental right (*State v. Skurdal*, 1988). The right to a public education, considered in Article X but not included in the Declaration of Rights and not yet determined to be a fundamental right, might be derived from this section. The principle of welfare, considered in Article XII, might be supported as a subset of the pursuit of "basic necessities." Case law denies welfare fundamental right status (*Butte Community Union v. Lewis*, 1986), the delegates having said that the right to pursue life's basic necessities was not intended to create a right to be provided with all of life's necessities at the expense of the public treasury (MCC Tr. 1636). But the provision was intended to assure that the public would provide assistance for those in genuine need (MCC Tr. 1637).

*State v. Bernhard* (1977) determined property rights to be secondary to police power, even as to aesthetics, upholding the requirement that motor vehicle wrecking facilities and graveyards be licensed and shielded. According to *State ex rel. Zander v. District Court* (1979), property rights are also subordinate to a compelling state interest in protecting against burglary, thereby justifying entrance into the privacy of one's home to protect the home even as against the wishes of the owner. The principal argument asserted by the homeowner was violation of the right of privacy provided by Article II, section 10. At the opposite extreme, the case of *State v. Bradford* (1984) cited this section to support a "stop and frisk" by a private security guard as "defense of property."

The guaranteed inalienable right to "a clean and healthful environment" will be fleshed out by subsequent administrative actions, legislation, and court decisions establishing standards by which to judge what is clean and healthful. While defining standards and determining limits is true of most rights, guarantees, and prohibitions found in the Declaration of Rights, there is less historical basis to draw from in defining "a clean and healthful environment." Article IX, sections (2) and (3) require the legislature to provide adequate remedies for enforcement of the right.

Because the statement is "new" and without historical gloss, the provision is in danger of being ignored, or being viewed as hortatory and not an enforceable guarantee of rights. Any new right facing generalized economic concerns as well as vigorous lobbying and legal attacks by powerful entities in the energy, agricultural, and extractive industries may be quickly eviscerated. Further, the text does not say whether the right is self-executing, although the delegates said that the right to a "clean and healthful environment" was intended to be self-executing for those whose health or property may be affected (MCC Tr. 1645), and that delegates intended to guarantee "a clean and healthful environment" for this and future generations (MCC Tr. 1637). It has been argued that "[T]he Montana Constitution's declaration of an inalienable right to a clean and healthful environment is self-executing. . . . [This] provision satisfies all the traditional criteria for self-execution: (1) it is a limitation on government; (2) it provides a standard for judicial review; and (3) it does not depend on legislation to be effective."[4] Other scholars are less certain.

The most significant case to interpret the provision supports the conclusion that the inalienable right to a clean and healthful environment is a self-executing fundamental right (*Montana Environmental Information Center et al. v. Dept. of Environmental Quality and Seven-Up Pete Joint Venture*, 1999). The opinion held that the right to a clean and healthful environment was complimentary to, interrelated with, and interdependent upon Article IX, section 1, subdivision (1), Environment and Natural Resources. By combining the "inalienable right to a clean and healthful environment" of this section with the obligation of the "state and each person to maintain and improve a clean and healthful environment," as stated in Article IX, the demanding strict scrutiny analysis associated with fundamental rights was transported to Article IX, and the embryonic standards found in section 1 of Article IX clarified and strengthened the environmental protection guarantee of Article II, section 3.

An earlier Montana Supreme Court case noted that a legislative purpose to preserve or enhance aesthetic values is consistent with the right to a "clean and healthful environment" (*State v. Bernhard*, 1977), and an Attorney General Opinion reported that the inalienable right of all Montanans to "a clean and healthful environment," as found in Article II, section 3, supports the purpose of the Montana Subdivision and Platting Act,[5] as against an apparent circumvention by a landowner (38 Op. Att'y Gen. 363 (1980)).

The constitution expresses elsewhere in more specific language and in more detail most of the ideas encompassed by this section; for example: Article IX on the environment and natural resources; Article II, section 29 on eminent domain; Article II, section 17 on due process relative to liberty and property; and Article XII, section 3 on basic necessities and economic assistance.

---

[4] Carl W. Tobias & Daniel N. McLean, "The Effect of the Environmental Policy Acts on Pre-Existing Agency Authority," *Montana Law Review*, 41 (1980): 255–256.

[5] Montana Code Annotated, Section 76-3-102 (1999).

## SECTION 4

**Individual Dignity.** The dignity of the human being is inviolable. No person shall be denied the equal protection of the laws. Neither the state nor any person, firm, corporation, or institution shall discriminate against any person in the exercise of his civil or political rights on account of race, color, sex, culture, social origin or condition, or political or religious ideas.

This section is a new approach to "equal protection"; even the title "individual dignity" is novel and the phrase "[t]he dignity of the human being is inviolable" has not been interpreted to mean anything in particular. The concept of "individual dignity" as a constitutional right is largely derived from the Puerto Rican Declaration of Rights (MCC Tr. 1642). As a practical matter, the vagaries of life coupled with the allure of power and privilege deny equality among persons, and make difficult the application and enforcement of equal protection before the law. Perhaps that is why "in recent years the equal protection guarantee has become the single most important concept in the Constitution for the protection of individual rights."[6]

Prior to passage of the Fourteenth Amendment to the U.S. Constitution (and perhaps the French Revolution), the idea of equality was limited to persons of power, usually free, white male property owners. Theoretically, blacks obtained equal protection of the law after the ratification of the Fourteenth Amendment; in practice the struggle for racial and ethnic equality under law continues. Women gained a measure of equality with the passage of the Nineteenth Amendment in 1920. Over time, the notion of equality under law has expanded, and theoretically most persons are now included. The 1972 Montana Constitution provides the most inclusive scheme of "equal rights" of any known constitution.

The 1889 Montana Constitution did not contain a plain statement as to equal protection of the law; however, Article III, section 3 stated that "all persons are born equally free, and have certain natural, essential, and inalienable rights." This language seems to imply some sense of government-recognized equality and cases interpreted the provision as a requirement of equal protection of the law (*State ex rel. Woare v. Board of Comm'rs*, 1924; *Kersey v. Nelson*, 1913; and *Stange v. Esval*, 1923). Further, Article III, section 27 of the 1889 Montana Constitution guaranteed "due process of law" which the U.S. Supreme Court has interpreted to encompass "equal protection" (*Boiling v. Sharpe*, 1954). Finally, Article V, section 26 of the 1889 Montana Constitution prohibited the legislature from passing any of an extended list of local or special laws, indicating an indirect concern about equality.

Article II, section 4 reaches beyond the boundaries of traditional equal protection. The language is unique to the extent it recognizes human dignity as a dimension of, or corollary to, the concept of equal protection of the law. The language also portends to create a right to equality within the realm of private activity, eliminating the

[6] John E. Nowak & Ronald D. Rotunda, *Constitutional Law*, 5th ed. (St. Paul, MN: West Publishing Co., 1995), p. 595.

"state action" requirement attached to the comparable provision of the U.S. Constitution. The private anti-discrimination "equal protection" guarantee is limited to the exercise of civil and political rights. The section enlarges the protected classes to include not only race but also color, sex, culture, social origin or condition, and political and religious ideas. Delegates understood that the scope of the prohibition against discrimination and its synthesis of human rights were unprecedented (MCC Tr. 1642, 1646). But it is unclear what the delegates perceived to be the definition and scope of the classes to be protected other than race and sex. The delegates noted that "culture" is intended to cover groups that are culturally distinct such as Native Americans (MCC Tr. 1642). "National origin," not included in the listed classes, may be embraced within race, color, or social origin. If race, color, or social origin are interpreted to include all who could be separately classified based on "national origin" then most identifiable groups or classes would be included. Insofar as race or color can be used, there is the advantage of existing case precedent to help in the definitional process.

Classifications based on sex, as an explicitly protected class, would presumptively be subject to the compelling state interest test, unlike its federal counterpart. Strangely, no state cases have raised the issue. One commentator has argued: "The starting point for sex discrimination analysis in Montana should always be the sweeping 'dignity clause'. . . . [T]he clause inextricably binds freedom from sex discrimination with equality and inviolable human dignity."[7] She says: "Montana lawyers should jettison federal discrimination analysis in favor of a Montana analysis free of gender-based standards."[8]

The idea of protecting human dignity, and the use of the undefined terms "civil" and "political" coupled with a prohibition against private discrimination and the enlargement of the classes required to be protected under this section would seem to guarantee extensive judicial interpretation. In fact, the prohibition against private discrimination; the meaning of political and civil rights that are to be protected; who or what might be included in classes of "social origin or condition," "culture," or "political or religious ideas"; and the significance of "human dignity" remain obscure.

The potential impact of this section on government action and social and economic interaction could be enormous. To date, the Montana Supreme Court has largely ignored the unique dimensions of the section and followed federal equal protection decisions. The clause in Article II, section 4, mimicking Fourteenth Amendment language (i.e. "[n]o person shall be denied the equal protection of the laws"), is the only clause the court has referenced.

---

[7] Wendy A. Fitzgerald, "Toward Dignity in the Workplace: *Miller-Wohl* and Beyond," *Montana Law Review*, 49 (1988): 147.

[8] Wendy A. Fitzgerald, "Toward Dignity in the Workplace: *Miller-Wohl* and Beyond," *Montana Law Review*, 49 (1988): p. 171.

The state supreme court posture relative to individual rights and equal protection is most clearly sculpted in the adjudicative pronouncements found in the following three areas: first, Article II, section 16, which guarantees both a speedy remedy for every injury of person, property, or character and "full legal redress"; second, Article X, section 1, which seems to require a system of free quality public elementary and secondary education and guarantees "equality of educational opportunity"; and third, Article XII, section 3(3), which originally required economic assistance to the needy, but was amended in 1988, changing the phrase from "the legislature *shall* provide economic assistance" to "the legislature *may* provide economic assistance" to those determined by the legislature to be in need. The cases in these three areas develop the general propositions that fundamental rights are limited to "right[s] found within Montana's Declaration of Rights or right[s] without which other constitutionally guaranteed rights would have little meaning" (*Butte Community Union v. Lewis*, 1986); that equal protection does not require that all persons be treated alike but only that all persons be treated alike under like circumstances (*Zempel v. Uninsured Employers Fund*, 1997); that the principal purpose of Article II, section 4 is to insure that persons are not subject to arbitrary and discriminatory governmental action (*McKamey v. State*, 1994); and that there are three levels of analysis. The three levels are: "rational basis," in which the court defers to other branches of government and asks only if it is conceivable that the particular classification is rationally related to a legitimate government purpose; "compelling interest" or "strict scrutiny," in which the court refuses to defer to other branches of government and requires a showing that the challenged law has as its objective a compelling government purpose, and the means used is either necessary or narrowly tailored to achieve the compelling government purpose; and "intermediate," which originally was formulated by the U.S. Supreme Court to require that a classification, to be constitutionally acceptable, must have a substantial relationship to an important government interest. Montana follows the federal analysis but not without differences. In Montana, rational basis does not always mean deference to the state legislature and strict scrutiny is not necessarily fatal (*Arneson v. State of Montana, 1993; Kaptein v. Conrad School District*, 1997; *In re C.H.*, 1984; *Meech v. Hillhaven West, Inc.*, 1989). Further, the intermediate test as developed and applied in Montana requires "the state to demonstrate two factors: (1) that its classification . . . is reasonable; and (2) that its interest in [the particular classification] . . . is more important than the . . . interests of the [persons disadvantaged by the classification]" (*Butte Community Union v. Lewis*, 1986).

Although the Montana Supreme Court has modified and to some extent enlarged traditional federal concepts of equal protection, the decisions have rarely protected the rights of persons charged with criminal conduct. For example, *In re C.S.* (1984) held that a sentence that was more severe than what would have been imposed on an adult for having committed the same act did not deny equal justice to a juvenile. This decision was in apparent violation of section 4 and in conflict with the specific command of Article II, section 15, that provides "persons under 18 years of age shall [have all the] fundamental rights of [Article II] unless specifically precluded by laws which enhance the protection of such persons." The court emphasized the difference between adults and minors in matters of sentencing, stating that the physical liberty interests of minors and adults are qualitatively different. The court also noted that the purpose of detention is not the same for adult and juvenile offenders.

The court has also addressed the problem of equal protection relative to the imposition of capital punishment, and determined that the constitution of the state of Montana provides no additional equal protection beyond that required by the Fourteenth Amendment to the U.S. Constitution as interpreted by the U.S. Supreme Court. The Montana Supreme Court held that a facially neutral statute that results in a disproportionate impact on a suspect class is not a denial of equal protection unless there is also proof of discriminatory purpose (*Fitzpatrick v. State*, 1981).

*State v. Pease* (1987) held that discretionary imposition of the costs of prosecution, without standards, by a district court judge does not violate the constitutional guarantee of equal protection. Presumptively, the imposition of costs based on race or sex would be a violation of equal protection. The court held in *State v. Carroll* (1986) that inability to pay restitution and subsequent incarceration was not violative of equal protection, although the court did determine that in this case there were other justifiable reasons for incarceration. According to the court in *State v. Herrera* (1982), disparate sentences for co-defendants (20 years versus suspended sentence) did not violate equal protection because of different personal histories.

In the area of economic classifications the court has been reasonably consistent in relying on the "rational basis" test, requiring that the classification be rationally related to a legitimate government objective. Sometimes the court has deferred completely to legislative classification, finding anything "conceivable" a justification to validate legislative actions. In *Federal Communications Comm'n v. Beach Communications, Inc.* (1993), Justice Thomas stated:

> In areas of social and economic policy, a statutory classification that neither proceeds along suspect lines nor infringes fundamental constitutional rights must be upheld against equal protection challenge if there is any reasonably conceivable state of facts that could provide a rational basis for the classification, (p. 313)

The Montana court, following Beach Communications in *Stratemeyer v. Lincoln County* (1993), stated: "The purpose of the legislation does not have to appear on the face of the legislation or in the legislative history, but may be any possible purpose of which the court can conceive" (p. 509). In *Arneson v. State of Montana* (1993), the court held that while a post-retirement increase in pensions of beneficiaries of the Teachers' Retirement System was a legitimate government purpose, a classification of teacher retiree beneficiaries excluding non-disability beneficiaries under age 55 was not rationally related to the legitimate government purpose. In a concurring opinion, Justice Treweiller noted that the majority neither followed, distinguished, nor overruled *Stratemeyer*, leaving the two cases decided the same year in direct conflict.

In most cases involving economic classifications the court takes a more careful look at the facts and occasionally concludes that legislative schemes are not rational. The decisions can best be understood by viewing the pragmatics of the individual case and by discerning the personal and political predilections of the members of the court. For example, tax exemptions for business inventories, but not for livestock, passed rational basis equal protection (*Montana Stockgrowers Ass'n v. State*, 1989). New tax valuations based on appraisals that raised taxes in one county above valuations of similar property in another county violated rational basis equal protection (*Montana Dept. of Revenue v. Sheehy*, 1993). Exempting local merchants from an anti-soliciting ordinance violated rational basis equal protection (*Tipco Corp. v. City of Billings*, 1982). Milk control quotas based on past records of milk production potentially violated equal protection (*Vita-Rich Dairy, Inc. v. Department of Business Regulation*, 1976). A variable retroactive increase in tax delinquent interest based solely on the dates of two conflicting Attorney General Opinions rendered within the space of three months did not violate rational basis equal protection. In *O'Shaughnessy v. Wolfe* (1984), the legislature had passed an amendment raising the rate of interest applied to delinquent tax payments. The attorney general subsequently issued two opinions as to whether the increase should be given retroactive application: the first opinion said "no" and the second opinion, issued two months later, said "yes." Appellant claimed that the effect of the Attorney General Opinions was to divide delinquent taxpayers into two groups, those to whom the increase was not applied retroactively, under the first opinion, and those to whom the increase was applied retroactively, under the second opinion. Therefore, retroactive application of the increase violated the Due Process and Equal Protection Clauses of the Montana Constitution as well as the Fourteenth Amendment to the U.S. Constitution. The Montana Supreme Court upheld the district court's dismissal of appellant's claim, ruling that the enactment itself rather than an administrative interpretation of it determines the constitutionality of a law. The court further held that the law is not discriminatory and a delinquent taxpayer does not have a vested right to application of a particular rate of interest. The court seemed to miss the point that a law may violate equal protection on its face or as applied.

## SECTION 5

**Freedom of Religion**. The state shall make no law respecting an establishment of religion or prohibiting the free exercise thereof.

This section purports to protect religious freedom in the state of Montana, guaranteeing the freedom to practice one's religion and the prohibition of statesponsored religion. The section is derived from and nearly identical with the religious freedom clause of the First Amendment to the U.S. Constitution, substituting the word "state" for "Congress." Article III, section 4 of the 1889 Montana Constitution, the predecessor provision guaranteeing religious freedom, was lengthy and detailed. It expressed a particular concern about, and antagonism toward, Mormon polygamy, specifying that "liberty of conscience hereby secured shall not . . . excuse acts of licentiousness by bigamous or polygamous marriage."

Little debate or serious philosophical discussion preceded the draft and passage of the guarantee of religious freedom. Perhaps this was because the identical phrase found in the U.S. Constitution was made applicable to all states (*Cantwell v. State of Connecticut*, 1940: free exercise clause; and *Everson v. Board of Education*, 1947: establishment clause). It is possible that the Montana Supreme Court could interpret the Montana provision to afford greater protection to the individual than does the U.S. Constitution. The two aspects of religious freedom, "establishment" on the one side and "free exercise" on the other, make the concept of religious freedom theoretically more difficult to enlarge by reference to a state constitution than most other personal freedoms. "Free exercise" can collide with "establishment" resulting in some unusual and difficult patterns of reconciliation. The few cases that the Montana Supreme Court has considered have followed U.S. Supreme Court precedent as precisely as such precedent could be understood.

Article X, section 6 of the 1972 Montana Constitution, a new section, prohibits aid to sectarian schools. The section is a specific and relatively broad prohibition against "establishment" of religion, declaring that "[t]he legislature, counties, cities, towns, school districts, and public corporations shall not make any direct or indirect appropriation or payment from any public fund or monies, or any grant of lands or other property for any sectarian purpose or to aid any church, school, academy, seminary, college, university, or other literary or scientific institution, controlled in whole or in part by any church, sect, or denomination."

In recent cases decided under the 1972 Constitution, the court has declined to intervene in what appeared to be internal church affairs. *Miller v. Catholic Diocese of Great Falls* (1986) involved the discharge of a parochial school teacher who claimed violations of due process and equal protection, alleging breach of the implied covenant of good faith and fair dealing. The court maintained

that to allow the lawsuit to go forward would impermissibly interfere with the free exercise of religion. Two U.S. Supreme Court cases (*Lemon v. Kurtzman*, 1971 and *Wisconsin v. Yoder*, 1972) were cited to support the court's reasoning.

In another case, the court denied a defamation claim, finding the publication of the questioned statements to have been made within the congregation and based on ecclesiastical doctrine. The court held that under the circumstances the statements were privileged under Montana defamation law, Montana Code Annotated, section 27-1-804, and the court would be violating the church leaders' right to free exercise of religion if it were to find the leaders' statements actionable (*Rasmussen v. Bennett*, 1987).

A most interesting interpretation of the prolix and detailed 1889 Montana constitutional provision on religious freedom was prescient of the U.S. Supreme Court decision denying the Native American Church religious sacramental use of peyote (*Employment Division v. Smith*, 1990). In 1926 the Montana Supreme Court decided that religious freedom did not restrict the state of Montana from prohibiting the possession of peyote for sacramental purposes (*State v. Big Sheep*, 1926). Minority disenchantment with the *Smith* free exercise test upholding any "neutral law of general application" resulted in Congress passing the Religious Freedom Restoration Act (RIFRA), Pub. L. 103–141, 107 Stat. 1488 (1993). RIFRA, an attempt to reinstate the compelling interest test, was found unconstitutional (*City of Boerne v. Flores*, 1997). It seems probable that the current Montana Supreme Court would employ the compelling interest test in the interpretation of the Montana free exercise provision, at least insofar as the particular facts before the court do not pose a conflict between free exercise and establishment.

An earlier case decided under the 1889 Montana Constitution upheld as constitutional a corporate license tax applied to a religious society created for the purposes of farming, stock growing, and other agricultural pursuits (*State v. King Colony Ranch*, 1960). The case is in harmony with more recent U.S. Supreme Court decisions on taxation and religious freedom (*Tony and Susan Alamo Foundation v. Secretary of Labor*, 1985; and *Jimmy Swaggart Ministries v. Board of Equalization of California*, 1990).

The only available evidence indicating that Montana might be more rigorous in prohibiting official support of a religion is an Attorney General Opinion stating that alternative renewable energy source grants may not be awarded to any church or to any school, academy, seminary, college, university, or other literary or scientific institution controlled in whole or in part by any church, sect, or denomination. The government may award grants to religious organizations if a substantial portion of their functions are secular and they will only use grants for such functions (37 Op. Att'y Gen. 683 (1978)). The opinion is more directly based on Article X, section 6 that specifically prohibits aid to sectarian schools, than on the provision for religious freedom found in Article II, section 5 of Montana's Declaration of Rights. The language of Article X, section 2 suggests that there could be constitutionally acceptable federal grants to sectarian organizations that would not be acceptable if the money originated within the state.

## SECTION 6

**Freedom of Assembly**. The people shall have the right peaceably to assemble, petition for redress or peaceably protest governmental action.

The section guarantees the basic right of the people to assemble, to petition, and to protest. It is derived from Article III, section 26 of the 1889 Montana Constitution and from the First Amendment to the U.S. Constitution. It is also traceable to the Case of the Seven Bishops in 1688 and the 1689 English Bill of Rights.[9] The provision is substantively similar to the last clause of the First Amendment to the U.S. Constitution. The limitation on the right to assemble "for the common good" found in the 1889 Constitution was eliminated, and the word "protest" included in this section is not found in either the federal constitution or the earlier Montana Constitution.

The freedom to assemble, protest, and petition for redress of governmental action is largely a subset of the freedom of speech and association as interpreted by the U.S. Supreme Court. The act of petition and protest against government was a special concern and subject to prosecution as seditious libel in early England. Freedom of assembly and protest emphasizes a particular kind of expressive action and gives added protection to group expression and the right of association. Article II, section 7 of Montana's 1972 Constitution uses the nominally broader phrase "speech or expression" in defining protected speech.

The court relied upon the provision to void legislation enacted by initiative that was intended to require disclosure of all private funding for state lobbyists (*Montana Automobile Ass'n v. Greely*, 1981). Failure to prove that disclosure of lobbyist funding met a compelling state interest rendered the law unconstitutional.

Subsequently, in *Dorn v. Board of Trustees* (1983), the Montana Supreme Court recognized that the state, by appropriate state law, could regulate the constitutional right to assemble and petition. In relying on the "compelling state interests" test to find the "lobbyist funding disclosure" legislation unconstitutional in *Montana Automobile Ass'n v. Greely* (1981), the court failed to discuss the extent to which the particular regulation infringed the right to petition. The lobbyist funding disclosure law did not eliminate the right to petition nor restrict the amount of money or the kinds of entities that could spend money for lobbying activities. It only required that secret lobbying sources be made public. The court emphasized freedom of speech, and its subset, the right to petition government. The court should have at least considered the competing constitutional

---

[9] Kermit L. Hall et al., *American Legal History: Cases and Materials* (New York: Oxford University Press, 1991), pp. 6–8.

rights of individual privacy, Article II, section 10, and the right to know, Article II, section 9.

Closely aligned with the freedom of assembly and an important part of the opinion in *Montana Automobile Ass'n v. Greely* (1981) is the Montana constitutional provision relating to initiatives, Article III, section 4. The freedom to petition is in Article II, the Montana Declaration of Rights, while the process of petition via initiative is in Article III. The Montana Supreme Court has categorically stated that rights not included in the Declaration of Rights of Montana's Constitution are to be afforded less protection (*In re S.L.M.*, 1997).

In *Dorn v. Board of Trustees* (1983), the Montana Supreme Court's discussion of time, place, and manner regulations on the right to use public places for expressive activity corresponded to the U.S. Supreme Court's discussions in *Groyned v. City of Rockford* (1972) and *Tinker v. Des Moines Indep. School District* (1969). The court noted that the right of public assembly may be regulated. The school district had a general policy prohibiting solicitation of any kind in school buildings. The policy prohibited gathering signatures for an initiative petition on election day in a school building used as a polling place. The court found that the school district's policy was not narrowly tailored to further its interests in undisrupted school functioning and that the fear of disrupting school functioning was unrelated to the facts in the case at bar and insufficient to overcome the right to freedom of expression.

Freedom of speech as separate from the freedom of association and freedom of assembly may have been a more appropriate basis for the decision in this case. The court cited First Amendment U.S. Supreme Court cases to support its decision and specifically used the language "expressive activity." Whereas the U.S. Constitution incorporates the concepts of speech, association, assembly, and religion in a single amendment, the Montana Constitution has separated the concepts into three sections: section 6, freedom of assembly and association; section 7, freedom of speech, expression, and the press; and section 5, freedom of religion.

Although the Montana Supreme Court has relied on U.S. constitutional decisions in interpreting this section, the thrust of the two cases that have been decided under the 1972 Montana Constitution indicate a tendency to enlarge the "right of assembly" beyond its parent provision in the U.S. Constitution.

## SECTION 7

**Freedom of Speech, Expression, and Press.** No law shall be passed impairing the freedom of speech or expression. Every person shall be free to speak or publish whatever he will on any subject, being responsible for all abuse of that liberty. In all suits and prosecutions for libel or slander the truth thereof may be given in evidence; and the jury, under the direction of the court, shall determine the law and the facts.

The first sentence is probably more protective of the right of speech than the federal counterpart, prohibiting "impairment" being more comprehensive than prohibiting "abridgement." The second sentence is theoretically less protective, since a requirement of responsibility not found in the U.S. Constitution modifies freedom of speech and the press. Freedom of expression is fundamental to a government based on representational democracy (*Montana Automobile Ass'n v. Greely,* 1981). It is fundamental to human dignity and to a sense of personal self-awareness and identification and, therefore, central to any Bill of Rights. Whether it is an important aspect of a state constitution is another question because the right is accorded substantial protection under the U.S. Constitution. It is doubtful that the state of Montana will expand the right beyond the parameters already specified by the U.S. Supreme Court. The convention committee wished to stress the primacy of these guarantees in the hope that their enforcement would not continue merely in the wake of federal case law (MCC Rep. 630).

This section is derived from and nearly identical to Article III, section 10 of the 1889 Montana Constitution. The addition of the words "or expression" expands the protection for speech, in theory if not in fact, and accords with the U.S. Supreme Court interpretation of "speech" as found in the First Amendment to the U.S. Constitution. Truth as a defense in all libel and slander cases was added, expanding the power of the jury to determine both the law and the facts in both libel and slander cases. The 1972 convention delegates apparently intended to invoke more populous control over speech and press cases; however, the delegates did not debate this issue in depth and there is no indication whether the delegates or the voters seriously considered either the historical background or the political justification for the particular language.[10] The Montana Supreme Court has admitted evidence of truth but refused to recognize any power in the jury to determine applicable law, with or without judicial direction (*State v. Barnes,* 1988).

The Montana Supreme Court has been cautious in interpreting the constitutional protection of freedom of speech and press. It has not pushed the limits of free speech beyond what the U.S. Supreme Court's interpretation of the First Amendment requires. In *Wurtzv. Risly* (1983), overruling *State v. Wurtz* (1981), the Ninth Circuit Court of Appeals held that the Montana criminal intimidation statute violated the First Amendment because the mere fact that communication induces or coerces an action in others does not remove it from First Amendment protection. The court determined that the statute was overbroad in that it regulated "pure speech" rather than conduct. A later Montana case,

[10] See *Bushell's Case,* 124 Eng. Rep. 1006 (C.P. 1670); and Paul Finkelman (ed.), *A Brief Narrative of the Case and Tryal of John Peter Zenger* (Union, NJ: Lawbook Exchange, 2000).

*State v. Lance* (1986), held a crime of intimidation that punishes threats of physical confinement and physical restraint is not an unconstitutional violation of free speech. Threats are not speech protected by the First Amendment to the U.S. Constitution, nor, evidently, by Article II, section 7 of the Montana Constitution.

Several Montana cases have relied on the U.S. Supreme Court's interpretation of the First Amendment to the U.S. Constitution. For example, a state agency refused to hire the plaintiff in *Taliaferro v. Department of Social and Rehabilitation Services* (1988) because of her support for certain legislation pending before the legislature. The court cited the U.S. Supreme Court case *Pickering v. Board of Education* (1968), which held that a public employee does not relinquish her First Amendment right to comment on matters of public interest by virtue of government employment. The *Pickering* decision involved firing a teacher for public expression, not for declining to hire. Although the Montana Supreme Court opinion mentioned discrimination, it discussed and relied on freedom of speech, not equal protection. *Small v. McRae* (1982) supported a similar argument, although the court did not reach a holding favorable to the protection of free speech because the complaint failed to state sufficient facts.

A majority of Montana free speech cases have supported regulations on speech. The court held that the necessity of orderly conduct justifies the use of force to physically remove disorderly persons from a public meeting and is not a violation of the freedom of speech (*State v. Lowery,* 1988). In State v. Woods (1986), the court found that a statute prohibiting solicitation of false testimony does not violate the freedom of speech because the right to freedom of speech is not absolute and may be regulated if the regulating statutes are narrowly and precisely drawn. The court maintained that the state's interest in prohibiting such solicitation must be balanced with the defendant's right to speak. Because witness tampering presents an imminent threat to the trial process, an aspect central to a Democratic society, the court held that prohibiting witness tampering does not violate either the U.S. or Montana constitutional guarantees of the right to free speech. According to the Montana Supreme Court, constitutional free speech does not include disturbing the peace by loud and obscene language (*Whitefish v. O'Shaughnessy,* 1985) nor "fighting words" (*Billings v. Batten,* 1985). It should be noted that neither of these decisions necessarily conform to minimum federal requirements for the protection of free speech. Other speech which may be regulated includes soliciting signatures for initiative in school (*Dorn v. Board of Trustees,* 1983); extraordinarily high licensing fees for adult movie video booths (*Great Falls v. M.K. Enterprises,* 1987); and a local ordinance prohibiting door to door solicitation (*Tipco Corp. v. City of Billings,* 1982).

Corporate and commercial concerns involving freedom of speech have been protected but the judicial pattern seems to be more reflective of a conservative political agenda than a concern for free speech. The court held that corporations are entitled to freedom of speech under both the First Amendment to the U.S.

Constitution and the parallel provision of the Montana Constitution. The Ninth Circuit Court of Appeals found that portion of Montana Code Annotated, Section 13-35-227, which prohibited contributions by corporations in support of or opposition to ballot issues, to be an unconstitutional restriction of corporate rights to free speech (*C & C Plywood Corp. v. Hanson*, 1978). In 1998 the Montana Federal District Court, relying on *First Nat'l Bank of Boston v. Bellotti* (1978), and *Buckley v. Valeo* (1976), held unconstitutional a historically and politically complicated initiative. As amended by the legislature, the initiative (statute) broadened the scope of prohibited expenditure in connection with ballot issues to include non-profit as well as for-profit corporations and added partnerships, associations, cooperatives, and other organizations. It appeared that the legislature amended the initiative, intentionally adding a "poison pill," threatening the constitutionality of the initiative without the politically difficult action of immediately countermanding the electorate (*Montana Chamber of Commerce v. Argenbright*, 1998). Assuming the finding of unconstitutionality is either affirmed or certiorary is denied, the Montana courts will almost surely face a number of suits relative to all initiatives and referenda. The Montana Supreme Court also found unconstitutional the lobbyists' financial disclosure law, a law strongly opposed by most corporations (*Montana Automobile Ass'n v. Greely*, 1981).

Free speech issues in drug cases are unlikely to be seriously considered. In upholding "The Montana Model Drug Paraphernalia Act" (Mont. Code Ann., Section 45-10-101), the Ninth Circuit noted that the only right arguably implicated by the Act was commercial speech, and that right was not constitutionally protected in this instance because the statute is expressly directed at commercial activity promoting or encouraging illegal drug use (*Stoianoff v. Montana*, 1983).

The court has been more rigorous in prior restraint cases. Prior restraint of speech is possible but must pass a rigorous test. In *Kuiper v. District Court* (1981), the Montana Supreme Court found protective orders precluding the use of certain documents to be unconstitutional. The case cited three criteria that must first be satisfied: "(1) the harm posed by dissemination must be substantial and serious; (2) the restraining order must be narrowly drawn and be precise; (3) there must be no alternative means of protecting the public interest that would intrude less directly on expression" (p. 698). Under the applicable free speech provision of the 1889 Montana Constitution, the court held that both the legislature and the courts were without authority to enjoin persons from speaking (*Empire Theatre Co. v. Cloke*, 1917).

Finally, the special problems of defamation have largely and necessarily followed U.S. Supreme Court decisions. This includes truth as a defense (*Lussy v. Davidson*, 1984); the concept of public figure (*Williams v. Pasma*, 1982); and the requirement of proof of negligence (*Madison v. Yunker*, 1978).

The final sentence of Article II, section 7, which charges the jury with a duty to determine both law and facts, has not had any significant impact on the law as interpreted. Case interpretations of similar language in the 1889 Constitution drained the language of all significant meaning. The court has never investigated nor analyzed the historical significance of the language, superficially concluding that the function of the court and jury is not greatly different in defamation than in other cases. The court, and not the jury, decides upon the admissibility of evidence and upon motions for non-suits, directed verdicts, new trials, setting aside verdicts, or vacating judgments. The court has held that defamation cases are subject to the same rules of practice generally employed in other cases (*Griffin v. Opinion Pub. Co., 1943; Manley v. Harer*, 1928).

The court has also noted that free speech does not include the right to cause substantial emotional distress by harassment or intimidation (*State v. Nye*, 1997). In addition, the court found that the stalking statute, Montana Code Annotated, Section 45-5-220, is not violative of free speech: the defendant stalker's conduct inflicted injury on the victim by causing substantial emotional distress and his conduct lacked any social value (*State v. Cooney, 1995*).

In a civil action for defamation, truth is an absolute defense barring any recovery by plaintiff. However, under the criminal defamation statute, Montana Code Annotated, Section 45-8-212, truth was not allowed as an absolute defense, impermissibly requiring the defendant to prove that the material, even if true, was communicated in good faith and for justifiable ends. However, the court said this statute was overbroad and that truth alone is sufficient as an absolute defense (*State v. Helfrich*, 1996).

## SECTION 8

**Right of Participation.** The public has the right to expect governmental agencies to afford such reasonable opportunity for citizen participation in the operation of the agencies prior to the final decision as may be provided by law.

This section creates the right of public participation in government decision making and suggests that the legislature will provide the means for and the scope of public participation. The section was a response not only to the perceived secrecy and insider deal-making in state government but to an elitist and secretive federal bureaucracy over which the state has no control. This section, in conjunction with Article II, section 9, the "right to know" provision, is intended to encourage open government in support of representational democracy and to maximize citizen access to the decision-making institutions of state government (MCC Rep. 630).

The provision is new. There is no comparable provision in the Constitution of 1889 nor is there a comparable provision in either the Virginia Bill of Rights or in the U.S. Constitution. In response to this section, the legislature has passed a number of laws that require governmental agencies to afford citizens an opportunity to participate in decision making.

None of the decisions interpreting the section have favored public participation in government decision making; each decision has justified the prohibition of participation or narrowing the scope of public participation (*Kadillak v. The Anaconda Co*, 1979; *Montana Consumer Counsel, Brazier v. Public Service Commission and Montana Power Co.*, 1975).

The most significant case focused on the "Hard Rock Mining Act." In *Kadillak v. The Anaconda Co.*, the court found that the Hard Rock Mining Act does not provide for public participation in the decision-making process preceding issuance of a permit. The court concluded that the constitutional right to participation and the contested hearing provisions of the Montana Administrative Procedure Act were not invoked.

The final phrase of the section "as may be provided by law" suggests legislative implementation is required and that the section is not self-executing. The public has a "right to expect" reasonable opportunity to participate in governmental decision making to the extent specified by the legislature.

The court has said that the open meeting law requires public notice of a meeting subject to that law. Without public notice, a meeting is open to the public in theory only, not in practice (*Common Cause of Mont. v. Statutory Comm. to Nominate Candidates for Comm'r of Political Practices*, 1994). An Attorney General Opinion concluded that the Montana Administrative Procedure Act, Title 2, ch. 4, part 3, fulfills the constitutional mandate that citizens of the state be afforded reasonable opportunity for participation in agency decision making in the context of rule making by providing notice and hearing (38 Op. Att'y Gen. 240 (1980)).

## SECTION 9

**Right to Know.** No person shall be deprived of the right to examine documents or to observe the deliberations of all public bodies or agencies of state government and its subdivisions, except in cases in which the demand of individual privacy clearly exceeds the merits of public disclosure.

The section is premised on the idea that government should be open and subject to public scrutiny. The only justifiable exception to the public's right to know is individual privacy and then only to the extent that individual privacy clearly exceeds the merits of public disclosure (MCC Rep. 632). This is a new provision. There is no comparable provision in the 1889 Montana Constitution and no right to know is mentioned in the U.S. Constitution, nor has the U.S. Supreme Court found one in the penumbras of the U.S. Constitution. Montana demands open government, and support for the right to know must be based exclusively on the Montana Constitution. This provision, in conjunction with Montana's constitutional right of participation, has helped bring state bureaucracy to an understanding that government is derived from the people, is intended for the benefit of the people, and the people have a right to know what their government is doing. The people have a right to participate and do participate in the process of government; the people have a right to know what government is doing, to demand information about government activities, and to obtain the information requested. Montana state government is more open and accessible as a direct result of this section.

Montana is one of only four states that have explicit constitutional right to know provisions, and Montana is the only state that does not dilute the right with open-ended exceptions. The only limitation placed on the right to know is the right of individual privacy.[11]

Several significant interpretations have helped clarify the contours of the section. First, the section is self-executing and legislation is not required to give it effect (*In re Lacy*, 1989). Second, a corporation, as well as a natural person, has a right to individual privacy and can assert the right to privacy as an exception to the constitutional right to know, although this is contrary to both the language and the apparent intent of the convention delegates (*Belth v. Bennett*, 1987; citing *Mountain States Tel. & Tel. v. Department of Public Service Regulation*, 1981). Third, a government agency cannot vicariously assert an individual's privacy interest without either obtaining authorization from the individual whose privacy is at risk or without notifying the individual. If notification is not possible the government agency "should independently weigh the privacy interests . . . and 'provide maximum access to the information while protecting the individual's right to privacy'" (p. 116) (*Worden v. Montana Board of Pardons and Parole*, 1998).

A number of cases have relied on this provision to open government operations, including the following: the public has a right to know what happens in the judicial system, including the filing of civil suits (*Cox v. Lee Enterprises*, 1986); the press and public may attend a voir dire examination which had been closed by the district court, thus imposing a more exacting standard to authorize closure of a trial than required by the U.S. Constitution (*Great Falls Tribune v. District Court*, 1980); an insurer was permitted to gain access to criminal justice information pertaining to the investigation of the death of an insured (*Allstate Ins. Co. v. Billings*, 1989); and evidentiary materials filed with the court fall within the public's constitutional right to know (*State ex rel. The Missoulian v. District Court*, 1997). In *Great Falls Tribune Co., Inc. v. Sheriff* (1989), the court approved the disclosure of the names of police officers who had been disciplined, noting that the people's right to know outweighs the officers' minimal right of privacy. In *Great Falls Tribune Co., Inc. v. Day* (1998), the state Procurement Act prohibiting

---

[11] Larry M. Elison & Deborah E. Elison, "Comments on Government Censorship and Secrecy," *Montana Law Review* 55 (1994): 190.

disclosure of proposals, in this case screening proposals for construction of a private prison, violated the constitution. The court stated:

> This case involves the perception of State officials that private negotiations are in the State's short-term economic interest. However, the delegates to the Constitutional Convention made a clear and unequivocal decision that government operates most effectively, most reliably, and is most accountable when it is subject to public scrutiny. It is that fundamental principle of this State's constitutional law which is the basis for this Court's decision, (p. 515)

Some earlier cases were more restrictive. For example, a graduate student doing research was denied sheriff's department information (*Engrav v. Cragun,* 1989); closure of a probation revocation hearing was constitutionally permissible to protect individual privacy (*State ex rel. Great Falls Tribune Co., Inc. v. District Court,* 1989); and job performance evaluations of university presidents could be withheld from public scrutiny based on the need to protect individual privacy (*Missoulian v. Board of Regents,* 1984). The non-disclosure of a university president's job performance evaluations seems based more on power and prestige than individual privacy balanced against the right to know.

The right to know, if read literally, prevails over all competing rights except individual privacy. However, in case decisions the court has held the right to know must be balanced against other competing constitutional interests in the context of each case. For example, the court held that a criminal defendant's right to a fair trial is paramount to the public's right to know (*State ex rel. Smith v. District Court,* 1982).

There are a number of Attorney General Opinions which have dealt with the right to know provision. Most of the opinions indicate that the right to know about government operations is a paramount right with which governmental agencies must conform.

## SECTION 10

> **Right of Privacy**. The right of individual privacy is essential to the well being of a free society and shall not be infringed without the showing of a compelling state interest.

The delegates realized that the Montana Supreme Court had recognized the right of privacy, but believed it important to explicitly include the right in the constitution (MCC Rep. 2484). During the debate the last clause, "shall not be infringed without the showing of a compelling state interest," was deleted. After the legal significance of "compelling state interest" was explained, the clause was restored. While the section guarantees the right of individual privacy, deducing the meaning and scope of privacy in concrete cases remains difficult. By reference to the constitutional convention transcripts, it is safe to assume that privacy protected by this section encompasses in some measure the right to be free from government observation, intrusion, or disclosure (MCC Tr. 1681, 1684, 1851); and the right to some level of personal autonomy (i.e., the freedom to choose) (*Gryczan v. State*, 1997). The word "individual" was added during debate on this provision and the phrase "individual privacy" was not intended to include corporations (MCC Tr. 1680, 1681). And finally, the convention transcripts indicate the delegates intended to protect citizens from private action that might impinge on individual privacy, as well as from governmental action that invaded the right (MCC Rep. 632).

Montana constitutional delegates favored an explicit right of privacy, apparently believing "Montana privacy" should be something special. Until recently, development of the right has tended to follow U.S. Supreme Court decisions. Non-public invasions of privacy have not been protected. Corporations have been afforded rights of "individual" privacy, and until 1997 there was no mention of the right of personal autonomy.

There was no explicit right of privacy in the former constitution, although Article III, section 7 of the 1889 Montana Constitution provided for a measure of privacy, guaranteeing that "[t]he people shall be secure in their persons, papers, homes and effects." Article II section II of the 1972 Montana Constitution duplicates this search and seizure provision.

The right to privacy is derived from federal and state case law that in turn found its genesis in scholarly writing.[12] The pivotal U.S. Supreme Court decisions were the dissent in *Poe v. Ullman* (1961) and the several opinions in *Griswold v. Connecticut* (1965). Although the U.S. Constitution makes no explicit mention of a right of privacy, the U.S. Supreme Court has found the right in the emanations from, and in the penumbras of, other constitutional rights; in the Ninth Amendment; and in some concept of fundamental liberty based on language from the Fourteenth Amendment coupled with ideas of natural law and substantive due process.

The Montana right of privacy in the area of sexual preference (*Gryczan v. State*, 1997) was expanded beyond the U.S. Supreme Court interpretation (*Bowers v. Hardwick*, 1986). In *Gryczan* the court reasoned that all adults have an expectation of privacy in non-commercial, consensual sexual conduct and, while society may disapprove of homosexual conduct, society still recognizes that expectation of privacy, including private homosexual acts (*Gryczan v. State*, 1997). The opinion focused on the objectively acceptable "reasonable expectation of privacy" derived from the U.S. Supreme Court decision in *Katz v. United States* (1967), a criminal procedure case concerned with the intrasional aspect of privacy. The personal autonomy dimension of privacy discussed in *Bowers v.*

---

[12] See Samuel Warren & Louis Brandeis, "The Right to Privacy," *Harvard Law Review*, 4 (1890): 193.

*Hardwick* was mentioned as an alternative basis for the decision. The Montana court said that "[r]egardless of whether *Bowers* was correctly decided, we have long held that Montana's Constitution affords citizens broader protection of their right to privacy than does the federal constitution" (p. 221).

In *Armstrong v. State* (1999), a case striking down a Montana statute (Montana Code Annotated, Section 37-20-103) that prohibited "physicians assistant-certified" from performing abortions, the court reiterated that "Montana adheres to one of the most stringent protections of its citizens' right to privacy in the United States—exceeding even that provided by the federal constitution" (p. 373). Later in the opinion the court added, "Montana's constitution affords *significantly* broader protection than does the federal constitution" (p. 375) (emphasis added).

The most interesting segment of the opinion discusses the meaning of personal autonomy, recognizing that "defining personal autonomy has and continues to challenge courts, philosophers and authors" (p. 374), and concludes that:

> while [personal autonomy] . . . may not be absolute, no final boundaries can be drawn around the personal autonomy component of the right of individual privacy. It is, at one and the same time, as narrow as is necessary to protect against a specific unlawful infringement of individual dignity and personal autonomy by the government—as in *Gryczan* (a case holding unconstitutional Montana's statute criminalizing homosexual conduct) and as broad as are the State's ever innovative attempts to dictate in matters of conscience, to define individual values, and to condemn those found to be socially repugnant or politically unpopular. (p. 375)

The court further notes that the Montana Constitution's declaration of rights is a "cohesive set of principles" of "overlapping and redundant rights and guarantees" (p. 383). Other concepts embedded in the constitutional declaration of rights that protect personal and procreative autonomy beyond privacy include respect for dignity, equality of right to follow one's conscience, the inalienable right to seek health and happiness, the right to accept or reject any religious doctrine, and the right to substantive due process inherent in the historical concept of "ordered liberty."

Most privacy cases, other than search and seizure, have focused on the request for information from government officials who claim, with the Montana Supreme Court upholding their claim, that the collection, use, and dissemination of private facts by government agencies threaten individual privacy rights. These include law enforcement records (*Engrav v. Cragun*, 1989); realty transfer records (*O'Neill v. Department of Revenue*, 1987); job evaluations of public officials (*Missoulian v. Board of Regents*, 1984); and medical records (*State v. Nelson*, 1997). Even harmless or generally known information is sometimes afforded constitutional privacy protection (*Goyen v. Troy*, 1996). However, it should be noted that *Worden v. Montana Board of Pardons and Parole* (1998) limited the vicarious assertion of individual privacy by public officials and may modify the conclusions reached in some earlier cases.

Other cases have determined that the constitutional right to privacy is not sufficiently compelling to shield information accumulated by government agencies or to keep official misconduct secret. These include the release of police records to an insurance company (*In re Lacy*, 1989), identification of disciplined police officers (*Great Falls Tribune Co., Inc. v. Sheriff*, 1989), and the report of an elected official's alleged misconduct in office (*Citizens to Recall Mayor James Whitlock v. Whitlock*, 1992).

Finally, some records have been released subject to protective orders. In an investigation of human rights violations the Human Rights Commission was allowed to access personnel files, but the Commission was prohibited from disclosing the information (*Montana Human Rights Division v. City of Billings*, 1982). The court required a telephone utility to release trade secrets to the Public Service Commission to aid in rate-making decisions, but issued a protective order preventing access to the secrets by the general public (*Mountain States Tel. & Tel. v. Department of Public Service Regulation*, 1981). In each case the requesting agency obtained the information allowing it to carry out its duties, but the information was not made available to the public and privacy prevailed over the right to know.

The Montana Supreme Court has stated that the privacy provision in the state constitution provides greater protection for individual privacy in search and seizure cases than the federal law; see, for example, *State v. Olson* (1979), *State v. Sawyer* (1977), *State v. Brackman* (1978), *State v. Solis* (1984), and *State v. Sierra* (1985). From the mid-1980s through the early 1990s, Montana cases provided no greater protection for individual privacy in search and seizure cases than parallel federal case law. The most significant retrenchment search and seizure privacy case decided under the 1972 Montana Constitution was *State v. Long* (1985), in which the court held that the privacy section of Article II applies only to state action, and the fruits of an illegal search conducted by a private citizen without governmental participation are not subject to exclusion. In so holding, the court overruled well-established Montana precedent that evidence obtained via an illegal private search invades protected privacy rights and must be suppressed (*State v. Brecht*, 1971; *State v. Helfrich*, 1979; and *State v. Van Haele*, 1982). Other cases such as *State v. Hawkins* (1989), *State v. Holzapfel* (1988), and *Helena v. Lamping* (1986) declined to expand search and seizure protection, but followed federal precedent in narrowing search and seizure protection. *State v. Brown* (1988), overruling *State v. Brackman* (1978), held that warrantless face-to-face electronic surveillance is constitutionally permissible.

Since 1995 the Montana Supreme Court has placed an increased emphasis on privacy as a mechanism to support interpretation of search and seizure cases. For example, a person may have an expectation of privacy in an area of land beyond the curtilage that society recognizes as reasonable and where the expectation of privacy is evidenced by no more than fencing or signs (*State v. Bullock*, 1995). The use of thermal imaging technology by the government in the absence of a search warrant requires the demonstration of a compelling state interest closely tailored to effectuate only that compelling interest, not simply enforcement of the criminal statutes (*State v. Siegal*, 1997).

## SECTION 11

**Searches and Seizures.** The people shall be secure in their persons, papers, homes and effects from unreasonable searches and seizures. No warrant to search any place, or seize any person or thing shall issue without describing the place to be searched or the person or thing to be seized, or without probable cause, supported by oath or affirmation reduced to writing.

This section is derived from and identical to Article III, section 7 of the 1889 Montana Constitution, except for minor changes in punctuation. The section is substantively identical with, and originally copied from the Fourth Amendment to the U.S. Constitution. Although unchanged, the convention committee did not intend that the section authorize, explicitly or implicitly, the interception of communications (wiretaps) by state officials (MCC Rep. 633).

The search and seizure provision in the U.S. Constitution was a direct response to the English "general warrant," which permitted agents of the British government to search homes of colonialists virtually at will, primarily in search of untaxed goods. State constitutions included it as a principal aspect of the criminal process to insure that the overwhelming power of government not be used in an arbitrary and discriminatory fashion and to guarantee some measure of individual privacy.

Immediately following the passage of the 1972 Constitution, court decisions broadened search and seizure power. *State v. Long* (1985) overruled the well-established Montana holding that private searches invade privacy rights. Under the federal constitution, evidence seized illegally by a private person is admissible (*United States v. Henderson*, 1983). Under Montana law prior to *State v. Long*, evidence seized illegally by a private, non-governmental agent was not admissible (*State v. Helfrich*, 1979). The *State v. Long* court held that the privacy section of the constitution contemplates privacy invasion only by state action. Similarly, in *State v. Brown* (1988), the Montana Supreme Court overruled *State v. Brackman* (1978) which had required a search warrant or prior showing of compelling state interest before the state was permitted to monitor or record a private conversation even where one of the participants had consented to the monitoring.

Generally, cases raising search and seizure questions under Article II, section 11 of the 1972 Montana Constitution have followed the lead of the U.S.

Supreme Court. The best example is *State v. Crain* (1986) in which the court held that the *Aguilar v. Texas* (1964) and *Spinelli v. United States* (1969) tests were met, and gratuitously added that the U.S. Supreme Court decision in *Illinois v. Gates* (1983) (the "totality of the circumstances" test for determining the sufficiency of the evidence to issue a search warrant) would replace the more stringent two-pronged *Aguilar-Spinelli* test. Another example is *State v. Burke* (1988) overruling *State v. Fogarty* (1980) on warrantless search of probationers' car and residence, adopting the "reasonable grounds" standard of *Griffin v. Wisconsin* (1987).

Since 1990, decisions have granted increased individual protection to privacy, limiting the scope of constitutionally permissible searches and seizures. In *Billings v. Whalen* (1990), the Montana Supreme Court held that a defendant was in his home because he had one foot inside his doorway, and an officer's restraining the defendant constituted an illegal, warrantless arrest of the defendant for a misdemeanor committed at some other place and time. Where a magistrate became an active participant in a police investigation, his impartiality ceased and he could no longer make a neutral evaluation of the evidence to determine whether probable cause existed, and therefore the search warrant was invalid (*State v. Wilson*, 1994). An investigatory stop must be justified by some objective manifestation that the person stopped is or is about to be engaged in criminal activity, and the totality of the circumstances must give the police a particularized and objective basis for suspecting the person of criminal activity. When the totality of the circumstances does not support a particularized suspicion, the investigatory stop is unjustified (*State v. Reynolds*, 1995). Because a search warrant application did not establish the existence of the fair probability that evidence would be found in defendant's residence, even though a reliable informant provided information of defendant's suspected criminal activity, the search warrant should not have been issued (*State v. Kaluza*, 1995). And in 1997 the court said that Montana's Constitution affords citizens broader protection from warrantless governmental intrusion in search and seizure cases than does the U.S. Constitution (*State v. Siegal*, 1997).

## SECTION 12

**Right to Bear Arms.** The right of any person to keep or bear arms in defense of his own home, person, and property, or in aid of the civil power when thereto legally summoned, shall not be called in question, but nothing herein contained shall be held to permit the carrying of concealed weapons.

The section is derived from and identical to Article II, section 13 of the 1889 Montana Constitution. The Second Amendment to the U.S. Constitution includes language that "the right of the people to keep and bear Arms, shall not be infringed." The U.S. Supreme Court has never held that the language of the Second Amendment to the U.S. Constitution guarantees the right of citizens to keep and bear arms. Further, the Second Amendment, whatever its meaning, has not been made applicable to the states (*United States v. Cruikshank,* 1876). The language of the state constitution is more clearly protective of the individual right to keep and bear arms as contrasted with a collective right (MCC Rep. 634). The only limitation on Montana's guarantee of the right to keep and bear arms is that permits may be required to carry concealed weapons.

The question of gun control is a very emotional issue in Montana. The right to bear arms is strongly supported by a number of small fringe political organizations, as well as the local chapters of the National Rifle Association, Montana hunters, and Montana gun dealers. The constitutional terms are unequivocal and unchanged from the parallel provision in the 1889 Montana Constitution. The only change suggested during the 1972 Constitutional Convention was adding the language that no "person's firearms [shall] be registered or licensed." The proposed language was debated and narrowly defeated: 53–42. Supporters of the additional language argued that the constitution could be in jeopardy if the anti-registration clause were not included. Delegate Arnold Jacobsen said: "There are 15,000 to 20,000 people who are pretty emotional about this" (quoted in the *Missoulian,* March 9, 1972).

Since the right to keep and bear arms is not specifically protected by current U.S. Supreme Court interpretation of the Second Amendment to the U.S. Constitution, this section of the state constitution is the primary protection of the right to keep and bear arms in Montana. In 1992 there was a serious attempt to amend the Montana Constitution to include a "fundamental right to hunt." The proposal called forth intense debate but never reached the ballot. In 1995, with the bombing of the federal building in Oklahoma City attributable to a militia organization, the tensions in Montana escalated. Montana is home to a number of persons identifying with the "militia movement." Precise identification of the ideology, policies, or goals of the individual organizations that are placed in this general category is impossible. Some groups are obviously revolutionary, others anti-United Nations or one-world, while others just like guns. A confrontation with the "Freemen" in 1997 triggered a series of civil and criminal cases and reignited concerns surrounding violence and guns.

There are no significant cases interpreting the section. Under the 1889 Constitution, the court relied on the right to "keep or bear arms" as justification for the killing of game animals out of season (*State v. Rathbone,* 1940). In 1991 an unusual and unique statutory provision was enacted (Mont. Code Ann., Section 1-1-224). The statute proclaims:

> The week beginning the first Monday in March is an official week of observance to commemorate Montana's valued heritage of the right of each person to keep and bear arms in the defense of his home, person, or property or in aid of civil power. During this week, all Montanans are urged to reflect on their right to keep and bear arms and to celebrate this right in lawful ways.

## SECTION 13

**Right of Suffrage**. All elections shall be free and open, and no power, civil or military, shall at any time interfere to prevent the free exercise of the right of suffrage.

The section is intended to guarantee free elections and the right to vote. It is derived from and identical to Article III, section 5 of the 1889 Montana Constitution. The value of the provision is minimal. It does not specify who shall have the right to vote and the basic format of the state constitution is based on representational democracy that necessarily presupposes "free elections." The specific provision might be useful in the case of emergency and the imposition of martial law.

The two cases citing the section were decided under the 1889 Constitution. Both cases considered the practical requirements of providing state citizens with the opportunity to exercise their right to vote. The first case considered the adequacy of voting facilities (*State ex rel. Bray v. Long*, 1898). The second case held that because newly created districts could not satisfy the statutory method of nominating judicial candidates, the statutory method was unconstitutional (*State ex rel. Holliday v. O'Leary*, 1911).

## SECTION 14

**Adult Rights**. A person 18 years of age or older is an adult for all purposes, except that the legislature or the people by initiative may establish the legal age for purchasing, consuming, or possessing alcoholic beverages.

The provision, as originally drafted and approved by the electorate, simply and arbitrarily established 18 as the age of adulthood. Subsequent amendments were in response to federal highway funding requirements. A 1978 amendment established the restriction on the use of alcohol by persons under 19 years of age. A 1986 amendment eliminated the 19-year-old restriction, leaving the authority to establish the legal age for the possession, consumption, and purchase of alcohol to legislative discretion.

This is a new provision. The source is found in the general social attitude as to when young persons should accept adult responsibilities and be entrusted with adult rights. It is probable that the arbitrary age of 18 was the result of the Twenty-Sixth Amendment to the U.S. Constitution giving 18-year-olds the right to vote. The Twenty-Sixth Amendment was an outgrowth of the draft of 18- year-olds who were required to fight for their country but not entitled to vote for its leaders.

In conjunction with Article II, section 15, which states that "the rights of persons under 18 years of age shall include, but not be limited to, all the fundamental rights of this Article [meaning Article II] unless specifically precluded by laws which enhance the protection of such persons," the provision establishes the constitutional foundation for the significant legal demarcation between juveniles and adults. The section is a significant factor in custody responsibilities, criminal charges and processes, and rights to participate in the political process. This provision also allows for someone 18, 19, or 20 years old to hold state office (MCC Tr. 296).

The one case citing the provision supports the conclusion that 18 years is a significant dividing line, removing custody claims and support obligations (*Chrestenson v. Chrestenson*, 1979). The attorney general has determined that the provision does not create such a rigid demarcation as to prohibit the Department of Institutions from continuing to exercise control over persons sentenced as juveniles (under 18 years of age) through age 20 (37 Op. Att'y Gen. 287 (1977)).

## SECTION 15

**Rights of Persons Not Adults.** The rights of persons under 18 years of age shall include, but not be limited to, all the fundamental rights of this Article unless specifically precluded by laws which enhance the protection of such persons.

The provision is intended to afford children all the fundamental constitutional rights of adults (MCC Rep. 636), and, perhaps, more. The additional "rights" include legislative enactments and administrative regulations designed to protect children, even though such laws or regulations may prohibit or limit a child's enjoyment of fundamental rights specified in the constitution. The two clauses may conflict in deciding the constitutionality of any number of statutes and regulations claimed to enhance the protection of young persons but appearing to limit Article II rights. As interpreted, the section leaves the state in a largely unfettered paternalistic role in relation to children. An objective of this provision is to prevent Montana's youth from becoming dissatisfied with the manner in which adults administer the laws that affect them in their everyday activities (MCC Tr. 296). This provision is new.

Two significant cases have applied and analyzed the section. The earlier case is more in keeping with both the language and the apparent intent of the drafters of the provision, and the later case did not overrule or discuss it. Neither case seems to be notably advantageous to juveniles. The court considered the issue of whether a youth "in need of supervision" by virtue of truancy and placed on juvenile probation who then violates her probation, and is thereby adjudged a "delinquent youth" and placed in a youth institution, has been denied due process, equal protection, and/or suffered cruel and unusual punishment in violation of the U.S. or Montana Constitutions (*In re C.H.*, 1984). The court concluded that the deprivation of the physical liberty of the youth for a period of 45 days was sufficient to constitute an infringement upon her constitutional right of physical liberty, but determined that there was a compelling state interest sufficient to warrant such an infringement. The court cited this section of the Montana Constitution as recognizing that the state's interest in protecting children may conflict with their fundamental rights. The court, looking to the Constitutional Convention Committee Report, found that in appropriate cases where the protection of the special status of minors demands it, exceptions can be made on "clear showing that such protection is being enhanced" (p. 940). The court then held "that a juvenile's right to physical liberty must be balanced against her right to be supervised, cared for and rehabilitated. This is precisely what the drafters of the 1972 Montana Constitution had in mind when they explicitly recognized that persons under 18 years of age would enjoy the same fundamental rights as adults, unless exceptions were made for their own protection" (p. 941). The court went on to determine that, in this case, there was a compelling state purpose to protect and rehabilitate youthful offenders likely to become adult criminals.

In the second case, *In re Wood* (1989), the court upheld the transfer of a juvenile to adult court for criminal prosecution and concluded that Article II, section 15 affords no special constitutional right for juveniles to be tried in juvenile court. The supreme court determined that no provision exists in the Montana Constitution that provides a youth with a fundamental right to special treatment, and thus the state's middle-tier analysis is inapplicable and only a rational relationship to a legitimate state interest is required to support removal of a juvenile to the adult criminal court.

## SECTION 16

**The Administration of Justice.** Courts of justice shall be open to every person, and speedy remedy afforded for every injury of person, property, or character. No person shall be deprived of this full legal redress for injury incurred in employment for which another person may be liable except as to fellow employees and his immediate employer who hired him if such immediate employer provides coverage under the Workmen's Compensation Laws of this state. Right and justice shall be administered without sale, denial, or delay.

The substance of the first and last sentences is derived from and identical to Article III, section 6 of the 1889 Montana Constitution and has roots tracing to the Magna Carta. The second sentence is new and was added at the urging of a lawyer-delegate to the 1972 Constitutional Convention to reverse a decision previously rendered by the Montana Supreme Court. This part of the section is uniquely detailed for a constitutional provision and should be read in conjunction with the case it overruled (MCC Rep. 636).

The section has aspects of equal protection, "every person to be afforded a remedy for every injury." It also has aspects of fairness and due process, "[r]ight and justice shall be administered *fairly*." The focus of equality, due process, and fairness is on the judicial system. The breadth of the protection is for every injury of person, property, or character. The practical limitation is that only those injuries recognized by law are to be included, and injuries recognized by law change over the years. While redress is provided for legally identified injuries, the legislature has the power to eliminate common-law rights, at least to the extent that the elimination does not interfere with vested rights, and, by implication, the legislature can create new causes of action (*Reeves v. Me Elec. Co.*, 1976). For example, alienation of affections is no longer an accepted cause of action while intentional infliction of severe emotional distress is now recognized as a cognizable injury (*McGregor v. Mommer*, 1986). The provision requires that recognized injuries are to be redressed in a manner insuring equality under the law and fairness within the court system, but the constitutional guarantee is limited to what the legislature or court currently defines as legally cognizable injuries.

In a narrow sense, some of the language overrules *Ashcraft v. Montana Power Co.* (1971), which denied recovery against Montana Power to a construction company's employee injured by a Montana Power Company utility pole. The court denied recovery on the basis that the Montana Power Company designated the construction company an independent contractor and required it to carry workman's compensation. Ashcraft was entitled to Workmen's Compensation only, and the power company was immune from liability for injuries which Ashcraft suffered. In a more general sense, the section guarantees protection for injuries and a fair legal process to correct harms done.

The broad language, which directs the judiciary to administer "right and justice" equally and fairly, is an available constitutional basis for infinite legal arguments addressed to the more or less subjective concepts of "justice," "equity," and "fairness." In this sense the provision is so broad as to have minimal significance, but like the equally broad term "due process," the court could give the terms definite and concrete meaning and use the section to decide many conflicts.

Constitutional Initiative No. 30, approved by the electorate on November 4, 1986, amended section 16 by narrowing or reversing decisions that had held legislative attempts to limit recovery for injuries unconstitutional. The specific language of the proposed amendment was:

> This section shall not be construed as a limitation upon the authority of the legislature to enact statutes establishing, limiting, modifying, or abolishing remedies, claims for relief, damages, or allocations of responsibility for damages in any civil proceeding; except that any express dollar limits on compensatory damages for actual economic loss for bodily injury must be approved by a 2/3 vote of each house of the legislature.

Although the electorate approved the amendment, it never became law. The Montana Supreme Court held that the proposed amendment was defective in the manner in which it had been presented to the electors *State ex rel Mont.*

*Citizens for the Preservation of Citizens' Rights v. Waltermire*, 1987). The language of the amendment, as filed and certified by the secretary of state, was not the same language submitted to the voters at the election. The difference in language was material.

Two years later, a reconstituted supreme court amended the section without an initiative and granted the legislature nearly unlimited authority to change remedies, to redefine injuries, and to limit recovery. In *Meech v. Hillhaven West, Inc.* (1989), the Montana Supreme Court held that the "Wrongful Discharge From Employment Act" does not wrongfully deprive an individual falling within its purview of the right to full legal redress or a speedy remedy within the meaning of Article II, section 16 of the Montana Constitution. The wrongful discharge act specifies the facts that an individual must establish to obtain redress for wrongful discharge. In analyzing the statute, the court held that Article II, section 16 creates no fundamental right to a particular cause of action, remedy, or redress. The court determined that the section does no more than guarantee a right of access to courts to seek a remedy for wrongs recognized by common law or statutory authority; that no one has a vested interest in any rule of common law; and that the legislature may alter common-law causes of action to promote legitimate state interests and may alter or abrogate causes of action sounding in tort.

Fundamental rights are those rights found in Article II of the Montana Constitution or rights without which other rights would have little meaning. Access to the courts seems to meet both tests, the right being found in Article II and a right without which enforcement of other rights would have little meaning. The Montana Supreme Court stated that constitutional mandates of due process and the administration of justice expressed in Article II, section 16 guarantee every person access to the courts (*State v. Perry*, 1988). However, in subsequent decisions, Peterson v. School District (1989), followed in *Miller v. Fallon County* (1989), the Montana Supreme Court held that "access to the court" is not a fundamental right. According to these two cases, the right of access to the courts is not violated by a statute granting immunity for certain acts of the legislature. An earlier case, *Merchants Association v. Conger* (1979), held that a statute requiring a deposit to perfect an appeal from justice court to district court violated an indigent appellant's right under both Fourteenth Amendment equal protection and this section. However, the opinion did not support the idea that court access, even in the sense of equal protection, is a fundamental right. The opinion relied on the rational basis test.

Access to courts has always been restricted by jurisdictional requirements and demands that administrative remedies be exhausted.[13] A number of cases citing Article II, section 16 have discussed jurisdictional questions relating to

---

[13] For example, an initial administrative handling of a racial discrimination complaint does not violate the requirement of a speedy court remedy (*Romero v. J & J Tire*, 1989).

standing and the proper court in which a case should be brought (*Butte-Silver Bow Local Gov't v. State,* 1989). Generally these limits have been subsumed under the headings of standing, ripeness, mootness, and justiciability (see *Grossman v. State,* 1984; *Tooke v. Miles City Production Credit Ass'n,* 1988). *Trankel v. State* (1997) held that a state employee has a right to full legal redress against the state.

## SECTION 17

**Due Process of Law.** No person shall be deprived of life, liberty, or property without due process of law.

This section is intended to guarantee reasonable and fair process before government deprives any person of life, liberty, or property. At a minimum, fair process includes notice as to what is at risk, an opportunity to be heard, and an impartial decision maker rendering a responsive and timely decision. The precise identification of what process is due, when it is due, and for what it is due is ultimately left to precedent, reason, history, and the legal philosophies of an ever-changing court.

This section is derived from and identical to Article III, section 27 of the 1889 Montana Constitution. The language is also identical to the due process language in both the Fifth and Fourteenth Amendments to the U.S. Constitution. It is a standard constitutional provision, found in every modern western constitution.

The U.S. Supreme Court requires every state to provide minimal procedural due process to every person. Because the Montana "due process" provision was not intended to afford greater procedural protection to Montana citizens than is required by the Fourteenth Amendment to the U.S. Constitution, its importance could be more symbolic than essential. As to "procedural due process," the federal scheme has been followed closely and variations from federal commands are de minimus. A second dimension of due process, "substantive due process," is of considerable significance in Montana, although there is no indication that the drafters or electorate perceived the idea of substantive due process as an essential part of this section. The phrase "substantive due process" is something of an internal contradiction in the first instance and, as a concept, is often derided as starkly subjective, applied or denied according to the personal philosophical predilection of each judge. Perhaps the phrase, if not the theory, should have been excised from the interpretation of this section. In fact, the phrase has been used and the theory recognized under both the 1889 Constitution and the 1972 Constitution, and as applied, substantive due process derived from this section has been unpredictable but generally more protective of individual rights than substantive due process recognized by the U.S. Supreme Court.

In *Newville v. State Dept. of Family Services* (1994), a case that considered the constitutionality of major statutory changes relating to joint and several tort liability, the court recognized and defined substantive due process in the following way:

> The theory underlying substantive due process reaffirms the fundamental concept that the due process clause contains a substantive component which bars arbitrary governmental actions regardless of the procedures used to implement them, and serves as a check on oppressive governmental action. Even though a plaintiff may have no property or liberty interest grounded in state law which is protected from arbitrary government action, such action still may be subject to review under substantive due process. Substantive due process primarily examines the underlying substantive rights and remedies to determine whether restrictions, such as those placed on both remedies and procedures in this case, are unreasonable or arbitrary when balanced against the purpose of the Legislature in enacting the statute, (p. 800)[14]

In *Plumb v. The Fourth Judicial District Court* (1996), the Montana Supreme Court stated that substantive due process required "that the law shall not be unreasonable, arbitrary, or capricious, and that the means selected shall have a real and substantial relation to the object sought to be attained" (p. 1016), citing the U.S. Supreme Court case *Nebbia v. New York*, 1934). Later in *Plumb* the court said that "substantive due process analysis requires that we decide (1) whether the legislation in question is related to a legitimate governmental concern, and (2) that the means chosen by the Legislature to accomplish its objective are reasonably related to the result sought to be attained" (p. 1016). As a practical matter the Montana cases show less deference to legislative or administrative bodies than federal courts do. For example, in *Plumb v. The Fourth Judicial District Court* (1996), the court held that statutory amendments permitting the assertion of a non-party defense violated substantive due process, and earlier the court held that a restrictive covenant which allowed disapproval of house plans based upon harmony of external design violated substantive due process and was not enforceable in view of existing mix of homes in subdivision (*Town and Country Estates v. Slater*, 1987).

A majority of the cases that raise issues of procedural due process are criminal, and most raise an additional constitutional issue in which due process plays a supportive and clarifying role rather than being a determinative consideration. Article II, sections 20 (initiation of proceedings), 21 (bail), 24 (counsel, notice, speedy trial, public trial, and impartial jury), 26 (jury trial), and

---

[14] The court cited J. McGuinness & L. Parlagreco, "The Reemergence of Substantive Due Process as a Constitutional Tort: Theory, Proof, and Damages," *New England Law Review*, 24 (1900): 1133.

25 (self-incrimination and double jeopardy) detail most recognized criminal procedural rights.

Theoretically, minimal procedural due process requirements include notice, hearing, decision, and an impartial decision maker. As the significance of the loss increases, the procedural requirements increase and may include a right to legal representation, special rules relative to admission of evidence, right of appeal, and more. In most of the procedural due process cases, the Montana Supreme Court has held that whatever government process has been followed is constitutionally adequate.

The cases finding a violation of due process are more helpful in describing state due process requirements. In *State v. Farrell* (1984), the supreme court ruled that sentencing violates the right to due process when a maximum sentence is given because a defendant is indigent and will therefore make restitution slowly. The court remanded the case for reconsideration of the sentence. *State v. Redding* (1984) held that the sentencing judge denied the defendant due process when the judge conferred with the presentence investigation officer behind closed doors with no opportunity for argument, rebuttal, or explanation. A number of the criminal due process cases have attempted to describe an acceptable process by which to invoke the death penalty (*State v. Smith,* 1985; *Fitzpatrick v. State,* 1981; and *State v. Coleman,* 1979), and mostly discuss the meaning and application of U.S. Supreme Court mandates. The taking of life or liberty by the state occurs almost exclusively in the criminal law context and federal due process generally controls.

Property, other than real property, requiring some measure of process before being taken, includes the right to carry on a business (*Billings Assoc. Plumbing, Heating, & Cooling, Contractors v. Board of Plumbers,* 1979), trade secrets (*Mountain States Tel. & Tel. v. Department of Public Service Regulation,* 1981) and employment (*Welsh v. Great Falls,* 1984). Neither employment at will (*Reiter v. Yellowstone County,* 1981) nor non-tenured employment is a property right protected by due process (*Akhtar v. Van de Wetering,* 1982). The Montana Supreme Court rarely considers the due process requirement in non-criminal taking of property apart from eminent domain. The eminent domain cases are discussed in conjunction with Article II, section 29.

The state drug forfeiture laws, patterned after federal laws, seem to threaten accepted minimum standards of procedural due process but to date have been upheld. A trial court judge released a forfeited vehicle allegedly used in a drug offense to protect the interests of an innocent lien holder, but the supreme court held the release was an abuse of discretion (*In re the Seizure of a 1988 Chevrolet Van,* 1991). Justice Trieweiler, dissenting, noted that:

> [P]ortions of the forfeiture statute relied upon by the majority turn traditional notions of fairness, due process, burden of proof, and presumption of innocence upside down. . . . Under our former system of justice, innocent people did not have

the burden of proving innocence. The State had the burden of proving their guilt before punishing them or seizing their property, (p. 864)

## SECTION 18

**State Subject to Suit.** The state, counties, cities, towns, and all other local governmental entities shall have no immunity from suit for injury to a person or property, except as may be specifically provided by law by a 2/3 vote of each house of the Legislature.

This section, as originally drafted and passed, eliminated sovereign immunity ("the King can do no wrong"). On its face the provision allowed any person to sue state and local governments for injuries caused by officials and employees of government. This was a new provision, having no comparable provision in the 1889 Constitution. In 1974 the provision was amended, adding language allowing the legislature to create and define areas of immunity by a two-thirds vote of each house.

In its original form the section was based on a commitment to the idea that government should be responsible for its derelictions, errors, and omissions; and that government responsibility and fairness should precede government largess (MCC Tr. 1763–64). The legislative response to the 1974 amendment, coupled with restrictive interpretation by the Montana Supreme Court, has defeated or reversed the original intent of the section. Governmental (sovereign) immunity in Montana is now more comprehensive than before this section was drafted and passed.

The Montana constitutional convention delegates had a unique attitude of openness. A sense of empowerment and not arrogance accompanied the open-mindedness. Open-mindedness and the sense of empowerment made it possible for the delegates to seriously consider issues without being irretrievably bound to precedent. Like the new protection for human dignity and environment, like the prohibition of some forms of private discrimination, and like the new right to know, this section rethought the relation between government and the people (MCC Rep. 638).

Sovereign immunity, a historical anachronism, has been slow to change. The change made by the section as proposed by the constitutional convention was dramatic. The people accepted the proposed change. Effective lobbying by tradition-bound politicians and frightened government employees quickly reversed the change.

Case interpretations coupled with an accumulation of statutory exceptions have drained the provision of any significant meaning. First, the court denied the statute its plain meaning in finding a common-law, non-statutory judicial immunity directly countermanding the constitutional language (*Knutson v. State*, 1984; citing *Butz v. Economou*, 1978). The court followed this with quasijudicial immunity for state boards (*Koppen v. Board of Medical Examiners*, 1988).

The court extended judicial immunity to the city and city employees who negligently carried out a judicial order (*Great Falls v. Price*, 1989). The court established prosecutorial immunity in *State ex rel. Dept. of Justice v. District Court* (1976) and extended it to county prosecutors in *Ronek v. Gallatin County* (1987). The court upheld legislative immunity in *Peterson v. School District* (1989) which *Miller v. Fallon County* (1989) followed. The court reasserted its pre-1972 interpretation that statutory waivers of immunity must be strictly construed (*W.D. Construction v. Board of County Commissioners*, 1985).

*Meech v. Hillhaven West, Inc.* (1989) overruled *White v. State* (1983), holding that statutory immunity providing the state protection from punitive damages was constitutional. According to *Jacques v. Montana Nat. Guard* (1982), even a statute could suspend an assessment of interest on a judgment against the state without offending the state constitution.

## SECTION 19

**Habeas Corpus**. The privilege of the writ of habeas corpus shall never be suspended.

The section guarantees, absolutely and unequivocally, the privilege of the writ of habeas corpus, primarily protecting the right to test the legitimacy of one's detention. Unlike the predecessor section in the 1889 Montana Constitution and the original habeas corpus provision in the U.S. Constitution, there is no provision for suspending the writ.

The section is derived from Article III, section 21 of the 1889 Montana Constitution.

That section states that the privilege of the writ of habeas corpus shall never be suspended, unless, in case of rebellion or invasion, the public safety requires it. This language is identical with the statement of the "Great Writ" found in Article 1, section 9 of the U.S. Constitution.

The reason for the provision is, at least partially, related to the historical significance of the Great Writ as a means to protect liberty against the tyranny of government. It was first expressed as part of the liberties contained in the Magna Carta, and remains as a primary process used to test the legality of any official detention.

Although the U.S. Constitution guarantees the privilege of the writ of habeas corpus, a state guarantee adds the protection of the availability of the writ via state court action. Further, this statement of the writ is more nearly absolute than its federal counterpart. Writs of habeas corpus to access the federal courts have been substantially limited.[15] While statutory schemes for testing detention are available in most states including Montana, the constitutional guarantee is important in both symbolic terms and in the sense of permanency.

There are no significant cases concerning the writ of habeas corpus in Montana. In large measure, the cases that do arise have followed federal precedents. Over the course of time, habeas corpus has become available to test more than the jurisdictional legitimacy of detention and now includes issues of constitutionality such as due process, right to counsel, and search and seizure questions. This broadening of the scope of habeas corpus first occurred in the federal system, which the Montana court has largely adopted.

To the extent that the Montana Supreme Court has made any significant interpretation of the meaning of habeas corpus, it may have thoughtlessly restricted its meaning to its original and ancient scope. In *Gates v. Missoula County Comm's* (1988), the court held that habeas corpus is not an appropriate remedy to test the physical conditions under which a prisoner is held, but only allows a prisoner to challenge the legal sufficiency of the cause for his incarceration. While this was the original scope of the writ of habeas corpus, it had come to be a primary means of testing the legitimacy of an incarceration in terms of constitutionality. In this case, the obvious constitutional question was whether the inadequate physical condition of the prison facility was a violation of the constitutional provision prohibiting cruel and unusual punishment. Because the U.S. Supreme Court has narrowed access to federal habeas corpus, this decision may be a significant restriction on the Great Writ.

## SECTION 20

**Initiation of Proceedings.** Criminal offenses within the jurisdiction of any court inferior to the district court shall be prosecuted by complaint. All criminal actions in district court, except those on appeal, shall be prosecuted either by information, after examination and commitment by a magistrate or after leave granted by the court, or by indictment without such examination, commitment or leave.

A grand jury shall consist of eleven persons, of whom eight must concur to find an indictment. A grand jury shall be drawn and summoned only at the discretion and order of the district judge.

The section outlines the constitutional requirements for commencing a criminal action, providing, for the accused, minimal protections from the enormous power of the state. It guarantees that no person shall be charged with a serious

[15] See, for example, Sharad Khandelwal, "The Path to Habeas Corpus Narrows: Interpreting 28 U.S.C. 2254(d)(l)," *Michigan Law Review*, 96 (1997): 434–439.

crime (felony) until after the state has established probable cause to believe that the defendant has committed the crime. Proof of probable cause must be made to the satisfaction of either a grand jury or judge, each of whom is, at least nominally, independent from the prosecutor. As to lesser criminal charges, the protection of the individual defendant is largely left to the discretion of the investigating officer and the prosecutor.

This section is derived from, and substantively comparable to, Article III, section 8 of the 1889 Montana Constitution, except that it increases grand jury membership from seven to eleven persons and requires a concurrence of eight jurors rather than five to find an indictment. The change is minimally significant, if for no other reason than that the grand jury, as a means of initiating a prosecution, is rarely used in the state of Montana. The provision does not require a grand jury indictment in all criminal cases as does the Fifth Amendment to the U.S. Constitution, with the exception of military cases.

In interpreting the comparable provision of the 1889 Constitution, the Montana Supreme Court held that one of the objects of this section was to eliminate the machinery and expense of a grand jury by substituting prosecution by information (*State v. Vinn*, 1914; *State v. Bowser*, 1898; *State v. Cain*, 1895; *State v. Brett*, 1895). The court has carried forward this arrangement for commencing a serious prosecution as part of the 1972 Constitution. In *State v. Cardwell* (1980), the court noted that Article II, section 20 of the 1972 Montana Constitution provides that: "[a]ll criminal actions in district court, except those on appeal, shall be prosecuted either by information, after examination and commitment by a magistrate or after leave granted by the court, or by indictment without such examination, commitment or leave." The court went on to say: "[r]eading this section of the Constitution broadly, all stages of the information filing process including amendments require judicial examination . . . to ensure a defendant receives a neutral determination of probable cause for detention under [all] . . . charges (pp. 1232–33).

In the only significant case interpreted under the 1972 Constitution, the court modified the language of the provision, holding that the constitutional discretion vested in district court judges to summon a grand jury is not an absolute unbridled discretion but may be reviewed by the supreme court (*State ex rel. Woodahl v. District Court, 1975*).

## SECTION 21

**Bail.** All persons shall be bailable by sufficient sureties, except for capital offenses, when the proof is evident or the presumption great.

The provision guarantees that all persons charged with having committed a criminal offense shall be bailable except when death is a possible punishment for the offense charged. This provision is derived from and identical to Article III, section 19 of the 1889 Montana Constitution, and assumes that there are capital offenses. Elimination of the death penalty was considered by the 1972 Montana Constitutional Convention but was ultimately submitted to the voters as a separate issue to avoid possible defeat of the constitution over such an emotional issue. The voters voted to retain the death penalty by a three-to-one margin.

Constitutional guarantee of bail prior to conviction is based on the presumption of innocence and is a shield against incarceration before the presumption of innocence is overcome and the accused is found guilty or pleads guilty. The comparable provision in the Eighth Amendment to the U.S. Constitution prohibits excessive" bail and has been interpreted to permit denial of bail altogether. Such linguistic sophistry should not be possible in interpreting the bail provision in the Montana Constitution. The spirit of the provision in the Montana Constitution has been perverted in a different way. Judicial officers regularly place bail so high that persons charged with a crime cannot make bail. The idea that all persons shall be bailable has come to mean that all wealthy persons shall be bailable. Some judges make no apology for effectively denying bail by setting it impossibly high and using preconviction incarceration to insure that the accused will get a taste of jail regardless of whether there is a conviction.

The Montana Supreme Court has opined that, in determining the amount of bail to be fixed, the judge should consider the unique facts of each case and take into account the enormity of the crime charged, the maximum penalty which the law authorizes, the pecuniary condition of the defendant, the probability of the defendant's flight to avoid punishment, the general character and reputation of the defendant, the apparent nature and strength of the proof as bearing upon the probability of conviction, and any other relevant matters (*State v. McLeod,* 1957). In the final analysis, the amount of bail is within the judge's sound legal discretion, but it must be reasonable (*State v. McLeod*) The Montana Supreme Court has never reviewed a case in which it found bail to be unreasonable and in violation of this provision. The court did hold that a statute providing for penalty assessment on bail violated the due process clause (*State ex rel. Sanders v. City of Butte,* 1968). In a case pre-dating the 1972 Constitution, the supreme court held that the district court erred in denying bail after a reversal of conviction for first degree murder and a remand for new trial (*Warwick v. District Court,* 1972). Evidently, conviction followed by reversal does not create the required presumption nor establish sufficient evidence to deny bail.

## SECTION 22

**Excessive Sanctions.** Excessive bail shall not be required, or excessive fines imposed, or cruel and unusual punishments inflicted.

The provision is intended to protect persons charged with crime from suffering pre-trial incarceration and to protect against disproportionate, cruel, and unusual punishments. This section is derived from and identical to Article III, section 20 of the 1889 Montana Constitution. The provision is a reflection of several important community and cultural values, deeply imbedded in the Anglo American history of criminal process, including: presumption of innocence, proof of guilt beyond a reasonable doubt before punishment, and humane punishment after conviction. The section has not been successfully interposed to modify, reduce, or change bail.

Perhaps the best approach to illuminating cruel or unusual punishment comes from the court's consideration of proportionality. In *State v. Bruns* (1984), the court found jail time for driving under the influence of alcohol not excessive since the sentence falls within the maximum authorized by statute and is not so disproportionate to the crime that it shocks the conscience and outrages the moral sense of the community or of justice. If shocking the conscience and causing moral outrage to some sense of justice is the standard, it is unlikely that many sentences will be overturned on a claim of cruel, unusual, or disproportionality. Sentencing a mentally ill defendant to 300 years in prison without possibility of parole or furlough is not cruel or unusual (*State v. Watson,* 1984). In *State v. Coleman* (1979), the court declared that death by hanging is not cruel or unusual and in *State v. McKenzie* (1980) the Montana Supreme Court upheld the death penalty, stating that the death penalty is not an excessive or disproportionate punishment for having taken a life. McKenzie was executed in 1995, the first execution in Montana since 1943 when a black man, charged and convicted of murder, was executed by hanging. In 1998, Langford became the second person executed in the 1990s.

In one case the court did determine that a sentence of death may be disproportionate to the crime and therefore unconstitutional (*Kills on Top v. State,* 1996). In that case, the defendant was charged with and convicted of deliberate homicide (murder) and sentenced to death. On appeal the state supreme court found that the defendant was not present when the killing occurred, the defendant did not inflict the death-causing injuries, there was no reliable evidence that the defendant intended the victim's death, and there was evidence that the defendant sought to prevent the victim's death; therefore, the sentence of death was disproportionate to the crime given the facts surrounding the criminal event.

In *State v. Langford* (1991), the Montana Supreme Court held that it was constitutionally acceptable for a sentencing judge to make reference to a victim impact statement in imposing a death sentence, distinguishing *Booth v. Maryland* (1987) in which the U.S. Supreme Court held that reference to a victim impact statement during the sentencing stage of a capital murder trial was a violation of the Eighth Amendment of the U.S. Constitution. (*Booth v. Maryland* has since been overruled by the U.S. Supreme Court.)

## SECTION 23

**Detention.** No person shall be imprisoned for the purpose of securing his testimony in any criminal proceeding longer than may be necessary in order to take his deposition. If he can give security for his appearance at the time of trial, he shall be discharged upon giving the same; if he cannot give security, his deposition shall be taken in the manner provided by law, and in the presence of the accused and his counsel, or without their presence, if they shall fail to attend the examination after reasonable notice of the time and place thereof.

The provision is intended to make the testimony of known witnesses available in the defense or prosecution of a criminal case while protecting the liberty interest of such witnesses. The section was derived from and is substantively similar to Article III, section 17 of the 1889 Montana Constitution. The propriety of introducing a deposition in a criminal trial under emergency circumstances was specified in the parallel provision of the 1889 Constitution. The primary difference is the deletion of language allowing depositions to be received in evidence in a trial if the witness who gave the deposition is dead or out of state.

More in the nature of a statute than a typical constitutional provision, the section protects against unnecessary restrictions on potential witnesses while insuring that witnesses are available for criminal trials. The first sentence announces the constitutional principle. The remainder of the provision details the implementation of the principle. Providing for the evidentiary sufficiency of a particular deposition should be a statutory embellishment, subject to the generalized requirements of the constitution that the defendant have adequate means of testing the validity of the testimony which is ordinarily done by confrontation and cross-examination.

There are no cases interpreting the section. Under the comparable provision found in the 1889 Constitution, the court held that admission of depositions provided for in this section did not violate other provisions of the constitution which require confrontation and cross-examination, providing that the witness was dead or not within the jurisdiction of the state (*Tooker v. State*, 1966).

## SECTION 24

**Rights of the Accused.** In all criminal prosecutions the accused shall have the right to appear and defend in person and by counsel; to demand the nature and cause of the accusation; to meet the witnesses against him face to face; to have process to compel the attendance of witnesses in his behalf, and a speedy public trial by an impartial jury of the county or district in which the offense is alleged to have been committed, subject to the right of the state to have a change of venue for any of the causes for which the defendant may obtain the same.

The provision lists a number of important constitutional protections afforded the accused in a criminal case. It includes the right to counsel, notice, confrontation, speedy trial, public trial, and impartial jury. Other constitutional protections afforded the defendant in a criminal case include sections 10 (right of privacy), 11 (search and seizures), 17 (due process), 19 (habeas corpus), 20 (initiation of criminal proceedings), 21 (bail), 22 (excessive sanctions), 25 (self incrimination and double jeopardy), 26 (jury trial), and 28 (purpose of punishment). The section is derived from and identical to Article III, section 16 of the 1889 Montana Constitution. The section guarantees, to every criminal defendant, some of the basic procedural requirements for a fair trial. This is a critically important aspect of any civilized scheme of justice. In an atmosphere of hysterical fear, the majority is capable of resorting to outrageous means of control and self-protection. This section is an important outline of a significant portion of criminal due process.

The case interpretations are divided among the various aspects of criminal due process outlined. The court, in considering the right to counsel, has discussed who, when, and for what counsel will be provided. For example, the right does not extend to civil cases (*In re Adoption of K.L.J.K.*, 1986), and it does not include a right to non-lawyer counsel (*State v. Barnes*, 1988). It requires that assistance of counsel be effective (*State v. Hoch*, 1988) and be available at every critical stage of the criminal process (*State v. Robbins*, 1985), but a defendant, when charged with murder, may represent himself if he understands the charges, the possible penalties, and the dangers of self-representation (*State v. Woods*, 1997).

Many cases have questioned the right of confrontation, most particularly those cases involving children victims and children as witnesses. While the right is generally protected, the supreme court has carved out a number of exceptions excusing potential witnesses from the rigors of confrontation and cross examination, even though the trial court has admitted testimonial evidence from these persons. In *State v. J.C.E.* (1988), a child abuse victim was excused. A co-conspirator was excused from testifying on the basis of a plea bargain in *State v. Stever* (1987). This determination followed the U.S. Supreme Court decision in *United States v. Inadi* (1986). In most areas of constitutional criminal process, the Montana Supreme Court has followed U.S. Supreme Court decisions, although not always required to do so.

There are many cases on the issue of speedy trial but, by and large, Montana has adopted and applied the federal standard created by the U.S. Supreme Court in *Barker v. Wingo* (1972). Court responses to questions of an impartial jury have been traditional, with the section reflecting the concern that the prosecution, as well as the accused, is entitled to an impartial jury. The petitioner must present specific evidence of prejudice to the court, and judges are not expected to intrude on jury deliberations to find out whether a decision was based on bias and prejudice (*Fitzpatrick v. State*, 1981). The cases do not presume prejudice, so the court decides each case on its unique facts.

## SECTION 25

**Self-Incrimination and Double Jeopardy**. No person shall be compelled to testify against himself in a criminal proceeding. No person shall be again put in jeopardy for the same offense previously tried in any jurisdiction.

The section prohibits both compelled self-incrimination and successive prosecutions for a single offense. The two protections, while different and distinct, limit the power of the state in criminal cases.

The first provision protecting against self-incrimination, an extremely important protection for persons charged with criminal conduct, is derived from and similar to Article III, section 18 of the 1889 Montana Constitution, which in turn was derived from the U.S. Constitution. Montana principles of constitutional and statutory self-incrimination are based on federal precedent. The cases and language of the federal judiciary have developed historically from the more obvious problems associated with admissions, confessions, and interrogation as well as from the constitutional right to counsel as defined in *Miranda v. Arizona* (1966) and its progeny, coupled with the exclusion of evidence remedy derived from *Wolf v. Colorado (1949) and Mapp v. Ohio (1961)*. Montana constitutional jurisprudence on self-incrimination has followed the lead and demands of the federal system.

The provision on self-incrimination has provided little, if any, added protection for Montana citizens, beyond what is already provided by the federal constitution. Fifth Amendment protection against self-incrimination covers not only criminal proceedings but other proceedings where compelled testimony could lead to future prosecution (*In re C.L.R.*, 1984). Fifth Amendment protections also include both incriminating statements and confessions of guilt. Comments on the accused's failure to take the stand and testify in his own behalf are not permitted (*State v. Gladue*, 1984;*State v. Johnson*, 1988; followed in *State v. Mix*, 1989). The court has noted that any "comment on the refusal to testify is a remnant of the 'inquisitorial system of criminal justice' which the right against self-incrimination outlaws" (p. 589), and that such comment "cuts down on the privilege by making its assertion costly" (*State v. Wilkins*, 1987). However, a majority of the Montana decisions that have considered prosecutorial comment on the accused's failure to testify have affirmed convictions, either by reliance on the harmless error rule which permits an appellate court to affirm a conviction although error is shown if the error does not affect substantial rights and did not influence the outcome of the case, as in *State v. Johnson* (1988); or as a fair response to claims made by defendant or defense counsel, as in State v. *Dawson*

(1988), which followed *United States v. Robinson* (1988); or by carefully distinguishing between comment that "the defendant has the right to remain silent" (which is permissible) and a comment on the accused's exercise of that right (which is impermissible), as in *State v. Gonyea* (1987). (See also *State v. Mix* 89.) Finally, the constitutional theory of self-incrimination does not require exclusion from evidence of defendant's refusal to submit to a breathalyzer test (*State v. Jackson*, 1983).

Seizure of physical evidence from the defendant is not subject to the constitutional protection of self-incrimination. This includes pubic hair (*State v. Armstrong*, 1980), neutron activation tests for gunpowder residues from defendant's hands (*State v. Ulrich*, 1980), and audio-video taping that generates objective physical evidence (*State v. Thompson*, 1989). The *State v. Thompson* decision held that a videotape that indicated the physical condition of the defendant at the time of arrest is not constitutionally prohibited testimonial evidence and is not protected by the Fifth Amendment. Under the holding of *State v. Jackson* (1983), neither the results of a breathalyzer test nor a defendant's refusal to submit to the test are communications protected by the Fifth Amendment of the U.S. Constitution or by Montana's constitutional prohibition against self-incrimination. Further, the Miranda warning does not apply to such non-testimonial conduct (*Missoula v. Forest*, 1989). Audio-video taping of a defendant arrested for driving while intoxicated was held to be physical evidence, outside the privilege against self-incrimination, because there was no evidence indicating the recording contained speech or gestures testimonial in nature (*State v. Finley*, 1977).

The determination of voluntariness relies on the totality of the circumstances and seeks to follow federal rulings (*State v. Grimestad*, 1979; *State v. Blakney*, 1982; *State v. Gleed*, 1986; *State v. Beach*, 1985). This issue is within the trial court's discretion; and if there is substantial evidence to support the trial court's finding of voluntariness, it must be affirmed (*State v. Davison*, 1980). The court has given little consideration to mental disease or defect determining voluntariness and upholds admissibility if the defendant is capable of understanding the meaning and consequences of his or her statements. It was held to be permissible to admit the confession of a 14-year-old boy with an I.Q. of 86, charged with the sexual assault of a 6-year-old child (*In re J.W.K.*, 1986: relying on *State v. Phelps*, 1985; see also*State v. Mercer*, 1981).

Arrests for traffic violation are non-custodial and the arresting officer need not give a Miranda warning to a person stopped for a speeding violation (*Billings v. Skurdal*, 1986; citing *Berkemer v. McCarty*, 1984). Non-custodial confessions without Miranda warnings are admissible (*State v. Holmes*, 1983; *State v. Lapp*, 1983; *State ex rel Berger v. District Court*, 1967).

The Montana cases on self-incrimination slavishly follow federal precedent. Early on, the court stated that the self-incrimination language used in Article II, section 25 of the Montana Constitution is substantially identical to the language in the U.S. Constitution and affords no basis for being interpreted more broadly than its federal counterpart (*State v. Jackson*, 1983).

The second provision of section 25, protecting against double jeopardy, is unlike the parallel provisions in the 1889 Montana Constitution and in the federal constitution. As interpreted, this section prohibits a second trial for the same offense in a different jurisdiction. The convention committee was aware that the Montana Constitution could not limit the federal government in this practice, but it did hope to induce cooperation (MCC Rep. 641).

Constitutional protection against double jeopardy, derived from and similar to Article III, section 18 of the 1889 Montana Constitution, traces its lineage to the Fifth Amendment to the U.S. Constitution. Montana has generally followed the minimum guarantees of federal constitutional double jeopardy and its supporting concept of collateral estoppel. While double jeopardy prohibits being tried twice or punished twice for the same offense, the companion concept of "collateral estoppel," not mentioned in either the U.S. Constitution or the Montana Constitution, but followed in both federal and state jurisprudence, prohibits relitigating an issue previously tried and decided, insofar as the same parties are involved (see *Ashe v. Swenson*, 1970).

Mistrial for manifest necessity does not invoke double jeopardy and the matter may be retried (*State v. Stringer*, 1994). Original jeopardy is not terminated following mistrial based on jury deadlock, hence retrial does not conflict with the constitutional mandates of double jeopardy (*State exrel. Forsyth v. District Court*, 1985). The Montana Supreme Court applied double jeopardy to reverse and dismiss a conviction for incest. The crime of which the defendant was charged and convicted had been enacted after the date of the alleged crime, iolating the ex post facto clause of the constitution. A retrial under a separate code provision, sexual assault, would violate constitutional double jeopardy (*State v. Hall*, 1986). The decision was reversed by the U.S. Supreme Court, per curiam with two dissents (*Montana v. Hall*, 1987). The per curiam opinion concluded that the Montana decision was not based on adequate and independent state grounds and applicable federal law holds "[t]he successful appeal of a judgment of conviction, on any ground other than the insufficiency of the evidence to support the verdict, poses no bar to further prosecution on the same charge" (p. 402). Retrial after reversal for failure to prove an essential element of the crime charged would be a violation of the constitutional protection against double jeopardy (*State v. Lundblade*, 1984). Note that the court did remand under its authority set forth in Montana Code Annotated, Section 46-20-703 to reduce the offense for which a defendant has been convicted to a lesser included offense because the record contained evidence establishing all of the elements of the lesser included offense which was sexual assault (*State v. Bad Horse*, 1980).

Double jeopardy does not protect against charging multiple counts arising from a single incident nor imposition of separate and consecutive sentences for each crime charged (*State v. Lindseth, 1983; State v. Wells*, 1983). Defendant argued that he could not be convicted of driving under the influence because he had already been punished when his driver's license was suspended for refusing to take the breathalyzer test and that to punish him for driving under the influence would constitute multiple punishments for the same offense (*Helena v. Danichek*, 1996). In *Danichek* the court held that the defendant's license was suspended for refusing the breathalyzer test and that it was the refusal that was the initial violation. That initial conviction had nothing to do with whether the person was actually driving under the influence, and, therefore, the "driving under the influence" conviction was a separate violation. The defendant was being punished for two separate infractions and was not placed in double jeopardy.

In *Crist v. Bretz* (1978), the U.S. Supreme Court held that Montana's statutory provision (Montana Code Ann., Section 46-11-503) that jeopardy did not attach when the jury was sworn but only after the first evidence was introduced violated minimum federal constitutional requirements.

While determinations about double jeopardy generally follow federal precedent, Montana has added to the minimum federal constitutional guarantees by the language of the state constitution, by court interpretation, and by enactment of an extensive legislative scheme outlining the application of double jeopardy. For example, the Montana State Constitution states: "No person shall be again put in jeopardy for the same offense previously tried in *any jurisdiction*." As interpreted, this clause protects a defendant from being tried in Montana for a criminal event for which he had been convicted or acquitted in another jurisdiction, either federal or another state (*State v. Zimmerman*, 1977; see also *State v. Sword*, 1987). While Montana law bars state prosecution following federal prosecution for the same conduct, Montana is without jurisdiction to bar a subsequent federal prosecution (*United States v. Engesser*, 1986). The convention committee was aware that the Montana Constitution could not limit the federal government in the practice of trying a defendant a second time in federal court after the defendant had been convicted or acquitted in Montana, but hoped to induce federal reconsideration and cooperation (MCC Rep. 641).

An example of the more protective posture of Montana's double jeopardy statutory scheme is the requirement that all known criminal events be charged at one and the same time and not be charged and tried seriatim (i.e., one by one in sequence). The theory, apart from an obvious concern about government efficiency, is that trying a single defendant for a series of criminal acts, one after another rather than all at once, unfairly exhausts the defendant mentally, physically and financially (Montana Code Ann., Section 46-11-501 et seq.).

These provisions are at the heart of any civilized scheme of criminal justice. If confessions can be obtained by torture or if a defendant is forced to defend repeatedly against the unlimited resources and power of a government, justice is gravely compromised.

## SECTION 26

**Trial by Jury.** The right of trial by jury is secured to all and shall remain inviolate. But upon default of appearance or by consent of the parties expressed in such manner as the law may provide, all cases may be tried without a jury or before fewer than the number of jurors provided by law. In all civil actions, two-thirds of the jury may render a verdict, and a verdict so rendered shall have the same force and effect as if all had concurred therein. In all criminal actions, the verdict shall be unanimous.

This section of the 1972 Montana Constitution provides the most comprehensive right to a jury trial imaginable. The section is similar to and derived from Article III, section 23 of the 1889 Montana Constitution, but unlike the 1889 Constitution, a defendant may waive a jury trial in felony cases as well as civil and misdemeanor cases and have his or her case tried by a judge. There may be instances where a defendant prefers to be tried before a judge without a jury (MCC Rep. 642). As applied, the defendant's preference for a bench trial is subject to prosecutorial veto. Montana Code Annotated, Section 46-16-110(3) provides that a criminal defendant may waive his right to jury trial, but to be effective the waiver must be in writing and the prosecutor must consent (*State v. Dahlin*, 1998). The section requires a unanimous jury verdict in a misdemeanor case, whereas the 1889 Constitution permitted a two-thirds jury concurrence to convict a defendant of a misdemeanor. The convention committee felt it necessary to strengthen the presumption of innocence in all criminal actions (MCC Rep. 642).

The basic right to jury trial derives from the U.S. Constitution and has its historical roots in the Magna Carta. The peculiar configuration of trial by jury has developed separately in the federal courts and the various state courts. In Montana the right to jury trial has been narrowed by court decisions. This narrowing has not been the result of following federal decisions, but has been an independent and separate development within the state of Montana.

Jury trials based on experience and the wisdom of history were intended to place the commonsense wisdom of the citizen between the criminal defendant and the awesome power of the state. It was further intended to make available the jury as a fact-finding instrument in non-criminal cases. Juries, as compared with legally trained judges, are deemed to be sufficiently able to ascertain facts and bring added compassion and sensitivity to the decision-making process. In civil cases this power is severely limited by the power of the judiciary to grant summary judgments and to change damage awards, notwithstanding what the jury finds. This is in addition to the general power the trial judge exercises in directing the course of a trial, admitting or denying evidence, and instructing. the jury.

The importance of the jury is the subject of passionate debate. Some members of the legal profession, judges in particular, argue strenuously for the elimination of the jury, emphasizing the difficulty juries have in dealing with complicated cases such as bank and security frauds, criminal conspiracies, and some product liability cases. This is apropos to all complicated cases, particularly cases involving extensive technical data. The Libertarian Party, having a considerable presence in Montana, supports an opposite point of view and seeks to expand the participation and power of the jury, urging passage of a "fully informed jury" amendment. The proposed amendment would require the court to advise the jury of its power to make a decision based on moral conviction apart from judicial instructions. A "fully informed jury" amendment could certainly wreak havoc in the civil law with the potential to undermine vested rights or to punish perceived advantage taking. The proposed amendment would be less damaging and more justifiable in the criminal law, insofar as the right was limited to the protection of the defendant. The 1972 Montana Constitution, as did the 1889 Constitution, requires the jury to determine both law and facts in libel and slander cases. The last sentence of Article II, section 7 states that "[i]n all suits and prosecutions for libel or slander the truth thereof may be given in evidence; and the jury, under the direction of the court, shall determine the law and the facts." The courts have consistently ignored or avoided the language (*Manley v. Harer*, 1928).

Notwithstanding the language of Montana's Constitution that says "[t]he right of trial by jury is secured to all and shall remain inviolate," the court has determined that the right to trial by jury is not available in all cases. The court has concluded that there is no constitutional right to jury trial in a racial discrimination suit (*Vainio v. Brookshire*, 1993). The adjudication of a new "public right" created by the legislature can be assigned to an administrative agency without violating the constitutional right to a jury trial (*Romero v. J & J Tire*, 1989). A jury trial is not required to establish aggravating circumstances necessary to impose a death sentence because aggravating circumstances are not elements of the crime charged and capital sentencing procedures do not require jury participation (*State v. Daw son*, 1988). The constitutional right to a jury trial is not applicable to revocation of a suspended sentence because the right is guaranteed in criminal prosecutions, but not necessarily in all criminal proceedings (*State v. Watts*, 1986). There is no right to a jury trial in termination of parental rights because the right to a jury trial is limited to cases in which the right was guaranteed when the 1889 Constitution was first adopted and at that time there was no right to a jury trial in cases terminating parental rights (*In re C.L.A.*, 1984). This interpretation, in effect, says new language in a new constitution can be ignored in reliance on the presumed intent of the drafters and ratifiers of a prior constitution and the history related to language used in that prior constitution.

Occasionally, the court has interpreted the right to jury trial more expansively. In *Gray v. Billings* (1984), overruling prior decisions, the Montana Supreme Court held that all parties in equity court are entitled to have their legal claims tried by a jury. The Montana Supreme Court has held that judicial increase of sentence in retaliation for demand to trial by jury violates the constitution (*State v. Baldwin*, 1981). A statute allowing a misdemeanor defendant to exercise his right to a jury trial, in either justice court or state district court in a trial de novo but not both, violated the defendant's constitutional right to a trial by jury (*Woirhaye v. Montana Fourth Judicial Dist. Court*, 1998). A number of cases discuss errors in empaneling, selecting, dismissing, and advising juries. The development of the law in these areas is generally in accord with prevailing theories of trial by jury.

## SECTION 27

**Imprisonment for Debt.** No person shall be imprisoned for debt except in the manner provided by law, upon refusal to deliver up his estate for the benefit of his creditors, or in cases of tort, where there is strong presumption of fraud.

The section is intended to protect every person from possible imprisonment for debt and is derived from and identical with the 1889 Montana Constitution, Article III, section 12. During the constitutional convention debates it was proposed that the section read: "[n]o person shall be imprisoned for debt" and the exceptions following the word "debt" be eliminated. The proposal was defeated by a vote of 44 to 34. The exceptions to imprisonment for debt are included to protect creditors from recalcitrant debtors and in victims of torts where there is a strong presumption of fraud. If fraud can be proved, criminal and tort law is available to right any wrong and that exception is unnecessary. Further, it is questionable whether a presumption should ever support imprisonment. Although important in theory, the provision has not been cited and has not had any notable effect in the law. Perhaps if it were not available persons would be imprisoned for debt.

In the criminal law there are some cases in which it appears that defendants have been incarcerated for failure to pay restitution or failure to pay fines where the defendant is financially unable to make the required payment. Suspended and deferred sentences, and parole or probation, conditioned on payment of fines or restitution, may appear like incarceration for indebtedness. The Montana Supreme Court has never held that financial conditions attached to a sentence are per se unconstitutional, but some cases touch on the idea (*State v. Fisch*, 1994; and *State v. Babbit*, 1978). The opinion in *State v. Carroll* (1986) suggested that incarceration based on the inability to pay restitution would not violate equal protection. The defendant argued that he had been sentenced to prison because of his indigence, but the court found sufficient reasons to support incarceration, noting that the sentence was well within the statutory parameters for felony theft.

The inability to make bail often results in incarceration. Persons with adequate financial backing will usually be allowed to bail themselves out of jail. People without sufficient assets are regularly held in jail, often for substantial periods of time until guilt or innocence is decided (*State v. Pease*, 1987).

## SECTION 28

**Criminal Justice Policy—Rights of the Convicted.** Laws for the punishment of crime shall be founded on the principles of prevention, reformation, public safety, and restitution for victims. Full rights are restored by termination of state supervision for any offense against the state.

The provision purports to lay a foundation for all criminal law, justifying punishment as the means to prevent crime, insuring public safety, providing restitution for victims, and reforming those convicted of crime. As a separate part, full rights are automatically restored to every convicted person after completion of state supervision. This section represents the vision of two distinctly different groups. The original language emphasized prevention, reformation, and restoration of rights. The change added by the referendum passed in 1998 (public safety and restitution) represented political pandering to public concern for public safety and restitution. The referendum has minimal, if any, practical impact since existing correctional and sentencing policy of the state of Montana, Montana Code Annotated, Section 46-18-101, includes provisions designed to "(b) protect the public by incarcerating violent offenders and serious repeat offenders; and (c) provide restitution [and] reparation . . . to the victim of the offense." Most courts include restitution as part of each sentence. Public demand to get tough on crime has resulted in more persons incarcerated for longer sentences than at any time in history. Montana reflects the same concerns, putting intense pressure on available correctional facilities and rehabilitation services.

The provision is derived from and similar to Article III, section 24 of the 1889 Montana Constitution, but deletes the reference to capital punishment that was addressed in the earlier version. Capital punishment was voted upon as a separate issue when the proposed constitution was presented to the people of Montana. Because capital punishment was being separately considered, it was necessary to remove any reference to capital punishment from the body of the constitution as submitted to the voters. The vote favored retention of capital punishment by a margin of nearly three to one.

Additionally, this section differs from the 1889 Constitution by providing for automatic restoration of rights. The 1972 Constitution restates this proposition in Article XII, section 3: "Suspended rights [due to commitment to a state institution] are restored upon termination of the state's responsibility." Article IV, section 2 excludes persons "serving a sentence for a felony in a penal institution" from being a qualified elector and section 4 adds that "no person convicted of a felony shall be eligible to hold office until his final discharge from state supervision." Thus a person convicted of a felony's right to seek public office is automatically restored after serving his sentence. Automatic restoration of rights is an attempt to facilitate the return of convicted criminal defendants (and persons committed to any state institution) to society in general and to the life of a given community. Under prior law, restoration of rights for convicted criminal defendants was accomplished by executive pardon. Full rights are not intended to be restored to those on probation, parole, or with suspended sentences because they are still considered to be under state supervision (MCC Tr. 39697).

In large measure, the state legislature and the Montana Supreme Court have ignored this provision. A variety of legislative acts prohibit the restoration of full civil rights upon termination of state supervision by restricting service and employment in a wide range of public and private activities. Upon termination of state supervision, former offenders (depending on the offense) are denied the right to: serve as jurors (Mont. Code Ann., Section 3-15-303); reside in Montana Veterans' Homes (Mont. Code Ann., Section 10-2-403); be employed as highway patrol officers, sheriffs, and game wardens (Mont. Code Ann., Sections 19-6-703, 19-7-703, and 19-8-803); be employed by disaster and emergency services organizations (Mont. Code Ann., Section 10-3-112); contract (Mont. Code Ann., Section 28-2-201); be elected as a bank director (Mont. Code Ann., Section 32-1-322); be licensed in horse racing, in gambling facilities, in sale of securities (Mont. Code Ann., Sections 23-4-201, 23-5-176, 30-10-201, and 37-1-2). Among the rights the delegates intended to be restored were the rights to vote, to hold office, and to enter occupations which require state licensing (MCC Tr. 1800–1801).

Montana Code Annotated, Section 45-7-401 requires forfeiture of office after conviction for misconduct. However, an Attorney General Opinion has determined that there is a right to run for a subsequent term of office from which a public servant has been removed for misconduct because the statute does not prohibit the officer from running for a subsequent term after the end of state supervision. To hold otherwise would violate this section's provision for full restoration of rights upon termination of state supervision for an offense against the state (39 Op. Att'y Gen. 226 (1982)).

In interpreting this section, the Montana Supreme Court has tended to emphasize the safety of society and not the requirement that punishment shall be based on prevention and rehabilitation. The court held that because of the violence associated with a defendant's crimes and the frequency of their commission, it was proper to restrict defendant's opportunity for parole to protect society (*In re Petition of Arledge*, 1988). Protecting society is undoubtedly that part of the justification for punishment that prevents criminal conduct. Cases have discussed prevention in a context that supports all incarceration within the parameters of an existing statutory design both in terms of warning future potential criminal law violators and in terms of removing the specific individual from society. The cases have not carefully or thoroughly addressed rehabilitation.

In *State v. Bruns* (1984), the defendant challenged her sentence on the theory that it violated Article II, section 28 because it failed to provide for rehabilitation. The court noted that Article II, section 28 requires that laws for punishment of crime be founded on the principles of prevention and reformation.

In a bit of sophistry the court reasoned that the defendant's sentence furthers the prevention principle through incarceration, and the order to abstain from the use of alcohol provides the avoidance of further incarceration as an incentive to reform, satisfying the constitutional requirement.

Article II, section 28 does not prevent increases in punishment for repeat offenders (*State v. Sanders*, 1984). While the section grants an offender who has served his sentence a fair opportunity to enjoy the rights of law-abiding citizens, it does not grant immunity from being treated as a persistent felony offender (*State v. Radi*, 1978; see also *State v. Gafford*, 1977). Persistent felony offender laws do not involve any civil or political rights, and increasing the sentence of a persistent felony offender is entirely consistent with the constitutional mandate that "laws for the punishment of crime shall be founded on the principles of prevention [and] reformation" (*State v. Maldonado*, 1978). About the only exception to the regular circumvention of the section was the determination that an escalating fine schedule for parking violations breaches the basic principle of law that punishment must be for the violation and proportional to the gravity of the offense, and hence is violative of Article II, section 28, which provides that laws for the punishment of crime shall be founded on principles of prevention and reformation (*Missoula v. Shea*, 1983).

## SECTION 29

**Eminent Domain**. Private property shall not be taken or damaged for public use without just compensation to the full extent of the loss having been first made to or paid into court for the owner. In the event of litigation, just compensation shall include necessary expenses of litigation to be awarded by the court when the private property owner prevails.

This section is a compromise between the protection of individual ownership of real property and the need for communities to provide for the public good. While private property may be taken for roads, bridges, and parks, and easements may be acquired for electric lines and pipelines, "just compensation" must be paid. No provision is made for compensating indirect regulatory takings. The 1972 Montana constitutional provision goes further than most in that it includes the necessary expenses of litigation when private property is taken. This language is intended to include appraisers' fees, attorneys' fees, and court costs (MCC Tr. 1825). This is more a clarification than a change. However, the section also says that just compensation shall be paid to the owner of private property whenever private property is "damaged" for or by public use to the full extent of the loss.

According to the philosopher John Locke, the protection of private property is a first principle of any free and effective system of government. While Adam

Smith might agree, many others would disagree, from Marx to supposedly ultra-conservative private power companies that have arranged to obtain great wealth as private monopolies with the power of eminent domain.

The section also provides for compensation for "damage to property" short of recovery of litigation expenses. The 1972 eminent domain section is derived from and similar to Article III, section 14 of the 1889 Montana Constitution. The basic provision is the same as the U.S. Constitution. This section does expand the protection afforded a landowner to include necessary expenses of litigation. The convention delegates did not intend to stop construction of highways while property value litigation is pending (MCC Tr. 1827).

In *McElwain v. County of Flathead* (1991), county regulations were changed after McElwain had purchased land on which to build a house. The property owner brought an action seeking damages for reduction in the value of her property caused by enactment of county septic regulations which required a 100- foot setback between the septic system drain field and the flood plain. The sole issue was whether the reduction in value of appellant's property was a taking for which compensation was due. The court held that the regulations did not constitute a "taking" of property for which compensation was due. This court reached this conclusion despite assuming that a diminution of two-thirds of the value of the property had occurred, stating that loss in values much greater than the two-thirds found here have been held not to constitute a taking. The court held the appropriate takings test was whether the land-use regulations were substantially related to the state interest in public health, safety, and general welfare and whether the regulations utilize the least restrictive means necessary to achieve their purpose without denying the owner the economically viable use of his or her land. The opinion did not discuss the meaning of the word "damaged."

Deemphasizing the "damage" provision of the section, the Montana Supreme Court has held that there can be no recovery if there is no actual taking. In the particular case, the plaintiff claimed damage as a result of increased noise, dust, traffic, and pollution; aesthetically, a change of view; and the inconvenience of ingress and egress (*Adams v. Department of Highways of State of Montana*, 1988). Although the provision was specifically intended to provide compensation for damage to private property as well as actual takings, *Yellowstone Valley Elec. Co-op., Inc. v. Ostermiller* (1980) also refused to evaluate damages as opposed to actual takings.

In *Howard v. State* (1982), the court concluded that an interference with the right to use property might constitute a taking but again failed to mention the "damage" concept of the provision. Only in *McCone County v. James* (1982) did the court find that damages could be recovered for diminution of land value. In this case there was a change of access rather than diminution caused by a regulation of use. Also, compensation by the state was required for diversion of vagrant surface water causing damage to private lands (*State v. Feenan*, 1988).

## SECTION 30

**Treason and Descent of Estates.** Treason against the state shall consist only in levying war against it, or in adhering to its enemies, giving them aid and comfort; no person shall be convicted of treason except on the testimony of two witnesses to the same overt act, or on his confession in open court; no person shall be attainted of treason or felony by the Legislature; no conviction shall cause the loss of property to the relatives or heirs of the convicted. The estates of suicides shall descend or vest as in cases of natural death.

The section both creates the crime of treason against the state of Montana and limits its scope. It also provides the additional procedural requirements of testimony by two witnesses or open court confession. Prohibiting the penalties of forfeiture or attaint (an accusation coupled with dishonor) and protecting the estates of suicides is traditional, laudable, and of marginal practical importance.

This section is derived from and nearly identical to Article III, section 9 of the 1889 Montana Constitution. Changes made were grammatical.

The reason for the section is more historical than currently significant. It has always been a part of constitutional law and certainly it is appropriate to continue the protection, although the treason portion seems pointless. The provision for descent of estates of suicides is appropriate, although it is equally unlikely that the legislature would provide otherwise. The apparently more civilized nature of legislative bodies coupled with the provision in the U.S. Constitution precludes the likelihood that penalties of forfeiture or attaint would be revived. Treason against the state that is separate and apart from treason against the national interest is difficult to imagine and unlikely to be punished. The provision is of significant theoretical value but of little or no practical value. Theonly case of any interest concluded that legislation prohibiting a woman, convicted of voluntary manslaughter, from inheriting property from the victim's estate, did not violate the parallel provision of the 1889 Montana Constitution (*Sikora v. Sikora*, 1972).

## SECTION 31

**Ex Post Facto, Obligation of Contracts, and Irrevocable Privileges.** No ex post facto law nor any law impairing the obligation of contracts, or making any irrevocable grant of special privileges, franchises, or immunities, shall be passed by the Legislature.

The section contains three distinct provisions with somewhat dissimilar objectives. The first, ex post facto, is traditionally a due process criminal notice provision and protects against making an act criminal which at the time of the act was not criminal, increases the punishment, aggravates the crime, or changes the evidence necessary to convict. The second, impairment of contract, as found in state constitutions, is designed generally to protect creditors; and the third, prohibition of special privileges, franchises, and immunities, is designed to avoid gross abuse of government power and to guarantee a measure of competitive equality.

The section is derived from and identical to Article III, section 11 of the 1889 Montana Constitution and in large measure parallels Article I, section 10 of the U.S. Constitution. dictable. The language seems to have been viewed as advisory rather than mandatory.

The idea of prohibiting special privileges, franchises, and immunities is appealing, both in the sense of abstract justice and the specifics of equal protection under law. Government grants of special privileges or franchises are at odds with an open, free economic system. To afford some citizens special privileges or immunities is, by definition, an affront to the ideal of equal protection and an abuse of both government power and government largesse. The singularly most provocative aspect of the section is the limitation that grants of special privileges not be irrevocable. Implicitly, the language seems to indicate that grants of special privileges could be made as long as the particular grant was not "irrevocable." However, without authoritative interpretation, what is meant remains obscure.

The interpretation of the 1889 Montana Constitution raised the "proper exercise of police power" to a position superior to all property and contract rights. *Butte v. Roberts* (1933) stated that if a city ordinance is a proper exercise of the police power it is of no consequence that it affects property rights or rights based upon existing contracts, since such rights must yield to the common welfare Under the 1889 Montana Constitution it was also established that the ex post facto provision applied only to criminal law, and the protection from retroactivity affecting private rights was protected, if at all, by some applications of due process and by the prohibition against the impairment of the obligation of contract (*Durocher v. Myers*, 1929). These positions have not changed under the 1972 Constitution, although they have been further explicated. As to the ex post facto clause, see *O'Shaughnessey v. Wolfe* (1984) and State v. Hall (1986). In at least two cases the Montana Supreme Court maneuvered around the ex post facto clause even in criminal cases: one involving a capital punishment law that was found to be unconstitutional (*State v. Fitzpatrick*, 1980); and a second, enhancing punishment for persistent felony offenders (*State v. Maldonado*, 1978). In both cases the Montana Supreme Court found that the ex post facto clause was not violated, even though the statute under which the defendant was originally sentenced was found to be unconstitutional and the defendant was subsequently sentenced under a new and revised statute (*State v. Fitzpatrick*). In *State v. Maldonado*, a persistent felony offender statute was invoked to enhance the defendant's sentence for a crime committed prior to the date of its enactment.

In interpreting the "impairment of obligation of contracts" clause as found in the 1972 Montana Constitution, the Montana Supreme Court established a threepart test relative to the impairment of contracts: (1) Is the state law a substantial impairment of a contractual relationship? (2) Does the state have a significant and legitimate purpose for the law? (3) Does the law impose reasonable conditions reasonably related to achieving a legitimate and public purpose? In the particular case the court found that the workmen's compensation law in question did violate the constitutional provision against the impairment of contracts. Although the language of the constitution seems absolute, the court's analysis relied on a series of prophylactic terms and phrases including "substantial," "significant," legitimate," and "reasonable conditions reasonably related." These terms would seem to leave the court with unlimited discretion (*Carmichael v. Workers' Comp. Court of State of Mont.*, 1988).

In *D & F Sanitation Serv. v. City of Billings* (1986), the Montana Supreme Court noted that Montana Code Annotated, Section 7-2-4736 conferred a special privilege or franchise upon garbage haulers, but since the franchise was revocable it was not unconstitutional.

## SECTION 32

**Civilian Control of the Military.** The military shall always be in strict subordination to the civil power; no soldier shall in time of peace be quartered in any house without the consent of the owner, nor in time of war, except in the manner provided by law.

The section subordinates military power to civil power and prohibits quartering soldiers in peacetime. The first phrase, civil power over military power, is a core protection of democracy but of limited significance in a state government which has minimal military presence or military authority, and the second phrase, quartering soldiers, was a concern of the colonists but not a concern of the citizens of Montana.

This section is derived from and similar to Article III, section 22 of the 1889 Montana Constitution. There are no substantive changes. It is also patterned after the U.S. Constitution, which was a response to the excesses of King George III and England. There is little or no reason for the provision. It has little relevance or value to the practical operation of the state government of Montana. It is unlikely to be cited in any Montana cases or to be determinative of the exercise of any individual rights. There are no cases interpreting the provision.

## SECTION 33

**Importation of Armed Persons.** No armed person or persons or armed body of men shall be brought into this state for the preservation of the peace, or the suppression of domestic violence, except upon the application of the Legislature, or of the governor when the Legislature cannot be convened.

The section prohibits bringing armed men into the state except upon official government request. It is derived from and identical to Article III, section 31 of the 1889 Montana Constitution. The substance of the section originally was proposed by a delegate with ties to organized labor. Friends of labor cited instances where companies employed bodies of armed men, ostensibly to preserve peace but in fact to intimidate workers. Pinkerton detectives had been brought to Butte to oppose strikers in labor disputes. Some delegates asserted that Montana was able to keep the peace and that armed men should be brought in only by the legislature or by the governor when the legislature was not in session.[16] The reason for continuing the section is dubious, rooted as it is in copper company power and nineteenth-century vigilantism. However, recent events may have rekindled fears relative to bringing armed persons into the state without government authorization. For example, self-proclaimed "Constitutionalist," Cal Greenup, a Montana rancher, challenged local law authorities and the Montana Fish and Game Department. According to newspaper reports, Greenup threatened to bring armed persons into the state to support his challenges to established authorities. There were some confrontations between Greenup, supported by friends and family, and duly constituted authority. In 1996, Greenup pled guilty to obstructing justice and was given a 15-year suspended sentence. A charge of criminal syndicalism was dropped.

The militant, anti-government "Freemen," located in eastern Montana, attempted to install a separate government and threatened various local officials. In 1998, a Montana federal district court jury convicted nine members of the Freemen on charges of bank and mail fraud and armed robbery. The "Montana militia" has received unfavorable notice, and finally, out-of-state terroristic activities such as the Oklahoma City disaster add to local fears and help justify the prohibition against bringing armed persons into the state. From the opposite political spectrum the prohibited activity seems to be directed toward private action and raises questions about the right to bear arms. In practice, the section is probably without significant value and there are no cases interpreting the provision.

---

[16] James M. Hamilton, *History of Montana: From Wilderness to Statehood* (Portland, OR: Binfords & Mort, 1970), p. 544.

## SECTION 34

**Unenumerated Rights.** The enumeration in this constitution of certain rights shall not be construed to deny, impair, or disparage others retained by the people.

The provision implies the existence of individual rights not otherwise specified in the constitution. This section is derived from and identical to Article III, section 30 of the 1889 Montana Constitution, and is nearly identical to the Ninth Amendment to the U.S. Constitution. The convention committee believed this section could be the source of innovative judicial activity in the area of civil liberties (MCC Rep. 645). The convention committee's belief has not been realized. There are no cases referencing or interpreting the section. Comparable language in the Ninth Amendment to the U.S. Constitution has rarely been referenced and never definitively. Some aspect of the idea of unenumerated rights might be found in the court's application of substantive due process.

The section could be used as the basis for the introduction of a theory of natural law or an expansion of the use of substantive due process or judicial finding of unstated individual rights hidden in the self-reliant, free-thinking, idiosyncratic Montanan mythology. Presumptively, this could limit state police power and enlarge existing rights or create new rights. Viewed in its historical context, the Ninth Amendment to the U.S. Constitution was drafted to prevent concentration of power in the federal government and to preserve individual or personal rights. The federal government was perceived as a government of limited, enumerated powers with all residual power resting in the states or the people. To the extent that the idea of a federal government of limited, enumerated power was implemented, the Ninth Amendment might be perceived as redundant or vestigial. Since the passage of the Fourteenth Amendment and the development of "incorporation" as a means of applying the first eight amendments to the U.S. Constitution to limit the exercise of state police power, the Ninth Amendment could prove a powerful addition to the judiciary's ability to protect individual rights if it were so inclined. While plenary state legislative power and unenumerated rights might appear to be in conflict or contradictory, they are not. In a state constitution a provision on unenumerated rights as a balance against state police power is a potentially useful idea, but something of an anomaly. Historically, within the context of state governments in a federal system, the limitations on plenary legislative power are the specific prohibitions and restrictions found in a constitutional declaration of rights. Adding unenumerated rights to specific prohibitions and restrictions could transfer to the people indirectly, and to the courts directly, additional means of checking plenary legislative power. There is no conflict or contradiction in the theory or nature of government so conceived. There is a tension in the balance of power between the legislative branch and judicial branch, in one dimension, and the degree of protected personal freedom versus the exercise of general police power of the legislature, in a second dimension. If "plenary" is perceived as without limit and if "unenumerated rights" are likewise perceived as without limit, then conflict or contradiction appears. Both theory and practice belie absolutist definitions in this context; rather, it is a matter of balance. The promise of protected unenumerated rights shifts the balance toward personal freedom and away from unfettered legislative prerogative.

The provision has had no practical value but could be a powerful tool in the hands of an activist and imaginative supreme court. While the Montana Supreme Court, in the decade following the enactment of the 1972 Constitution, might be considered activist in its interpretation of the plain language of the constitution, its substitution of traditional theories of the common law for the language of the constitution and its reliance on a subjective sense of fairness in evaluating the facts of a given case rather than a rigorous application of statutory language or constitutional principle were not imaginative or creative in the sense of limiting state police power or expanding individual rights. The Montana Supreme Court, in the years approaching 2000, was more creative and less activist while directed toward both enlarging individual rights and curbing the excesses of state police power.

## SECTION 35

**Servicemen, Servicewomen, and Veterans.** The people declare that Montana servicemen, servicewomen, and veterans may be given special considerations determined by the Legislature.

The section announces a patriotic commitment to Montana service personnel, circumventing the equal protection clause of Article II, section 4, without direct cost or sacrifice and without specific meaning. The legislature is instructed that it may implement the proclamation.

This is a new provision and has no parallel or comparable provision in the 1889 Montana Constitution. It was a response by the constitutional delegates to a general sense of guilt, patriotism, and concern in the aftermath of the Korean conflict and in the wake of protests against the Viet Nam conflict; Nixon's Vietnamization plan; and the tedious Viet Nam peace initiatives. It was a means to honor and repay veterans for military service and give added advantages to those still in the military.

Payment for service to country should be direct and consistent. It should be related to the sacrifice made. This does neither. Many of those who sacrificed most have been forgotten, while generalized, indiscriminate special privileges defy the ideal of equal protection.

The cases conclude that any right created by this provision is permissive only; that is, it may be acted upon by the legislature but there is no requirement that the legislature enact any special considerations for servicemen or servicewomen

(*Femling v. Montana State Univ.*, 1986). Once the legislature grants special considerations, such considerations are neither vested rights (*Conboy v. State*, 1985) nor property rights (*Nick v. Montana Department of Highways*, 1985). This section, as implemented, seems to frustrate the idea of equal protection as expressed in Article II, section 4, and to violate Article II, section 31, prohibiting the grant of irrevocable privileges although, since the court has determined that privileges once granted do not vest, any privileges are not irrevocable (*Conboy v. State*). The Montana Supreme Court has held that the provision does not infringe the rights of due process or equal protection and the issue of irrevocable special privileges has not been raised directly (*Nick v. Montana Department of Highways*).

# Article III

## *General Government*

### SECTION 1

**Separation of Powers.** The power of the government of this state is divided into three distinct branches—legislative, executive, and judicial. No person or persons charged with the exercise of power properly belonging to one branch shall exercise any power properly belonging to either of the others, except as in this constitution expressly directed or permitted.

This section is intended to insure a separation of powers among the branches of government. It is an explicit statement of the structure of government to be followed in the state of Montana. The specific allocation of power among the branches of government is outlined in Articles V (the legislature), VI (the executive), and VII (the judiciary). Separation of powers is generally conceded to be the most effective structural design to limit accumulation of power in the hands of a single person or a single group of people.

The section is indirectly derived from the idea of separation of powers implicit in the U.S. Constitution and is immediately derived from and substantively identical to Article IV, section 1 of the 1889 Montana Constitution. There are minor word and punctuation changes. "Department" as used in the 1889 Constitution has been changed to "branches" in the 1972 Constitution. The word "branch" is used in the 1972 Constitution to identify the legislative, executive, and judicial divisions of government. The word "department" is used in the 1972 Constitution to identify the various divisions within the executive branch of government.

The idea that power allocated to one branch of government shall not be exercised by a different branch of government seems implicit in the grant of power in Articles V, VI, and VII. Power granted to one branch of government cannot be exercised by another. Such separation of power helps restrain the centralization and abuse of power, but with the loss of efficiency and the fragmentation of responsibility.

Three cases decided under the 1889 Montana Constitution succinctly outlined the purpose of constitutionally mandated separation of powers. They noted that the separation of powers constituted each department (branch under the 1972 Constitution) as an exclusive trustee of the power vested in it, accountable to the people alone for its faithful exercise, so that each department acts as a check upon the other to prevent the tyranny and oppression which would be the result of a lodgment of all power in the hands of one body (*State ex rel. Smith v. District Court*, 1914; *O'Neill v. Yellowstone Irrigation District*, 1912; *Schneider v. Cunningham*, 1909). A fourth case noted that the separation of the government into three departments does not mean that there shall be no common link of connection or dependence but only that the powers properly belonging to one shall not be exercised by the others (*State ex rel. Hillis v. Sullivan*, 1913).

The several cases discussing legislative branch powers display few unexpected conclusions. However, an equal protection case challenging mandatory early retirement as age discrimination reached a somewhat unusual conclusion, holding the determination of discrimination was a legislative function and not a judicial function. The court held that resolution of the case required a (legislative) fact-finding hearing to determine whether there was a basis for age discrimination (*Taylor v. Department of Fish, Wildlife & Parks*, 1983). In another case the Montana Supreme Court held that a judicial law clerk could also be a legislator without violating this section (*State ex rel. Paugh v. Bradley*, 1988).

The cases discussing judicial powers and the possible intrusions on judicial powers are standard and expectable decisions. One case held a statute providing termination of a police judge at the will of the city commission was an unconstitutional violation of the separation of powers provision (*State ex rel. Morales. City Comm'n*, 1977). Other cases have held that the establishment of time requirements for rendering judicial opinions is exclusively a judicial function (*Coate v. Omholt*, 1983); that a statutory provision for automatic transfer of older youth from youth court to district court for prosecution for some offenses does not usurp judicial power (*In re. Wood*, 1989); and that commitment of a delinquent juvenile by youth court to the Department of Family Services for placement was not a violation of the separation of powers section and did not infringe on the judicial decision-making power (*In re Peterson*, 1989).

A number of cases have discussed the problem of delegating power (i.e., the transfer of power) from one branch of government to a second branch. Statutes that delegate legislative authority to executive branch administrative agencies are required to provide policy directives as well as clear, definite guidelines prescribing the agencies' authority (*Douglas v. Judge*, 1977).

## SECTION 2

**Continuity of Government**. The seat of government shall be in Helena, except during periods of emergency resulting from disasters or enemy attack. The Legislature may enact laws to insure the continuity of government during a period of emergency without regard for other provisions of the constitution. They shall be effective only during the period of emergency that affects a particular office or governmental operation.

The state constitution designates Helena as the permanent capital of the state of Montana. The emergency clause gives the legislature an effective trump card over all other constitutional provisions during the course of an emergency resulting from unnamed disasters or enemy attack. The only stated limitation on the power of the legislature is the determination that an emergency exists, and the duration of the emergency.

Location of the state capital was one of the most hotly disputed issues surrounding the drafting and ratification of the 1889 Montana Constitution. Article X, sections 2 and 3 of the 1889 Montana Constitution provided that Helena would be the temporary location of the capital; that the permanent location of the capital would be determined later, by vote of the electors; and that the location of the capital of the state might thereafter be changed by two-thirds vote of the qualified electors. The elimination of the 1889 constitutional provision allowing the seat of government to be moved by a vote of two-thirds of the people was the most significant change made by this section. After 100-plus years the commitment to having the temporary and permanent capital of the state of Montana located in Helena is uncontested. The remainder of the section was derived from and similar to Article V, section 46 of the 1889 Montana Constitution that provided for continuity of government in periods of emergency.

The provision is probably necessary but no longer interesting or controversial. There is a minimum of continuing activity in preparing for government during periods of emergency, but there is no concern about relocation of the capital during periods of emergency or otherwise.

There are no cases interpreting this provision.

## SECTION 3

**Oath of Office**. Members of the Legislature and all executive, ministerial and judicial officers, shall take and subscribe the following oath or affirmation, before they enter upon the duties of their offices: "I do solemnly swear (or affirm) that I will support, protect and defend the constitution of the United States, and the constitution of the state of Montana, and that I will discharge the duties of my office with fidelity (so help me God)." No other oath, declaration, or test shall be required as a qualification for any office or public trust.

The provision is intended to specify a required oath for government officers and to both identify the scope of the oath and to constitutionalize the limits of the oath. This section was derived from and substantively similar to Article XIX, section 1 of the 1889 Montana Constitution. The oath required in the 1889 Constitution was considerably longer and more detailed than required by this section.

The required oath is more a historical relic than an enforceable moral commitment. An amoral or immoral, traitorous villain would not hesitate to take an oath to uphold the constitution and the law. The person most likely to hesitate or object to an oath or affirmation would be someone of deep philosophical and moral commitment. There may be a measure of value to the moment of formality surrounding the oath-taking ceremony. The moment of formality may impress some persons, and does stress the responsibilities they are assuming and the commitment they have made.

There are no cases interpreting the section. Under the 1889 Constitution members of the legislature were prohibited from accepting grants or gifts even as members of a specially created "Legislative Council" (*State ex rel. Mitchell v. Holmes*, 1954; overruled in *State ex rel.* James v. Aronson, 1957). While such a limitation is not a part of the 1972 Constitution, limitations on acceptance of gifts or grants by government officials is now statutory (Mont. Code Ann., Section 45-7-104: gifts to public servants by persons subject to their jurisdiction).

## SECTION 4

**Initiative.** The people may enact laws by initiative on all matters except appropriations of money and local or special laws.

Initiative petitions must contain the full text of the proposed measure, shall be signed by at least five percent of the qualified electors in each of at least one third of the legislative representative districts and the total number of signers must be at least five percent of the total qualified electors of the state. Petitions shall be filed with the secretary of state at least three months prior to the election at which the measure will be voted upon.

The sufficiency of the initiative petition shall not be questioned after the election is held.

This section is a broad authorization for enactment of laws by initiative, excluding only appropriation laws and local or special laws. Constitutional amendment by initiative is provided for separately in Article XIV. This section requires that an initiative petition be signed by 5 percent of the electors (voters) in each of at least one-third of the 100 legislative districts, and by 5 percent of the total qualified electors, and be filed with the secretary of state at least three months prior to election. This much detail is unusual in a constitution, but significant in emphasizing the objective of the convention delegates and the voters that government operation be accessible to the people, not only in a representative sense but by direct action.

This section was derived from and similar to Article V, section 1 of the 1889 Montana Constitution. Although the original 1889 provision limited the means by which the constitution could be amended, the voters approved an amendment in 1905 that provided for initiatives and referenda. The 1889 Constitution, as amended, excluded from the initiative process appropriation laws, local and special laws, and constitutional amendments; it also was more demanding in the numbers and geographical location of signatures required. It required 8 percent rather than 5 percent of the total qualified electors, and 8 percent rather than 5 percent of the electors (voters) in each of at least two-fifths of the 28 counties, rather than one-third of the electors in each of the 100 legislative districts.

At the turn of the century, concern over corporate control of state legislatures prompted the Progressive Party to crusade for constitutional authorization of initiatives and referenda. Montana mining companies exerted inordinate influence over legislators, first by providing bill drafting services and prepaid "watering holes." When subtle influences were inadequate, monied individuals and powerful corporations resorted to bribery, fraud, collusion, and blackmail (see K. Ross Toole, *Montana, An Uncommon Land*, p. 188 et seq.). Company lobbyists were often indistinguishable from the legislators; indeed, many were legislators. "Lobbying in the Montana Legislature was part art, part cold cash, part rubber-hose bludgeoning and part cajolery" (K. Ross Toole, *Twentieth-Century Montana: A State of Extremes*, p. 259). After ten years of vigorous crusading, with support from the Montana Federation of Labor and various progressive leaders, the Progressive Party secured, via constitutional amendment, the initiative and referendum (Malone, Roeder, Lang, *Montana: A History of Two Centuries*, pp. 255–256).

While initiatives and referenda are perceived as progressive or liberalizing mechanisms and the signature requirement in the 1972 Montana Constitution is more liberal than in its 1889 counterpart, still the need to obtain signatures in at least one-third of 100 legislative districts, as contrasted with obtaining signatures in two-fifths of 28 counties, causes problems for individuals or groups seeking to have an initiative or referendum qualified and placed on the ballot. Voters rarely know legislative district boundaries and often do not know the legislative district of their residence. Finally, in a somewhat unexpected turn, initiatives and referenda have proved useful to conservative foes of government and taxation.

This section is intended to insure that the citizens of the state of Montana have the ability to initiate changes in the law. This section does not provide for constitutional change by initiative, but unlike the comparable section of the 1889 Constitution it does not prohibit such change, and Article XIV, section 9 does provide for constitutional change by initiative. The entire tenor of the 1972 Constitution encourages public participation in government, including in this instance changing law by initiative. "[T]he similarity between the process required to amend the Montana Constitution and the initiative process gives an aura of constitutionality to laws passed by initiative."[17]

This is an important provision, expressing the populous spirit that pervaded the constitutional convention. The response by the public has been notable. By the end of the millennium 59 petitions proposing laws had been attempted; 30 had been completed, filed, and voted upon; and 17 had passed and become law (see Figure 1). Among the more notable initiatives are the following:

1-84: forbidding the disposal of radioactive waste material within the state of Montana (1980), passed by a vote of 172,909 to 172,493.
1-85: requiring public disclosure of money spent to influence action of a public official (lobbyist disclosure) (1980), passed by a vote of 259,698 to 76,358.
1-92: expanding gambling to include blackjack, punch boards, and certain electronic or mechanical gambling devices (1982), rejected by a vote of 191,334 to 115,297.
IR-112: rejecting, by referendum, a proposed income tax passed by the legislature (1994), 246,368 to 83,813.
1-121: increase minimum wage (1996), rejected by a vote of 227,975 to 175,769.

The principal case decided under this section was *Montana Automobile Ass'n v. Greely* (1981). In that case the court held that parts of Initiative 85 requiring disclosure of non-lobbying expenses, providing exemptions for Montana citizens, and restricting voters from making promises to support elected officials were unconstitutional as violative of free speech and the privileges and immunities clause of Article IV, section 2 of the U.S. Constitution. The balance of the initiative dealing with the licensing, eligibility, arid record keeping of lobbyists; specific accountings of lobbyists; reimbursements by public officials to lobbyists; disclosure by elected officials; the authority of the Commissioner of Campaign Finances and Practices to promulgate the necessary administrative rules; and civil penalties and enforcement for the various provisions was held to be sufficient to carry out its purpose, and was sustained.

---

[17] Larry M. Elison & Dennis NettikSimmons, "Right of Privacy," *Montana Law Review*, 48 (1987): 43.

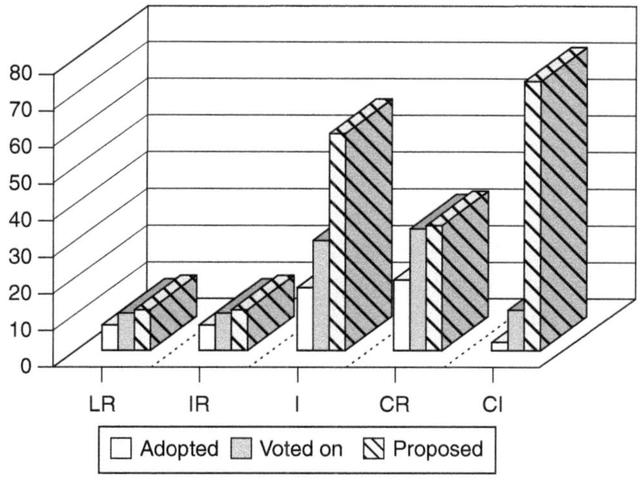


***Figure 1*** *Direct Democracy in Action: 1972–1998.*

LR = Legislative Referendum. A legislative referral of a proposed law to the people in their capacity as the "third branch of the state legislature."
IR = Initiative Referendum. A referendum initiated by electors by which petitioners may secure voter review of a legislative enactment. If there are enough signatures, the measure is suspended until the election.
I = Initiative. This is a law originating with a petition and then passed by the voters. The legislature is not involved.
CR = Constitutional Referendum. This is a proposed constitutional amendment referred to the voters by the legislature. The legislature cannot independently amend the constitution but must refer constitutional amendments to the people for a referendum.
CI = Constitutional Initiative. This is a constitutional amendment proposed by petition. The legislature is not a part of this process. Most are not brought to a vote because petitioners are unable to secure the required number of signatures.

In an important aside the court noted that the absence of fact-finding capabilities in the initiative process is not proof of the absence of a compelling state interest in the enactment of an initiative. An affirmative statewide vote on an initiative is a demonstration of a compelling state interest in enactment of the initiative (*Montana Automobile Ass'n v. Greely,* 1981).

Under the 1889 Constitution the Montana Supreme Court approved an initiative generating and appropriating money for a discrete, special group, holding that the prohibition against appropriating state funds by initiative was directed to appropriations from the general funds. The section did not prohibit an additional cigarette tax to pay a soldiers' bonus since the tax was to go into a special fund and was to be used only for a special purpose (*State ex rel. Graham v. Board of Examiners,* 1952).

## SECTION 5

**Referendum.** (1) The people may approve or reject by referendum any act of the Legislature except an appropriation of money. A referendum shall be held either upon order by the Legislature or upon petition signed by at least five percent of the qualified electors in each of at least one third of the legislative representative districts. The total number of signers must be at least five percent of the qualified electors of the state. A referendum petition shall be filed with the secretary of state no later than six months after adjournment of the Legislature which passed the act.

(2) An act referred to the people is in effect until suspended by petitions signed by at least 15 percent of the qualified electors in a majority of the legislative representative districts. If so suspended the act shall become operative only after it is approved at an election, the result of which has been determined and declared as provided by law.

Continuing the goal of open government and citizen participation, this section insures the power of citizen review of legislation by referendum. Referendum petitions need to be signed by only 5 percent of the electors in one-third of the legislative districts and 5 percent of the qualified electors in the state. These percentages are reduced from parallel requirements in the 1889 Montana Constitution and have recently come under attack as being too liberal and an unnecessary imposition on the representative nature of state government.

This section was derived from Article V, section 1 of the 1889 Montana Constitution but unlike this section, the comparable 1889 constitutional provision excepted, from approval or rejection by public referendum, laws "necessary for the immediate preservation of the public peace, health, or safety." The court defined the exception to extend no further than to matters arising out of some unforeseen menace, public calamity, accident, sudden emergency, extraordinary occurrence, or unprecedented climatic condition rendering immediate action imperative to prevent serious or irreparable injury to the public (*State ex rel. Goodman v. Stewart*, 1920). Both this section and the parallel provision in the 1889 Constitution except appropriations from approval or rejection by referendum. The provision allows the citizens of the state to exercise a more direct control on the actions of elected representatives.

The section broadens the scope of the referendum and makes it easier to use. As such, the section is an important check on legislative action. Special interest groups often exercise notable control over elected officials without broad-based support for their positions. While these same special interest groups may be able to sway public opinion and obtain the same result at the polls, it is a more difficult challenge and the public is provided an avenue for direct participation in the decision-making process. By the end of 1998 there had been 11 legislative referenda in which the legislature referred a proposed law to the people. The people approved seven. There had also been seven referenda initiated by electors in which petitioners sought voter review of a legislative enactment. Ultimately, two were submitted to the voters and one was approved.

Four cases have interpreted the section. The first determined that the referendum, if passed, would have no effect on the "fait accompli"—the legislative ratification of the proposed "Equal Rights Amendment." At the time the referendum was attempted, the ratification was an accomplished fact and could not be rescinded by referendum (*State ex rel. Hatch v. Murray,* 1974). The second case held that a proposed referendum to prevent the use of funds to pave a county road was an attempt to overrule an administrative decision, not a legislative act, and was therefore an inappropriate use of the referendum (*Chouteau County v. Grossman,* 1977). The third case (*State ex rel. Gould v. Cooney,* 1992) said that the governor's signature was not required on a legislative referendum and that a referendum measure redirecting the coal trust fund was not an appropriation. The fourth case (*Nicholson v. Cooney,* 1994) said: (1) the suspension of a new income tax passed by the legislature pending the referendum on it did not violate equal protection of the laws, even though the suspension of the law by petition was caused by only a minority of the people; and (2) a tax increase is not an appropriation and therefore is subject to a referendum.

## SECTION 6

**Elections.** The people shall vote on initiative and referendum measures at the general election unless the Legislature orders a special election.

## SECTION 7

**Number of Electors.** The number of qualified electors required in each legislative representative district and in the state shall be determined by the number of votes cast for the office of governor in the preceding general election.

Section 6 describes the method for determining when initiatives and referendums shall be voted upon. Section 7 describes how the number of qualified electors shall be determined, primarily in response to Article III, sections 4 and 5, that address percentages of "qualified electors" necessary to place initiatives and referendums on the ballot. The section does not refer specifically to initiatives and referendums and is a separate subdivision of the Article on General Government. It outlines the method of determining the number of qualified electors required for any purpose and for initiatives and referenda in particular.

The substance of both sections is derived from Article V, section 1 of the 1889 Montana Constitution, a lengthy section encompassing legislative power, initiatives, referenda, and details relating to each. The 1972 Constitution generally followed the pattern established in the 1889 Constitution, but separated the several subjects and liberalized the numbers required to place initiatives and referenda on the ballot.

Both sections are necessary. Also, they are necessarily arbitrary, technical, and specific but unlikely to create substantial controversy, although initiative and referendum activity in the 1990s triggered renewed debate on the number of signatures that should be required. There are no cases interpreting the 1972 provision and no significant cases interpreting the comparable 1889 provision.

## SECTION 8

**Prohibition**. The provisions of this Article do not apply to Constitutional Revision, Article XIV.

This is a new provision intended to differentiate the general initiative and referendum requirements found in this section from the special initiative and referendum requirements for amending the constitution, found in Article XIV.

The section is clarifying and cautionary, as it endeavors to avoid potential confusion between general initiatives and referenda provided for in this Article and constitutional amendatory initiatives and referenda provided for in Article XIV. Since this section and Article XIV, sections 1, 8, and 9 use the identical words "initiative" and "referendum," it was advisable to explain what was intended and avoid the potential argument that the two articles addressed the same subject matter.

There are no cases interpreting this provision.

## SECTION 9

**Gambling**. All forms of gambling, lotteries, and gift enterprises are prohibited unless authorized by acts of the Legislature or by the people through initiative or referendum.

This section prohibits gambling unless authorized by the legislature or the people. It was approved at the same time the body of the constitution was ratified but appeared as a separate ballot issue.

Article XIX, section 2 of the 1889 Montana Constitution addressed the issue of gambling, prohibiting the legislature from authorizing lotteries or gift enterprises for any purpose. This section changes the constitutional prohibition against "lotteries and gift enterprises" and allows the citizens of the state of Montana and their legally elected representatives to determine the issue of gambling without constitutional restraint. Although lotteries and gift enterprises were prohibited under the 1889 Constitution, there was a measure of legal circumvention as well as erratic enforcement. For example, legislation permitting and implementing parimutuel gambling on horse racing was enacted in 1965.

The 1972 provision opened the door to gambling in Montana. Over the course of 25 years, legislation has been enacted permitting live and video poker, keno, and bingo. Other permitted gambling includes card games, sport pools, Calcutta pools, and lottery tickets. Gambling on live horse racing has continued and mule racing has been added as well as simulcast betting on horse racing and greyhound racing. Live greyhound racing is prohibited, and in 1982 the voters rejected Initiative 92 which would have allowed blackjack, punch boards, and other electronic or mechanical gambling devices.

In interpreting section 9 the supreme court denied local governments the right to pass local gambling laws, holding that "People," as used in Article III, section 9 of the Montana Constitution is synonymous with the voters of the entire state of Montana and not the voters of a single local unit of government. Only the state legislature or "the people" of the entire state are authorized to legalize gambling (*Anaconda-Deer Lodge County v. Lorello*, 1979).

# Article IV

*Suffrage and Elections*

## SECTION 1

**Ballot.** All elections by the people shall be by secret ballot.

The section guarantees that all elections shall be by "secret" ballot and is derived from and nearly identical to Article IX, section 1 of the 1889 Montana Constitution. The only modification of the comparable 1889 provision is the use of the term "secret ballot" in place of the term "ballot." Elections under the 1889 Constitution were in fact secret, although the former constitutional provision did not specify that ballots were to be secret. It is an important but non-controversial provision, unlikely to be tested in the courts. The word "secret" was added to guarantee secrecy (MCC Tr. 391).

There are no cases interpreting the 1972 constitutional provision. Under the 1889 provision the court held that "secrecy" is the essence of voting by ballot even though there was no mention of a "secret" ballot in the constitution (*State ex. rel. Van Horn v. Lyon*, 1946), and further, that the use of voting machines was not in contravention of the ballot requirement of Article IX, section 1 of the 1889 Montana Constitution (*State ex rel. Fenner v. Keating*, 1917).

## SECTION 2

**Qualified Elector.** Any citizen of the United States 18 years of age or older who meets the registration and residence requirements provided by law is a qualified elector unless he is serving a sentence for a felony in a penal institution or is of unsound mind, as determined by a court.

The section insures the basic right of suffrage for all persons residing in the state of Montana. It specifies constitutional minimums of age (18), and citizenship (U.S.). It excludes persons incarcerated for conviction of a felony and persons of unsound mind, as determined by a court of law. Otherwise the section assigns authority to define registration and residence requirements to the legislature. The 18-year-old vote is provided to comply with the Twenty-sixth Amendment (1971) to the U.S. Constitution (MCC Tr. 392).

The section is derived from parts of a number of sections of Article IX of the 1889 Montana Constitution, including sections 2, 3, 6, 8, and 12. Sections 2 and 3 of Article IX of the 1889 Constitution provided for the qualification of electors in Montana, whereas under this section qualification to vote is established by the legislature. Further, part of Article IX, section 2 of the 1889 Constitution proviso was negated by the Twenty-sixth Amendment to the U.S. Constitution which lowered the voting age for all U.S. citizens to 18. The U.S. Supreme Court held invalid the provisions of Article IX, section 2 of the 1889 Montana Constitution restricting, to taxpayers, the right to vote on measures creating a debt or liability (*State ex rel. Ward v. Anderson,* 1971).

The 1972 constitutional provision changed the felony conviction limitation on voting, providing that only those persons currently serving a sentence for a felony in a penal institution are constitutionally prohibited from voting rather than any person convicted of a felony who has not received gubernatorial pardon. The objective of no longer requiring pardons is to remove participation of the governor's office from decisions regarding reinstatement of citizens' rights under conditional paroles and conditional sentences. This was too cumbersome and expensive a process (MCC Tr. 398).

Persons of unsound mind, as determined by a court, are denied the right to vote under this section, whereas under Article IX, section 8 of the 1889 Montana Constitution "idiots and insane" persons were denied the right to vote (see Article IX, section 8 of the 1889 Constitution). The real significance of the change is in limiting the exclusion to persons who have been found by a court to be of unsound mind rather than use the generalized and undefined terms of idiocy and insanity. As a result of new developments in mental health, the delegates thought it unwise to set arbitrary mental disqualifications with labels and felt it wiser to leave decisions to judges (MCC Tr. 392).

The basic scheme of representational democracy presupposes citizen participation in government. The provision is important in designing the basic format for suffrage. The section is neither novel nor controversial. Perhaps it implies a responsibility of citizenship and not just a right of citizenship. (See Article II, section 1, stating that "[i]n enjoying these rights, all persons recognize corresponding responsibilities.")

There are no significant cases interpreting section 2.

## SECTION 3

**Elections.** The Legislature shall provide by law the requirements for residence, registration, absentee voting, and administration of elections. It may provide for a system of poll booth registration, and shall insure the purity of elections and guard against abuses of the electoral process.

This section, along with Article IV, section 2 of the 1972 Constitution, authorizes the legislature to establish general voting requirements and to administer elections. Poll booth registration is intended to make it easier to vote. Pre-registration to vote can act as a deterrent to voting fraud (MCC Tr. 401).

This section is derived from Article IX, sections 2 and 9 of the 1889 Montana Constitution, but unlike the earlier provision this section does not attempt to fix the specifics of voter qualification or the administrative details for elections. Authorizing the legislature to provide the means to secure generalized constitutional objectives such as voter registration, residency requirements, absentee voting, and the administration of elections in a manner to avoid abuses is in accord with the general tenor of a constitution. The constitution guarantees the right to vote and access to the polls, encourages voter participation, and maintains individual safeguards, while transferring to the legislature the responsibility for arranging the details. The provision makes it easier to comply with federal changes in the law, and, within the limits of constitutional protections, allows for practical changes toward enhancing voter participation.

There are no cases interpreting the 1972 provision.

## SECTION 4

**Eligibility for Public Office.** Any qualified elector is eligible to any public office except as otherwise provided in this constitution. The Legislature may provide additional qualifications but no person convicted of a felony shall be eligible to hold office until his final discharge from state supervision.

The section establishes the basic qualifications necessary to hold public office. Since all qualified electors are generally eligible to hold any public office, the intent is for maximum citizen participation in government. The two exceptions, "as otherwise provided in this constitution" and as the "Legislature may provide," could be significant limitations. For example, the constitution prescribes additional qualification for some public offices: most judicial officers must be admitted to the practice of law (Article VII, section 9) and the governor must be at least 25 years of age (Article VI, section 3). The section also adds the special proviso prohibiting felons from holding office until after final discharge, although they may vote after release from incarceration (*Emery v. State*, 1978).

This section is derived from Article LX, sections 2, 10, and 11 of the 1889 Montana Constitution. Excluding felons from holding public office was an indirect prohibition in the 1889 Montana Constitution. Convicted persons were prohibited from voting unless they were pardoned or restored to citizenship by the governor, and the right to hold public office was limited to qualified voters.

To organize government it is essential that requirements for holding public office be established, and it seems appropriate that general qualifications, as well as some specific qualifications, be included in the constitution. The specific qualifications for public office, although necessarily arbitrary, are rarely contested.

There are no cases interpreting this section of the 1972 Constitution. The cases under the comparable 1889 constitutional provision have no value as precedent, but are of historical relevance as they record and symbolize the struggle for equality by women who sought to become citizens, which encompassed the right both to vote and to hold public office. The determinative case was *Rose v. Sullivan* (1919), holding that adoption of the suffrage amendment to the U.S. Constitution eliminated gender as a qualification to hold office in the state of Montana, and the use of the word "male" in any statute prescribing a qualification for office was of no consequence.

## SECTION 5

**Result of Elections.** In all elections held by the people, the person or persons receiving the largest number of votes shall be declared elected.

The section provides for traditional majority rule and perhaps it implies a "one person, one vote" rule. (See the U.S. Supreme Court case *Reynolds v. Sims,* 1964.)

This section was derived from and is substantively identical to Article IX, section 13 of the 1889 Montana Constitution. There are minor changes in language. The idea of majority rule is a premise of the theory of constitutional democracy. The identification of persons to be considered in the idea of "majority rule" has been a continuing conflict, commencing with the federal constitution and the exclusion of slaves, women, and Native Americans. Perhaps the rule is now so fundamental that it is unnecessary to include the provision in the constitution, but it seems appropriate to do so.

There are no cases decided under the 1972 Montana constitutional provision and no significant cases decided under the 1889 Montana Constitution.

## SECTION 6

**Privilege from Arrest.** A qualified elector is privileged from arrest at polling places and in going to and returning therefrom, unless apprehended in the commission of a felony or a breach of the peace.

The provision is intended to protect the voting process and avoid abuse by legal authorities in delaying or stopping people from voting for minor infractions or by delaying arrests for prior offenses until election day. A voter is privileged from arrest during the voting process unless "apprehended in the commission of a felony or breach of peace."

This section is derived from Article IX, section 4 of the 1889 Montana Constitution. The substance of the provision is nearly identical to the comparable 1889 Montana Constitution, although it deletes the term "treason" that presumably is included in felony; it also broadens the privilege by narrowing the exception to current criminal conduct. It is possible that in response to historic abuses there is a continuing concern that legal authorities could use unsubstantiated charges to deter people from voting. The historical tradition of voting freedom in Montana is sufficiently strong that such blatant abuse of the legal system seems unlikely, short of revolution or other complete breakdown of the system, and control by unforeseen tyranny or unrestrained corruption.

The provision has marginal value. Arranged arrests, sufficient to affect the electoral process, are unlikely short of mass arrests signifying the destruction of the entire governmental system. If the system is destroyed, this provision seems unlikely to save it.

There are no cases interpreting this section or its predecessor in the 1889 Montana Constitution.

## SECTION 7

**Ballot Issues—Challenges—Elections**

1. An initiative or referendum that qualifies for the ballot under Article III or Article XIV shall be submitted to the qualified electors as provided in the Article under which the initiative or referendum qualified unless a new election is held pursuant to this section.
2. A preelection challenge to the procedure by which an initiative or referendum qualified for the ballot or a postelection challenge to the manner in which the election was conducted shall be given priority by the courts.
3. If the election on an initiative or referendum properly qualifying for the ballot is declared invalid because the election was improperly conducted, the secretary of state shall submit the issue to the qualified electors at the next regularly scheduled statewide election unless the Legislature orders a special election.

This section, enacted in 1990 by Constitutional Amendment Number 21, was a direct response to the court decision *State ex rel. Mont. Citizens for the Preservation of Citizens'* Rights v. Waltermire (1987). In this case the court held a purported amendment void because publication of the amendment by initiative did not follow constitutional mandates. The language of the amendment as filed and certified by the secretary of state was not the same as the language submitted to the voters at the election and the difference was material. Voter upset with the decision triggered this addition to the constitution.

This provision is intended to provide a special procedural design to protect and implement initiatives and referendums. The provision emphasizes the importance of legislation that is supported by a majority vote of the people, commanding judicial priority in resolving challenges to initiatives or referendums and requiring immediate resubmission of any initiative or referendum that is invalidated because the election was held to be improper.

There are no cases interpreting the section.

## SECTION 8

### Limitation on Terms of Office

1. The secretary of state or other authorized official shall not certify a candidate's nomination or election to, or print or cause to be printed on any ballot the name of a candidate for, one of the following offices if, at the end of the current term of that office, the candidate will have served in that office or had he not resigned or been recalled would have served in that office; (a) 8 or more years in any 16-year period as governor, lieutenant governor, secretary of state, state auditor, attorney general, or superintendent of public instruction; (b) 8 or more years in any 16-year period as a state representative; (c) 8 or more years in any 16-year period as a state senator; (d) 6 or more years in any 12-year period as a member of the U.S. house of representatives; and (e) 12 or more years in any 24-year period as a member of the U.S. senate.
2. When computing time served for purposes of subsection (1), the provisions of subsection (1) do not apply to time served in terms that end during or prior to January 1993.
3. Nothing contained herein shall preclude an otherwise qualified candidate from being certified as nominated or elected by virtue of write-in votes cast for said candidate.

This section was Constitutional Initiative Number 64, which the voters approved in 1992. There were no term limit provisions in the 1972 Constitution.

The U.S. Supreme Court in U.S. Term Limits v. Thornton (1995) said that the U.S. Constitution prohibits states from imposing congressional qualifications additional to those enumerated in the text of the U.S. Constitution. Thus subsections (1)(d) and (1)(e) of section 8 are void.

A Montana Attorney General Opinion, 47 Op. Att'y Gen. No. 9 (1997), dealt with how this section affects a potential candidate who has served eight years in office and then left office for a period of eight years. This rather confusing opinion says that such a candidate would not be eligible to run for office again after having been out of office for eight years. The opinion does not say whether the individual would ever be eligible to run for office again.

There are no cases interpreting this section.

# Article V

## *The Legislature*

### SECTION 1

**Power and Structure.** The legislative power is vested in a Legislature consisting of a senate and a house of representatives. The people reserve to themselves the powers of initiative and referendum.

The section vests the legislative power, an essential attribute of any government, in a bicameral legislature. The particular design selected by the 1972 Montana Constitution is traditional and similar to that followed in most states. The specific language for the section is derived from and substantively identical to the first two phrases of the first sentence of Article V, section 1 of the 1889 Montana Constitution. A proposal for a unicameral legislature was separately submitted to the electorate and defeated.

It is essential to designate the source of state legislative authority, because, unlike the U.S. Constitution, there is no specific enumeration of the powers granted to the legislature. The theoretical difference is significant. The practical difference is more ephemeral since the limited, delegated, enumerated powers of the federal government as originally conceived have grown to enormous proportions in large measure based on Supreme Court Justice John Marshall's interpretation of the "commerce clause" and the "necessary and proper" clause.

Historically, state governments within the U.S. federalist system have assumed general police powers with the power to enact any law that advances the general welfare, health, and safety. The only limitations on the Montana legislature are the specific prohibitions and restrictions upon government power found in the Montana Constitution and the limitations imposed by the U.S. Constitution.

Article I, section 1 of the 1972 Montana Constitution states that "All political power is vested in and derived from the people. All government of right originates with the people, is founded upon their will only, and is instituted solely for the good of the whole." Unlike the original states, heirs to the historical power derived from the 13 colonies, Montana might be perceived as really different and without some vestigial implied powers. If the literal language of Article I, section 1 were followed, it might be assumed that, insofar as all political power is vested in and derived from the people, until specific grants of power are transferred from the people to the government, the government is without power. The only power the state government could legitimately exercise would be the power specifically granted in the state's organic document, the Montana State Constitution. Whether a general grant of legislative power includes all that is not prohibited or only that which is specified is theoretically important but pragmatically insignificant. The historical assumption of implied power, the concept of state police power and the general deference by the state judiciary to discretionary legislative determination means that as a practical matter state government is limited only by specific constitutional prohibitions. An increasingly expansive application of substantive due process or serious judicial consideration of unenumerated constitutional rights, as found in Article II, section 34, could change the equation.

Several cases have considered the issue of delegation of legislative power. In *White v. State*, (1988), the court focused on the authority delegated by the legislature and whether limits on that authority are clearly prescribed, holding that constitutional law does not permit an administrative board to determine the limits of its power. In this case the administrative board would have been required to legislate the limits of its power to give meaning to the vague terms of the bill.

In most cases the court has found challenged legislative enactments complete and sufficiently clear, definite, and certain to enable the agencies to know their respective rights and obligations. Guidelines as amorphous as "economic and environmental feasibility" have been sustained (*Grossman v. State*, 1984; see also *Huber v. Groff*, 1976).

An Attorney General Opinion states that the orderly gathering of initiative petition signatures at primary election polling places that does not interfere with the election process may not be prohibited. Any interference with the initiative process must be narrowly construed in light of the state constitution's provisions guaranteeing an open initiative process (39 Op. Att'y Gen. 229 (1982)).

There was only one case interpreting the parallel section in the 1889 Montana Constitution. The case dealt with the effect of voter disapproval of a legislative enactment and is not of continuing significance (*State ex rel. Esgar v. District Court*, 1919). The particular problem is now the subject of another provision. (See Article III, sections 4 and 5.)

## SECTION 2

**Size.** The size of the Legislature shall be provided by law, but the senate shall not have more than 50 or fewer than 40 members and the house shall not have more than 100 or fewer than 80 members.

This section establishes, within designated limits, the size of the state Senate and House. As a result the number of senators was reduced from 56 to 50 and the number of representatives was reduced from 104 to 100. The policy determination as to the optimum size of a legislature and of each house of a bicameral legislature is necessarily arbitrary. The decision limiting the total number to not more than 150 and not less than 120 was an obvious attempt to keep the two chambers small enough to be efficient and at the same time adequately represent the people of the state, according to geographical distribution, special interests, and existing political units. Montana has a population of less than 800,000, making it possible to represent the various geographical areas, special interests, and existing political units with comparatively few representatives. Because the number of elected representatives is restricted, operational costs are minimal and greater efficiency is possible, although efficiency in the legislative process is not necessarily a positive attribute.

The section covers the same area of constitutional law as Article V, section 4 in the 1889 Montana Constitution, which was repealed in 1966, leaving the determination of the number and distribution of persons in the legislature to be determined by statute. The repeal was in part a response to the decision in the U.S. Supreme Court case *Reynolds v. Simms* (1964), requiring equal representation, giving each vote roughly equal weight.

There are no cases interpreting the section. The explicit position of this section became law in 1974 when the Montana Attorney General certified to the Montana Secretary of State: "The first redistricting and reapportionment plan . . . [providing for 100 House districts and 50 Senate districts has been] filed with the Secretary of State."

## SECTION 3

**Election and Terms.** A member of the house of representatives shall be elected for a term of two years and a member of the senate for a term of four years each to begin on a date provided by law. One-half of the senators shall be elected every two years.

The provision establishes terms of office for each person elected to the state legislature. Two-year terms for members of the House of Representatives in effect means service during the course of one legislative session plus any special sessions that may be called in the course of the biennium. Staggering the four-year terms for senators was intended to guarantee some continuity and experience for each legislative session. Two-year limitations for members of the House of Representatives and four-year limitations for senators is an arbitrary policy decision based on tradition.

This section is derived from and similar to Article V, section 2 of the 1889 Montana Constitution. The 1972 Montana Constitution changes the grammar and otherwise revises the 1889 Montana Constitution by adding the requirement for staggered terms for senators.

Specifying length of terms for members of the legislature seems to be an essential obligation of a constitution, although it is conceivable that terms of office could be left to the decision of subsequent legislatures. The relative short terms for members of the House of Representatives insures maximum responsiveness to the political process, while four-year staggered terms for senators insures some measure of continuity.

There are no cases interpreting this provision. The principal difficulty remaining after reapportionment was completed and after this provision went into effect was scheduling senatorial terms of office. The attorney general issued an opinion concluding that the commission provided for in Article V, section 14 had the responsibility of satisfying the requirements of this section and reapportionment, but could not shorten the term of office of Montana state senators who were elected in 1982 (40 Op. Att'y Gen. 7 (1983)).

## SECTION 4

**Qualifications**. A candidate for the Legislature shall be a resident of the state for at least one year next preceding the general election. For six months next preceding the general election, he shall be a resident of the county if it contains one or more districts or of the district if it contains all or parts of more than one county.

The section establishes residency qualifications for the state legislature. No other qualifications are specified. The section dictates that candidates running for the legislature will reside in the district or county from which they are elected. It responds to the fear that outsiders, not familiar with the local problems, might be elected to office. If the people want an outsider as their candidate and want to elect her to represent them, there is no substantial reason why the people should be denied this power. Preventing a legislator from changing residency during the term of office would seem to be a more legitimate concern.

This section is derived from and similar to Article V, section 3 of the 1889 Montana Constitution. The 1972 Montana Constitution has no minimum age requirement for state legislators as did the 1889 Montana Constitution. The section requires one-year state residency and six months' residency within the county, or within the district, if an election district contains all or parts of more than one county.

There are no cases interpreting this section. An Attorney General Opinion has attempted to describe the intended meaning of the section relative to who may be a candidate for a given district or county. Concluding that:

[a] legislative candidate who resides in a district crossing county boundaries may run in another district in the county of residency which is wholly contained within that county, but may not run in another district in the county of residency which also crosses into another county. A legislative candidate who resides in a district wholly contained within the county of residency may run in another district in the county of residency which is also wholly contained within that county, but may not run in another district in the county of residency which also crosses into another county. (35 Op. Att'y Gen. 76 (1973))

## SECTION 5

**Compensation.** Each member of the Legislature shall receive compensation for his services and allowances provided by law. No Legislature may fix its own compensation.

The provision establishes the method by which legislative compensation shall be determined. It also prohibits the legislature from raising or lowering the compensation to be received by the members of the legislature during a session of the legislature. All changes in compensation must be prospective, commencing after the session during which the change was made.

This section is derived from and similar to Article V, section 5, paragraph 3 of the 1889 Montana Constitution. The changes are mostly grammatical, although the 1972 constitutional provision includes "allowances" in addition to "compensation" as provided by law.

The policy determination to compensate members of the legislature rather than have an unpaid, voluntary legislature seems important in permitting a cross-section of the community to participate directly in the legislative process. Leaving the amount of compensation and allowances to the discretion of the legislature permits the necessary increases or decreases in both compensation and allowances as dictated by economic conditions and political determinations of the time. The original provision in the 1889 Montana Constitution provided that each member of the first legislative assembly receive six dollars for each day's attendance. As of June 1998, legislators received $58.50 per day when the legislature was in session and $70 per day for meal and lodging expenses.

The prohibition against legislative members increasing their own compensation exhibits the inherent distrust of politicians and the sense that a constitution should guard against the private greed of those in power.

In *Gehring v. Members of 1993 Legislature* (1995), the Montana Supreme Court held that the 1991 legislature had fixed the amount of compensation for the 1993 legislature and that the appropriation of money by the 1993 legislature to pay itself the compensation set by the previous legislature did not violate the constitution.

## SECTION 6

**Sessions.** The Legislature shall meet each odd-numbered year in regular session of not more than 90 legislative days. Any Legislature may increase the limit on the length of any subsequent session. The Legislature may be convened in special sessions by the governor or at the written request of a majority of the members.

The provision establishes the time frame within which the legislature is permitted to meet, including special sessions, and provides the means for calling special sessions. The provision reduces the likelihood of having full-time professional legislators. It retains a measure of flexibility in providing for special sessions, affording the legislature the option of increasing the length of future legislative sessions. Under the 1889 Constitution only the governor could convene special sessions. Allowing the legislature to convene a special session was thought to restore the balance of power between the legislature and the governor (MCC Rep. 385). However, the lawmakers have never succeeded in calling themselves into special session. The power to do so remains and over time the legislators may exercise the power and convene a special session.

Originally, Article V, section 6 of the 1972 Montana Constitution provided for annual sessions of 60 days. This section was amended by Initiative Number 1 in 1974. The amendment eliminated annual sessions and deleted the language that "The Legislature shall be a continuous body for two-year periods." The 1974 amendment also increased the number of days that the legislature was to be in session from 60 days in annual session to 90 days in each biennium.

The section is derived from and similar to Article V, sections 5 and 6 of the 1889 Montana Constitution.

There are no cases interpreting this section of the 1972 Montana Constitution. The cases interpreting the parallel provision of the 1889 Montana Constitution validated a bill passed after the 60-day session limit had expired. The legislative journal entries, on their face, showed compliance with the 60-day provision. In other words, the journal entries, although erroneous, were binding on the court (*Standard Oil Co. v. State Board of Equalization*, 1940).

An Attorney General Opinion concluded that a majority of members of the legislature, and not a majority of each house, is required to call a special session (41 Op. Att'y Gen. 99 (1985)).

## SECTION 7

**Vacancies.** A vacancy in the Legislature shall be filled by special election for the unexpired term unless otherwise provided by law.

The provision emphasizes a policy choice made by the 1972 Constitution in favor of electing rather than appointing most public officials. In this case the cost of special elections and the short terms involved in legislative office encouraged the constitutional drafters to defer to existing law on the subject of filling vacancies, providing a constitutional choice if the legislature removed the existing law and declined to replace it.

This is a new provision. The manner of filling vacancies has been and continues to be provided by statutory law (appointment by Board of County Commissioners) and there was no separate provision in the Montana Constitution of 1889 that provided for filling vacancies in the legislature. The provision has no purpose unless the statutory law providing for the filling of an unexpired legislative term were to be repealed.

There are no cases interpreting this provision.

## SECTION 8

**Immunity**. A member of the Legislature is privileged from arrest during attendance at sessions of the Legislature and in going to and returning therefrom, unless apprehended in the commission of a felony or a breach of the peace. He shall not be questioned in any other place for any speech or debate in the Legislature.

The section seeks to protect the members of the legislature from the harassment of having criminal process invoked against them during the course of the sessions that they are obligated to attend. The exceptions are broad enough to protect the public from immediate felonious acts by legislators and grant no ultimate immunity for criminal acts by members of the legislature. The same protection from harassment justifies the freedom from questioning for any statements made in the legislature.

It is possible that the last sentence of the section conflicts with Article II, section 7, if it means that a legislator could not be questioned by members of the general public about comments, indicating positions taken, made in the legislature. Presumptively, the questioning protected against relates to questioning by officials of government with the ability to sanction a legislator.

This section is derived from and, except for grammatical changes, identical to Article V, section 15 of the 1889 Montana Constitution.

The value of the provision is questionable. It is archaic. Legislators are generally subject to the law, possessing the same civil and political rights as other citizens of the state. Legislators are harassed to no greater or lesser extent in public or other forums as a result of this provision.

There are no cases interpreting this provision of the 1972 Montana Constitution and no cases interpreting the parallel provision in the 1889 Montana Constitution.

## SECTION 9

**Disqualification**. No member of the Legislature shall, during the term for which he shall have been elected, be appointed to any civil office under the state; and no member of congress, or other person holding an office (except notary public, or the militia) under the United States or this state, shall be a member of the Legislature during his continuance in office.

The provision prohibits individuals from violating the separation of powers doctrine by holding positions in the executive or judicial branches of government while serving as legislators. It also prohibits individuals from breaching the separation inherent in the theory of federalism, denying state legislators the right to contemporaneously hold office in the federal government. It limits individual power and reduces some potential conflicts of interest.

This section prohibits a legislator from creating an office or job and appointing a legislator to that position (MCC Tr. 595). It also prevents an official from bribing a legislator with the promise of an appointed position in exchange for that legislator voting a certain way on a bill (MCC Tr. 597).

This section is derived from and, except for minor grammatical changes, identical to Article V, section 7 of the 1889 Montana Constitution.

One of the most important determinations made by the Montana Supreme Court was interpreting this section to prohibit members of the legislature from serving as delegates to the 1972 Constitutional Convention (*Legislative Assembly v. Lennon,* 1971). This decision discouraged most long-term members of the state legislature from seeking to become delegates to the 1972 Constitutional Convention. Delegates to the 1972 Constitutional Convention brought a large measure of creative energy and independence. Most of the delegates were not indebted to special interests; and few of the delegates were indebted to other delegates or had a history of antagonism toward other delegates.

In interpreting a similar provision of the 1889 Constitution in *State ex rel. Barney v. Hawkins* (1927), the court held that a public office of a civil nature is: (1) an office created by the state constitution or by the legislature or by a municipality pursuant to delegated authority; (2) an office that has been delegated a portion of the sovereign power of government; (3) an office that exercises independent power; (4) an office that has permanency and continuity; and (5) an office requiring the incumbent to take and file an oath, hold a commission, and give an official bond, if required, by proper authority.

In specific terms, the court has held that neither a "law clerk" nor "master" is a public officer (*State ex rel. Paugh v. Bradley,* 1988); and under nearly identical language in the 1889 Constitution, the court held that a state"boiler inspector" is not a state officer (*State ex rel Nagle v. Page,* 1934). On the other hand, the attorney general said that a mayor (41 Op. Att'y Gen. 348 (1986)) and other municipal officers are prohibited from serving as members of the legislature (40 Op. Att'y Gen. 184 (1984)).

## SECTION 10

### Organization and Procedure

1. Each house shall judge the election and qualifications of its members. It may by law vest in the courts the power to try and determine contested elections. Each house shall choose its officers from among its members, keep a journal, and make rules for its proceedings. Each house may expel or punish a member for good cause shown with the concurrence of two thirds of all its members.
2. A majority of each house constitutes a quorum. A smaller number may adjourn from day to day and compel attendance of absent members.
3. The sessions of the Legislature and of the committee of the whole, all committee meetings, and all hearings shall be open to the public.
4. The Legislature may establish a legislative council and other interim committees. The Legislature shall establish a legislative post audit committee which shall supervise post auditing duties provided by law.
5. Neither house shall, without the consent of the other, adjourn or recess for more than three days or to any place other than that in which the two houses are sitting.

The provision establishes the procedural and organizational structure for the legislature. Subsection (1) grants the legislature authority to provide for judicial intervention in contested elections, thereby reversing a decision interpreting the parallel provision under the 1889 Montana Constitution. In *State ex rel. Ford v. Cutts* (1917), the court held that since each house of the legislature is the judge of the right of persons to seats as members of the legislature, the Montana Supreme Court is without jurisdiction to determine such right.

This section is derived from and similar to Article V, sections 9, 10, 11, 12, and 13 of the 1889 Montana Constitution. Subsection (1) is similar to Article V, sections 9, 11, and 12 of the 1889 Montana Constitution. Subsection (2) is nearly identical to Article V, section 10 of the 1889 Montana Constitution, with minor grammatical changes. Subsection (3) is similar to Article V, section 13 of the 1889 Montana Constitution but requires that all sessions and committee meetings be open to the public. The predecessor section in the 1889 Montana Constitution permitted secrecy if the business at hand so required. Subsection (4) is new, specifically permitting the legislature to create committees to work during periods when the legislature is not in session. Subsection (5) is identical to Article V, section 13 of the 1889 Montana Constitution, except for minor grammatical changes. The lieutenant governor is not intended to be head of the Senate as he was under the 1889 Constitution (MCC Tr. 599).

The policy choices are minimal except the provision for opening to the public all legislative sessions and committee meetings. Delegates debated this policy choice during the consideration of Article II, sections 8 and 9, creating a public right of participation and a public right to know. The 1995 legislature revisited the problem in a debate over whether party caucuses are to be open to the public.

The 1889 Constitution allowed secret proceedings (MCC Tr. 603). The basic procedural and organizational structure is traditional.

It is necessary to provide basic procedural and organizational schemes for the function and operation of the state legislature. It is appropriate that this be done in the state constitution, thereby insuring greater stability in the procedure. Opening all sessions and committee meetings to the public indicates a greater trust in the people and is a positive development of democratic government. The provision for interim committees is managerially advantageous if not absolutely necessary in a state like Montana where the legislature is not continuously in session but meets every other year for 90 days.

The delegates thought it important that the legislature have the authority to continue to conduct legislative post audits. They further concluded that a provision on legislative post audits must be included in the state constitution to avoid constitutional challenges based on any perceived conflict with the duties of the Executive Branch Auditor (MCC Tr. 1005).

The objectives of subsection (5) are to prevent the legislators from using delaying tactics and to prevent one house from passing its bills and then adjourning (MCC Tr. 730).

The court has imposed limits on what an interim committee can constitutionally do. In *State ex rel. Judge v. Legislative Fin. Comm.* (1975), the Montana Supreme Court held that an interim legislative finance committee could not approve budget amendments. The power to approve budget amendments is properly exercisable only by the entire legislature or by an executive officer or agency. Such power vested in an interim legislative committee is an unconstitutional delegation of legislative power.

## SECTION 11

### Bills

1. A law shall be passed by bill which shall not be so altered or amended on its passage through the Legislature as to change its original purpose. No bill shall become law except by a vote of the majority of all members present and voting.
2. Every vote of each member of the Legislature on each substantive question in the Legislature, in any committee, or in committee of the whole shall be recorded and made public. On final passage, the vote shall be taken by ayes and noes and the names entered on the journal.
3. Each bill, except general appropriation bills and bills for the codification and general revision of the laws, shall contain only one subject, clearly expressed in its title. If any subject is embraced in any act and is not expressed in the title, only so much of the act not so expressed is void.
4. A general appropriation bill shall contain only appropriations for the ordinary expenses of the legislative, executive, and judicial branches, for interest on the public

debt, and for public schools. Every other appropriation shall be made by a separate bill, containing but one subject.
5. No appropriation shall be made for religious, charitable, industrial, educational, or benevolent purposes to any private individual, private association, or private corporation not under control of the state.
6. A law may be challenged on the ground of noncompliance with this section only within two years after its effective date.

Subsection (1) establishes the requirement of a majority vote for the passage of legislation. This traditional democratic, majoritarian approach to passing, amending, or repealing laws is a foundational policy choice. It should be noted that there are other provisions in the constitution that require more than a simple majority for some legislative action. (See, for example, Article IX, section 5, dedicating not less than one-fourth of the coal severance tax to a trust fund and requiring a vote of three-fourths of the members of each house of the legislature to change it.) The remaining portion of subsection (1) and all of subsections (3) and (4) are intended to compel the legislature to enact laws in a straightforward and efficient manner. It is intended that the objects of each piece of legislation should be known to the legislators charged with voting for or against the legislation and further, that the public be advised as to the nature of the legislation that is under consideration. Interested persons should be able to understand and follow the course of pending bills. The section is designed to prevent legislators and the people from being misled by false or deceptive titles and to guard against legislative fraud or deceit by incorporating into a law provisions concerning which neither legislators nor the public have any knowledge. It also prevents including unrelated and incongruous subjects in a single bill or including material in a bill that has no relation to the subject specified in the title.

Subsection (1) is derived from and similar to Article V, section 19 of the 1889 Montana Constitution. There is no change except in the grammar. Subsection (2) is derived from and similar to Article V, section 24 of the 1889 Montana Constitution, but unlike the parallel provision in the 1889 Montana Constitution, the 1972 Montana Constitution requires a recorded vote on all substantive questions, both on the floor and in committee. Subsections (3), (4), and (5) are derived from and similar to Article V, sections 23, 33, and 35 of the 1889 Montana Constitution with only minor grammatical changes. Subsection (3) requiring that "[e]ach bill . . . shall contain only one subject clearly expressed in its title" was approved by the delegates by a vote of 52 to 37. Nearly identical wording in the 1889 Constitution had been a frequent source of litigation and at least one delegate to the 1972 convention expressed concern that the nearly identical language would invite continuing litigation. This has not been the case, although the problem did arise in connection with initiative CI-75, *Marshall v. State ex rel. Cooney* (1999). Subsection (4) could be construed to be a substantive change. The parallel provision in the 1889 Montana Constitution appears to absolutely prohibit any appropriation to any denominational or sectarian institution whereas the 1972 Montana Constitution prohibits appropriations for religious purposes to any private association or private corporation. Apparently, appropriations can be made to private religious associations for any purpose which is not religious, charitable, industrial, educational, or benevolent. The listing seems comprehensive and it is difficult to imagine an acceptable purpose. Subsection (6) is a new provision and, according to the explanation provided by the constitutional convention delegates, means that after a law is two years old it cannot be challenged for technical errors based on how it was passed.[18] The language of subsection (6) appears to be much broader and on its face would prohibit a substantive challenge of unconstitutionality to a law that was more than two years old if the law appropriated money"for religious, charitable, industrial, educational, or benevolent purposes to any private individual, private association, or private corporation not under control of the state."

Appropriation bills and bills for codification are excepted as a matter of efficiency and practicality. The process of balancing the state budget makes it almost impossible to attempt to identify each appropriation under a separate title. Less informality as to general appropriations for the continued operation of government is tolerated, although some risk of unidentified spending is possible. As to the codification of general laws, such a process is extraordinary in character and it is impracticable, if not impossible, to formulate a title that would cover every subject embraced in such a bill. Interested members of the legislative body and the public will generally know the overall subject matter being codified. Such bills create a risk of uninformed public support and votes by representatives with less than complete knowledge of what the codification accomplishes. The efficiency of the process is deemed to justify the decreased explanation of the meaning of the legislation.

The difficulty of accurately encompassing the substance of a bill in the title of a bill and of keeping different subject matter separated among bills is attested to by the substantial number of cases that have challenged laws on this ground. A partial answer to the large number of challenges on this ground, while still attempting to prevent legislators and special interest groups from deceiving the public or fellow legislators about the content of bills under consideration, is subsection (6) that limits the time period available in which to challenge a bill on the grounds provided in Article V.

Subsection (5) is an attempt to protect the public purse from benefitting private persons or private associations in a direct financial way rather than bestowing the benefits of government largesse on all citizens, pursuant to acceptable generalized classifications. The language "private corporations" is intended to

[18] *Proposed 1972 Constitution for the State of Montana Official Text with Explanation*, p. 10.

distinguish between private corporations and municipal corporations because of the need to appropriate funds to incorporated towns and cities (MCC Tr. 659).

The provision generally accomplishes its purpose of avoiding the passage of legislation that is unknown to either the legislators or interested members of the public. People drafting bills are generally aware of the requirements and rarely attempt to deceitfully or secretly pass bills with concealed and inappropriate attachments. The process of political compromise generates enough confusion in the meaning of legislation without intentional deception. By the same token the exceptions provided allow for a measure of efficiency in both recodification of the law and in balancing the budget.

There are a number of cases interpreting section 11. The decisions accord with the apparent meaning of the provision. For example, loans and leases to private persons or private associations do not violate the prohibition against making appropriations to private persons or private associations. In the case of *Grossman v. State* (1984), the Montana Supreme Court held that as long as the provisions relating to the expenditure of the funds derived from the proceeds of the bonds are under the control of the state, the constitutional mandate is satisfied. In the *Grossman* case, a state agency was authorized to spend state funds for construction of hydroelectric projects. Subsequent leasing of the completed hydroelectric projects to private associations or private corporations was not unconstitutional.

Guaranteeing loans for the benefit of private persons or private associations does violate the provision. In *White v. State* (1988), the Montana Supreme Court held that pledging the credit of the state to secure the bonds issued by a state agency, the proceeds of which are to be used for the benefit of private businesses, violates this provision of the constitution. Likewise, in *Hollow v. State* (1986), the court held that permitting the use of in-state investment fund money derived from taxation to guarantee loans or bonds of private individuals or private entities, either directly or through the capital reserve account or through the economic development guaranty fund, was unconstitutional under subsection (5) of this section.

There are a number of cases on the sufficiency of "bill titles" and "titles of initiatives." The cases interpret the specific laws or initiatives and the titles attached to each, and determine the sufficiency of the titles in meeting the demands of subsection (3) of Article V. No unusual interpretations or interpretive techniques are to be found in these cases.

## SECTION 12

**Local and Special Legislation.** The Legislature shall not pass a special or local act when a general act is, or can be made, applicable.

This section is derived from and similar to Article V, section 26 of the 1889 Montana Constitution. The parallel provision in the 1889 Montana Constitution attempted to enumerate all of the instances in which local or special laws were prohibited. This section is a general prohibition of special or local legislation.

The provision protects against the legislature imposing burdens or creating benefits that are directed toward individuals separately rather than directed toward all persons over whom jurisdiction is exercised, or directed toward rationally related and legitimately distinguishable classes of persons. The purpose of the section largely parallels the purpose attributed to the equal protection clause of Article II, section 4 in the Montana Constitution and the Fourteenth Amendment to the U.S. Constitution. Both sections have been interpreted to require that similarly situated persons be treated similarly before the law. Section 12 seeks to accomplish the same goal by prohibiting "special" legislation. Section 31 of Article II touches on the same general principle, providing that "[no law] making any irrevocable grant of special privileges, franchises or immunities, shall be passed by the Legislature."

A number of cases have considered the question of local or special legislation as prohibited by this section of Article V of the 1972 Montana Constitution, and all of the cases have found the challenged legislation constitutional. The areas of law considered under this section are diverse, from annexation (*D & F Sanitation Serv. v. City of Billings*, 1986) and gambling (*Palmer v. State*, 1981) to revenue bonds (*Grossman v. State*, 1984) and medical malpractice panels (*hinder v. Smith*, 1981). The judicial response, in practical effect, is much like the equal protection rational basis test. The supreme court has relied on an earlier test for special or local legislation, first announced by *State ex rel. Redman v. Meyers* (1922): "Does [the legislation] . . . operate equally upon all of a group of objects which, having regard to the purpose of the Legislature, are distinguished by characteristics sufficiently marked and important to make them a class by themselves" (p. 1066). Under the parallel provision in the 1889 Montana Constitution the Montana Supreme Court noted that the provision against special and local laws is not absolute. Special laws are prohibited only where general laws can be made applicable (*State ex rel. Ford v. Schofield*, 1917). Most of the cases decided by the Montana Supreme Court in interpreting the provision under the 1889 Montana Constitution indicate a strong deference to classifications made by the legislature.

## SECTION 13

### Impeachment

1. The governor, executive officers, heads of state departments, judicial officers, and such other officers as may be provided by law are subject to impeachment, and upon

> conviction shall be removed from office. Other proceedings for removal from public office for cause may be provided by law.
> 2. The Legislature shall provide for the manner, procedure, and causes for impeachment and may select the senate as tribunal.
> 3. Impeachment shall be brought only by a two-thirds vote of the house. The tribunal hearing the charges shall convict only by a vote of two-thirds or more of its members.
> 4. Conviction shall extend only to removal from office, but the party, whether convicted or acquitted, shall also be liable to prosecution according to law.

This section is derived from and similar to Article V, sections 16, 17, and 18 of the 1889 Montana Constitution.

The provision provides a means for removal of certain high officials from office for whatever reasons may be established by the legislature. This section lists the following officials as subject to impeachment: governor, executive officers, heads of state departments, and judicial officers. It further authorizes but does not mandate the legislature to pass laws enlarging the list of officials subject to impeachment. The section mandates the legislature to define the causes for impeachment and to provide a procedure to be followed in all cases of impeachment. Impeachment can only be brought by two-thirds vote of the House of Representatives but can be tried in any tribunal, and the legislature may select the Senate to try an impeachment. If the legislature does not select the Senate as the tribunal to try impeachments, there is no suggestion as to what other tribunal might be called upon to try an impeachment or who should select the tribunal. Presumptively, the task would fall to the legislature under the requirement that the legislature provide the manner and procedure to be followed. Whatever the tribunal selected, conviction requires two-thirds vote of the members of the tribunal. The punishment for conviction is limited to removal from office although there may be a subsequent charge and prosecution for any crime committed. Unlike a criminal conviction the object of impeachment is removal from a position of power and trust, and punishment beyond removal must derive from the formal criminal code of the state.

The provision is an unusual amalgam of self-executing clauses, clauses authorizing legislative action, and clauses mandating legislative action. The legislature has responded to the constitutional mandates and authorizations by passing a comprehensive law on impeachment. The statutory law generally hews close to the constitutional authorizations, mandates, and suggestions. It repeats the constitutional list of officials subject to impeachment; it selects the Senate as the body to try impeachments; and it provides that the named officials are liable to impeachment for felonies and misdemeanors or malfeasance in office (Mont. Code Ann., Sections 5-5-401 to 5-5-433). However, where the constitution says that "upon conviction [the officer] shall be removed from office," the statute states that the defendant may be suspended or removed from office and disqualified to hold any office of honor, trust, or profit under the state. The language of "suspension" and "disqualification to hold any office" could be found unconstitutional. The language of the constitution is both clear and mandatory. Further, as to future disqualification, Article II, section 28, referring to rights of the convicted, states that "[f]ull rights are restored by termination of state supervision for any offense against the state." Impeachments may be different but the language used is "conviction" and convictions are based on proof of felonies and misdemeanors or malfeasance in office.

Since procedures, other than impeachment, for removal from public office for cause may be provided by law, a number of criminal laws include removal from public office as part of the penalty to be imposed. For example, officials convicted of "Bribery in Official and Political Matters" shall be imprisoned in the state prison for any term not to exceed 10 years or be fined an amount not to exceed $50,000, or both, and shall forever be disqualified from holding any public office in this state (Mont. Code Ann., Section 45-7-101). A conviction of the offense of "Official Misconduct" carries a potential penalty of fine and/or imprisonment and orders forfeiture of office, and expressly states that this statute does not affect any power conferred by law to impeach or remove any public servant or any proceeding authorized by law to carry into effect such impeachment or removal (Mont. Code Ann., Section 45-7-401).

The provision is important to the extent that it affords a method of removing dishonorable officials from office. To maintain public confidence in government, it is essential that officials who abuse their position of trust and power be removed fairly and expeditiously. The impeachment process generally conforms with traditional notions of due process or a sense of fairness but is not likely to be expeditious. Other approaches, such as reliance on the criminal law or the political process as the means for removing officials from public office, are not necessarily faster or more fair.

There is a single case that considers Montana's impeachment provision. While the opinion discusses the almost unlimited authority of the legislature in establishing the procedure for impeachment, the focus of the case is on the Judicial Standards Commission created in Article VII, section 11 (*State ex rel. Shea v. Judicial Standards Comm'n*, 1982).

Under the parallel provision of the 1889 Montana Constitution many cases discussed the problems of determining who are officers subject to impeachment and defining what is "misconduct" sufficient to justify impeachment. The 1972 Constitution left the determination of what misconduct might justify impeachment and what procedures should be followed in an impeachment to the legislature. The primary constitutional limitation is the requirement that impeachment shall be brought by the legislature and by two-thirds vote.

Another customary way to remove dishonorable officials from public office in advance of the time scheduled for their possible re-election is by recall. Twelve other state constitutions have recall provisions. The majority committee report contained a proposal for recall. The minority report characterized recall as "an unnecessary and dangerous harassment provision that would hinder an elected official in performance of his duties. . . . The intent of recall is also basically covered under the . . . electoral system, as elected officials are subject to recall each time their office is up for election" (MCC Rep. 824). The recall proposal was defeated by a vote of 54 to 38.

## SECTION 14

### Districting and Apportionment

1. The state shall be divided into as many districts as there are members of the house, and each district shall elect one representative. Each senate district shall be composed of two adjoining house districts, and shall elect one senator. Each district shall consist of compact and contiguous territory. All districts shall be as nearly equal in population as is practicable.
2. In the legislative session following ratification of this constitution and thereafter in each session preceding each federal population census, a commission of five citizens, none of whom may be public officials, shall be selected to prepare a plan for redistricting and reapportioning the state into legislative districts and a plan for redistricting the state into congressional districts. The majority and minority leaders of each house shall each designate one commissioner. Within 20 days after their designation, the four commissioners shall select the fifth member, who shall serve as chairman of the commission. If the four members fail to select the fifth member within the time prescribed, a majority of the supreme court shall select him.
3. Within 90 days after the official final decennial census figures are available, the commission shall file its final plan for congressional districts with the secretary of state and it shall become law.
4. The commission shall submit its plan for legislative districts to the Legislature at the first regular session after its appointment or after the census figures are available. Within 30 days after submission, the Legislature shall return the plan to the commission with its recommendations. Within 30 days thereafter, the commission shall file its final plan for legislative districts with the secretary of state and it shall become law.
5. Upon filing both plans, the commission is then dissolved.

Subsection (1) is a new provision creating single-member house districts, and senatorial districts composed of two house districts for each senator. Subsections (2), (3), and (4) are also new. They create a five-member commission to prepare, submit, and file a plan for redistricting and reapportioning after each U.S. census. The language in Article V, section 14 was the result of Constitutional Amendment Number 14, which passed in 1984. This section is derived from former Article V, section 4 of the 1889 Montana Constitution and

Article VI, which replaced Article V. Section 2 of Article VI was passed in response to the decision by the U.S. Supreme Court in the case of *Reynolds v. Sims* (1964), requiring that state legislatures reflect population: one person—one vote. (See *Herweg v. Thirty-Ninth Legislative Assembly of Mont.*, 1965.)

The provision arranges for legislative districts coinciding as nearly as possible to both existing geographical configurations and the commands of equal protection of the U.S. Constitution.

The section removes the power of redistricting and reapportioning from the legislature and the judiciary, placing legislative redistricting in the hands of persons other than the affected public officials. Persons entrusted with the power to redistrict and reapportion are selected anew, prior to each national census. This salutary policy decision minimizes both personal political control and party control, thereby increasing the likelihood of fair, objective redistricting and reapportionment. Without such a commission, the Montana Supreme Court or a federal district court could end up performing the task of redistricting and reapportionment (MCC Tr. 694).

Commission reapportionment criteria were challenged in 1983. The U.S. District Court, District of Montana, held that the criteria would have to be balanced; that the commission was judge of its own criteria; and that failure to keep the population deviation within 5 percent of the ideal did not invalidate the reapportionment plan. Some population deviations were over 10 percent (*McBride v. Mahoney*, 1983). The criteria established by the reapportionment commission included governmental boundaries, geographic boundaries, communities of interest, consideration of existing district boundaries, and an attempt to stay within a 5 percent plus-or-minus deviation from the ideal district population.

An Attorney General Opinion concluded that the adoption of the new constitution divested the legislature of all power concerning apportionment of the legislature, except for the power of recommendation in Article V, section 14 of the 1972 Montana Constitution (35 Op. Att'y Gen. 24 (1973)). That same opinion added that the "Commission to Redistrict and Reapportion" has the exclusive power to determine the size of the legislative houses and the geographical makeup of the legislative and congressional districts, subject only to the restrictions of Article V of the 1972 Montana Constitution.

# Article VI

*The Executive*

## SECTION 1

### Officers

1. The executive branch includes a governor, lieutenant governor, secretary of state, attorney general, superintendent of public instruction, and auditor.
2. Each holds office for a term of four years which begins on the first Monday of January next succeeding election, and until a successor is elected and qualified.
3. Each shall reside at the seat of government, there keep the public records of his office, and perform such other duties as are provided in this constitution and by law.

The section establishes constitutional executive branch officers; fixes their term of office; and specifies where each shall reside during their term of office. It is a key provision in arranging the practical organization of the executive branch as one of the branches of government.

This section is derived from and substantively similar to Article VII, sections 1, 8, and 20 of the 1889 Montana Constitution. The 1972 Constitution simplifies the language establishing constitutional executive branch officers. It eliminates state treasurer and state examiner as identified constitutional officers and the board of examiners as a constitutional office, although the positions of treasurer and examiner and the office of the board of examiners remain as a result of statutory law.

There are no decisions interpreting the section under the 1972 Montana Constitution. The cases decided under the comparable provision of the 1889 Montana Constitution are primarily involved with the scope of power and responsibility legitimately held by the named executive branch officers, including the governor (*Gildroy v. Anderson,* 1973), the attorney general (*Woodahl v. Highway Comm'n,* 1970; *State ex rel. Ford v. Young,* 1918; *State ex rel. Nolan v. District Court,* 1899), and the auditor (*State ex rel. Pearl Assurance Co. v. Holmes,* 1942).

## SECTION 2

### Election

1. The governor, lieutenant governor, secretary of state, attorney general, superintendent of public instruction, and auditor shall be elected by the qualified electors at a general election provided by law.
2. Each candidate for governor shall file jointly with a candidate for lieutenant governor in primary elections, or so otherwise comply with nomination procedures provided by law that the offices of governor and lieutenant governor are voted upon together in primary and general elections.

The section states which executive branch officers should be constitutional officers subject to election. The choice was largely dictated by tradition and pressed by persons currently holding the named offices. Which executive branch officers should be of constitutional stature, which should be elected, and which appointed are important policy choices. Guaranteeing an elected auditor is intended to keep people's trust in government and its financial affairs (MCC Tr. 845). Keeping the attorney general an elected official assures his independence and his allegiance to the people rather than to the governor (MCC Tr. 844).

The section is similar to and derived from parts of sections 1 and 2 of Article VII of the 1889 Montana Constitution. The requirement that the candidates for governor and lieutenant governor run as a team and be elected as a team is new. Otherwise the section is less detailed than the parallel provision in the 1889 Constitution. This section leaves the details to the legislature.

There are no cases interpreting the section. The one Attorney General Opinion that is at least partially based on the section determined that the governor has the statutory authority to represent all executive branch agencies for the purpose of collective bargaining with public employee unions (37 Op. Att'y Gen. 702 (1978)).

## SECTION 3

### Qualifications

1. No person shall be eligible to the office of governor, lieutenant governor, secretary of state, attorney general, superintendent of public instruction, orauditor unless he is 25 years of age or older at the time of his election. In addition, each shall be a citizen of the United States who has resided within the state two years next preceding his election.
2. Any person with the foregoing qualifications is eligible to the office of attorney general if an attorney in good standing admitted to practice law in Montana who has engaged in the active practice thereof for at least five years before election.
3. The superintendent of public instruction shall have such educational qualifications as are provided by law.

This section is derived from Article VII, section 3 of the 1889 Montana Constitution. The qualifications for the named constitutional officers were revised by the 1972 Constitution. The age requirement for all named officers was set at 25, whereas the 1889 Constitution required that the governor, lieutenant governor, the superintendent of public instruction, and the attorney general be at least 30 years of age. Residency requirements remain the same but the attorney general is now required to have engaged in legal practice for at least five years and the superintendent of public instruction must meet whatever educational requirements may be established by the legislature. The residency requirement is intended to insure that elected officials are well acquainted with Montana's unique characteristics (MCC Tr. 861).

The provision establishes qualifications for named constitutional officers and is an important, arbitrary, and generally non-controversial statement of qualifications for executive branch leaders in state government.

There are no cases interpreting the provision. It is possible that Article II, sections 4, 14, and 15 imply a constitutional intent that adults should be treated as equals in all regards and that there should be no age requirements or age limitations. However, Article II, section 4, the Montana constitutional provision on non-discrimination and equal protection, does not specifically protect against age discrimination.

## SECTION 4

### Duties

1. The executive power is vested in the governor who shall see that the laws are faithfully executed. He shall have such other duties as are provided in this constitution and by law.

> 2. The lieutenant governor shall perform the duties provided by law and those delegated to him by the governor. No power specifically vested in the governor by this constitution may be delegated to the lieutenant governor.
> 3. The secretary of state shall maintain official records of the executive branch and of the acts of the Legislature, as provided by law. He shall keep the great seal of the state of Montana and perform any other duties provided by law.
> 4. The attorney general is the legal officer of the state and shall have the duties and powers provided by law.
> 5. The superintendent of public instruction and the auditor shall have such duties as are provided by law.

This section is derived from and similar to Article VII, sections 1,5, 15, and 17 of the 1889 Montana Constitution. The only significant change is subsection (2), which is a new provision allowing the legislature to make the lieutenant governor a full-time office. The governor's increasing responsibilities justified a full-time lieutenant governor to be trained as a successor and to provide additional staff support for the governor (MCC Tr. 843). Provision for the lieutenant governor to be president of the Senate was deleted.

The provision designates the general authority of the governor, the secretary of state, and the attorney general. The provision does not suggest any particular responsibilities for the lieutenant governor, the superintendent of public instruction, or the auditor other than the names attached to the office. Detailed responsibilities for each constitutional office are to be provided by the legislature. The post-audit function is intended to stay with the Legislative Audit Committee, which the delegates thought to be more dependable. This was the intent behind not specifying post-audit duties for the auditor (MCC Tr. 922).

The authorization of executive authority is an essential attribute of government as understood in a traditional constitutional democracy. The designation of constitutional officers and the division of executive authority among them is an important guide to the legitimate exercise of executive authority. Further, in a limited constitutional democracy which emphasizes a separation of powers among branches of government, it is significant that the constitution, in establishing the structure of government, specify the scope of executive authority and identify who is to exercise the authority granted.

Only two cases have arisen under this section since the adoption of the 1972 Constitution. One discussed the authority of the attorney general of the state of Montana to effectuate an appeal from a Public Service Commission order to which the attorney general was not a party. The attorney general was denied the right to appeal on behalf of the state of Montana (*Montana Power Co. v. Department of Pub. Serv. Regulation*, 1985). The second case restated an earlier position that held that a constitutional office, such as an auditor, appointed to serve on an executive board, is not in violation of the commands and limitations of the constitution. The appointment to an executive board authorizes no activity which invades the province of power granted to either the legislative or judicial branch of government (*Mountain States Ins. Co. v. State*, 1985).

## SECTION 5

### Compensation

1. Officers of the executive branch shall receive salaries provided by law.
2. During his term, no elected officer of the executive branch may hold another public office or receive compensation for services from any other governmental agency. He may be a candidate for any public office during his term.

The section is derived from Article VII, section 4 of the 1889 Montana Constitution but substantially revises the provision. There is no prohibition against increasing or decreasing salaries of executive branch officers during their term of office and salaries are to be set by the legislature.

The section limits government-paid compensation of each elected officer in the executive branch. It seeks to focus responsibility and to avoid conflicts of interest by restricting the compensation of elected constitutional officials to a single office and to a specified salary for a designated job. These limitations are helpful in allowing voters to better understand the nature and limitations of each office and the total money paid to each elected constitutional officer.

If a sitting legislator is elected to a new office, he must either resign his old office or decline the new (MCC Tr. 927). A constitutional officer is not restricted from serving on a board, such as the Board of Hail Insurance, or from carrying out the duties imposed by the legislature. The basic constitutional limitation is a separation of power among the executive, legislative, and judicial branches. As long as the position on the board has neither legislative nor executive duties, there is no constitutional prohibition. In this instance the court upheld the state auditor's membership on the Board of Hail Insurance as provided by law (*Mountain States Ins. Co. v. State*, 1985).

An Attorney General Opinion (43 Op. Att'y Gen. 93 (1989)) concluded that a national guard member engaged in state service and compensated by the state is subject to state regulation. Pursuant to this section an elected member of the executive branch is prohibited from accepting compensation from the state for service in the Montana Army National Guard. Receipt of dual compensation must be repaid to the state and the state auditor has a right to compel repayment of the unauthorized compensation (43 Op. Att'y Gen. 144 (1989)).

The Montana Supreme Court decided one of the more significant cases on this issue just prior to the 1972 Constitutional Convention. The court held that state constitutional officers could not serve as delegates to the constitutional convention (*Legislative Assembly v. Lennon*, 1971). This decision denied to most entrenched politicians the opportunity to serve as members of the 1972 Montana

Constitutional Convention. The result was a convention composed of concerned citizens rather than career politicians. Old political alignments were avoided; the impact of paid lobbyists was diminished; and pre-existing personal antagonisms and personal obligations were the exception rather than the rule.

## SECTION 6

**Vacancy in Office**

> 1. If the office of lieutenant governor becomes vacant by his succession to the office of governor, or by his death, resignation, or disability as determined by law, the governor shall appoint a qualified person to serve in that office for the remainder of the term. If both the elected governor and the elected lieutenant governor become unable to serve in the office of governor, succession to the respective offices shall be as provided by law for the period until the next general election. Then, a governor and lieutenant governor shall be elected to fill the remainder of the original term.
> 2. If the office of secretary of state, attorney general, auditor, or superintendent of public instruction becomes vacant by death, resignation, or disability as determined by law, the governor shall appoint a qualified person to serve in that office until the next general election and until a successor is elected and qualified. The person elected to fill a vacancy shall hold the office until the expiration of the term for which his predecessor was elected.

The section is derived in part from Article VII, sections 7, 15, and 16 of the 1889 Montana Constitution, but changes and simplifies filling a vacancy in the constitutionally created offices of lieutenant governor, secretary of state, attorney general, auditor, and superintendent of public instruction. The section eliminates the requirement of Senate confirmation.

The section simplifies the process of filling vacancies in constitutionally designated offices. Because the Senate is not continuously in session, Article V, section 6 provides that the legislature shall meet biannually for 90 legislative days. Special sessions, as provided for in the constitution, extend the time the legislature may be in session. Senate confirmation of gubernatorial appointments, if required, could be delayed, generating an increased aura of uncertainty about interim appointments of constitutional officers.

While interim appointments of various executive officers are essential, the precise method employed is rarely a hard-fought policy choice. Simplification of the process seems desirable. Obviously, the less involvement the legislature has in the process, the greater the power lodged in the executive branch of government. In pragmatic terms, the relative shift of power to the executive by eliminating Senate confirmation of some gubernatorial appointments is de minimis.

There are no cases interpreting the provision and only one insignificant case decided under the 1889 sections from which the 1972 provision was at least partially derived. As pointed out by a 1978 Attorney General Opinion, the provisions of the 1972 Montana Constitution compel officials appointed to vacant offices to submit to the electorate as soon as possible within the constraints of election schedules (37 Op. Att'y Gen. 492 (1978)).

## SECTION 7

**20 Departments.** All executive and administrative offices, boards, bureaus, commissions, agencies and instrumentalities of the executive branch (except for the office of governor, lieutenant governor, secretary of state, attorney general, superintendent of public instruction, and auditor) and their respective functions, powers, and duties, shall be allocated by law among not more than 20 principal departments so as to provide an orderly arrangement in the administrative organization of state government. Temporary commissions may be established by law and need not be allocated within a department.

This section is similar to Article VII, section 21 of the 1889 Montana Constitution. Article VII, section 21 was adopted in 1970 and the 1972 constitutional provision made only minor grammatical changes.

Prior to 1970 there had been substantial support for executive branch reorganization with particular emphasis on streamlining government bureaucracy. The constitutional provision establishes the maximum number of departments in the executive branch and encourages a sensitivity to the people's desire that the bureaucracy be not only limited absolutely in number but that the bureaucracy be streamlined in fact. A constitutional limit on the number of departments was perceived as an important guarantee to insure that the executive branch be streamlined and to limit subsequent growth in the executive branch. Presumptively, the same goal could have been accomplished without a constitutional provision, although fixing a limit in the constitution gives increased prominence and permanence to the choice.

There are no cases interpreting this provision.

## SECTION 8

**Appointing Power**

1. The departments provided for in section 7 shall be under the supervision of the governor. Except as otherwise provided in this constitution or by law, each department shall be headed by a single executive appointed by the governor subject to confirmation by the senate to hold office until the end of the governor's term unless sooner removed by the governor.
2. The governor shall appoint, subject to confirmation by the senate, all officers provided for in this constitution or by law whose appointment or election is not

otherwise provided for. They shall hold office until the end of the governor's term unless sooner removed by the governor.

3. If a vacancy occurs in any such office when the Legislature is not in session, the governor shall appoint a qualified person to discharge the duties thereof until the office is filled by appointment and confirmation.

4. A person not confirmed by the senate for an office shall not, except at its request, be nominated again for that office at the same session, or be appointed to that office when the Legislature is not in session.

Subsections (1) and (4) are new provisions. Subsections (2) and (3) are derived from and are similar to Article VII, section 7 of the 1889 Montana Constitution, with only minor grammatical changes.

The language in subsection (1) places supervisory authority over all executive appointments in the governor with the power to appoint and remove. Supervisory power seems implicit and probably adds nothing of substance. The second paragraph of subsection (1) states the traditional and perhaps obvious proscription against appointing more than one person to head a department, although this language would prohibit increasing the number of departments, sub rosa, by dividing the department by placing two persons in charge of a single executive department. Subsections (2) and (3) provide for governor appointment of department heads and legislative confirmation, which is the traditional design. Placing administrative control in the executive branch secures efficiency and responsibility. Legislative veto power over appointments checks politically outrageous appointments.

Subsection (4), prohibiting nomination or appointment of persons previously rejected by the Senate, gives increased significance to the refusal of the legislative branch to confirm. In point of fact almost all gubernatorial appointments are confirmed without challenge.

It is a traditional and necessary outline or description of executive appointment powers. It is not a provision that generates difficult policy choices after the initial decisions to create a constitutional democracy and to structurally limit government power by dividing the power among the legislative, executive, and judicial branches. The increasing size of administrative government, nominally under the control of the governor, has changed the balance of power from the legislative branch to the executive branch and from elected government to appointed government, more often controlled by professionally and technically trained full-time, permanent civil servants. However, this is much more prevalent in the federal government and large states than in Montana.

There are no cases interpreting this provision of the 1972 Montana Constitution. The cases interpreting the parallel provisions of the 1889 Montana Constitution are generally not relevant. However, an interesting 1906 case held that the power to appoint or delegate the appointing power is reserved to the people acting through the legislature. That is, the legislature could appoint or provide for the appointment of officers not otherwise provided for by the constitution. This would seem to be not only a circumvention of the limits on government placed there by the power of the people, but also to endorse the creation of an administrative bureaucracy under the control of the legislative branch of government. In the particular case the legislature designated three stockbrokers in each county to appoint bounty inspectors (*In re* Terrett, 1906).

## SECTION 9

**Budget and Messages**. The governor shall at the beginning of each legislative session, and may at other times, give the Legislature information and recommend measures he considers necessary. The governor shall submit to the Legislature at a time fixed by law, a budget for the ensuing fiscal period setting forth in detail for all operating funds the proposed expenditures and estimated revenue of the state.

This section is derived from and similar to Article VII, section 10 of the 1889 Montana Constitution. There are minor grammatical changes but the only substantive change from the 1889 Constitution is to make mandatory that the governor send a budget to the legislature.

The section outlines the obligation and authority of the governor to generate and lead government policy by informing the legislature about the condition of government and recommending action to be taken by the legislature. The obligation imposed upon the governor to prepare a budget and estimate revenue provides the initial projection for financing state government, to which the legislature responds by preparing a separate budget and a separate estimate of revenue.

This is an important specification of governmental budgetary authority and responsibility. The provision does not control the budget but requires that someone take the initial responsibility for the budget and, perhaps more important, estimate revenue, to comply with the demand, in Article VIII, section 9, that "[a]ppropriations . . . shall not exceed anticipated revenue."

While the language of this section of the Montana Constitution requires the governor to prepare a budget, only the legislature has the power to appropriate money for state government. Further, the legislative branch has the power to create an interim committee to gather information from other branches of government necessary to form a rational basis for its budget determinations (*State ex rel. Judge v. Legislative Fin. Comm.*, 1975).

In *Huber v. Groff* (1976), the court held, in interpreting the mandatory language in the Housing Act of 1975 that required the governor to include the Board of Housing's appropriation request in his budget, that the governor's constitutional obligation to prepare and submit a budget does not prohibit the legislature from requiring the governor to include a specific and identified appropriation request.

## SECTION 10

**Veto Power**

1. Each bill passed by the Legislature, except bills proposing amendments to the Montana constitution, bills ratifying proposed amendments to the United States constitution, resolutions, and initiative and referendum measures, shall be submitted to the governor for his signature. If he does not sign or veto the bill within 10 days after its delivery to him, it shall become law. The governor shall return a vetoed bill to the Legislature with a statement of his reasons therefor.
2. The governor may return any bill to the Legislature with his recommendation mendation for amendment. If the Legislature passes the bill in accordance with the governor's recommendation, it shall again return the bill to the governor for his reconsideration. The governor shall not return a bill for amendment a second time.
3. If after receipt of a veto message, two-thirds of the members of each house present approve the bill, it shall become law.
4. (a) If the Legislature is not in session when the governor vetoes a bill approved by two-thirds of the members present, he shall return the bill with his reasons therefor to the secretary of state. The secretary of state shall poll the members of the Legislature by mail and shall send each member a copy of the governor's veto message. If two-thirds or more of the members of each house vote to override the veto, the bill shall become law. (b) The Legislature may reconvene as provided by law to reconsider any bill vetoed by the governor when the Legislature is not in session.
5. The governor may veto items in appropriation bills, and in such instances the procedure shall be the same as upon veto of an entire bill.

Subsections (1) and (3) are derived from Article VII, section 12, and Article V, section 40 of the 1889 Montana Constitution. Subsections (2) and (4) are new provisions. Subsection (5) is derived from and similar to Article VII, section 13.

The section delineates the governor's post-recommendatory legislative authority, which is primarily the requirement to sign bills before they become law and the power to veto bills, stopping them from becoming law. The traditional two-thirds requirement to override a governor's veto is retained. The interde pendent nature of the legislative process in the structure of a constitutional democracy is derived from the U.S. Constitution. The specific pattern provided in the 1972 Montana Constitution is fairly traditional. Legislative resolutions, state and federal constitutional amendments, initiatives and referenda are all excluded from the governor's veto. A governor may return bills with suggestions for changes, in effect an amendatory veto (available in only seven states). Among other potential values, the amendatory veto permits a final review of technical and constitutional problems with pending legislation. The governor may veto items in an appropriations bill, the so-called line-item veto. Arrangement is made for restricting the so-called pocket veto. First, the legislature may be reconvened to consider vetoed bills; and second, if the bill vetoed was originally passed by a two-thirds majority and the legislature is not in session, the legislature may override the governor's veto by a two-thirds mail vote.

Constitutional Amendment C-26, ratified by the voters in 1993, changed the time frame for the governor to sign or veto bills to ten days after delivery, whether the legislature was in session or not. Previously, the section required the governor to sign or veto a bill within five days after delivery, if the legislature was in session, and within 25 days after delivery, if the legislature was not in session. Under the former arrangement, post-session gubernatorial delay in vetoing bills which had passed by two-thirds vote could delay the known fate of the legislation for two months or more.

A second problem solved by the amendment was whether the bill had been delivered to the governor during or after a legislative session. Regardless of whether the legislature is in session, the governor now has 10 days to sign or veto any bill. Previously, there had been shenanigans by the legislature in claiming delivery by leaving a bill outside the governor's office or recording, as a journal entry, delivery of a bill to the governor in an effort to complete delivery before the end of a session. Likewise, the governor sometimes locked his office, refusing receipt of a bill to avoid delivery prior to the end of a session and thereby avail himself of the 25-day period in which to veto or sign a bill. Timing and deadlines are of increased concern in a state that has brief biennial legislative sessions.

The underlying value of interdependency between the legislature and the executive branch of government might be questioned. It is certainly not the most efficient operational method. But it does give an added measure of protection to the people by making it more difficult for either branch of government to act in a tyrannical fashion. The particular design created by the 1972 Montana Constitution seems to be a thoughtful balance between legislative and executive branches.

The plain language of Article III, section 5, and Article IV, section 10, makes it clear that referenda, whether initiated by the legislature or the public, do not require gubernatorial signature (*State ex rel. Gould v. Cooney*, 1992). In 1975 the Montana attorney general issued an opinion that a gubernatorial veto may be overridden by a vote of two-thirds of the members present in each house of the legislature, but may not be overridden by two-thirds of the members present in the whole legislature (36 Op. Att'y Gen. 309 (1975)).

An interesting early case disapproved any gubernatorial power to scale down appropriations by a certain percent which, because of adjournment, could not be returned to the legislature for further action (*Veto Case*, 1924).

There are no other significant cases decided under the 1889 Montana Constitution or the 1972 Montana Constitution.

## SECTION 11

**Special Session.** Whenever the governor considers it in the public interest, he may convene the Legislature.

This section is derived from Article VII, section 11 of the 1889 Montana Constitution. It covers the same subject matter but in a different method. The governor is authorized to call special sessions of the legislature but, unlike the parallel provision in the 1889 Constitution, the governor cannot restrict the purposes for which the legislature is convened. From 1889 to 1998, governors called 26 special sessions.

The section is intended to allow government to meet exigent circumstances in a pre-arranged and orderly fashion. It is essential to provide for the convening of the legislature in extraordinary session where the regular legislative sessions are limited to 90 days biennially. As the chief administrative office in the state, responsible for the conduct of state government as well as being intricately connected to the legislative process, it is appropriate that the governor should have this power. The policy determination that the governor should not have the power to limit the purposes for which the legislature is convened is an arbitrary judgment. Focusing legislative attention on problems the governor perceives to be critical is logical and meritorious. On the other hand, since legislators are required to provide the necessary response, perhaps they should be free to address problems of state government in whatever fashion they deem best, especially during times of crises when the governor has called a special session.

There are no cases interpreting Article VI, section 11 of the 1972 Montana Constitution. Cases that interpreted the parallel provision, Article VII, section 11, of the 1889 Montana Constitution continuously raised the issue as to whether the legislative action taken pursuant to the governor's proclamation calling the special session of the legislature was within the scope of the governor's proclamation. This series of cases encouraged the constitutional convention delegates to modify the provision in the 1972 Constitution, removing the power of the governor to limit the scope of legislative action and thereby eliminate the problem. See *Pierson v. Hendricksen* (1934); *State v. Dishman* (1922); *State ex rel. Anaconda Copper Mining Co. v. Clancy* (1904).

## SECTION 12

**Pardons.** The governor may grant reprieves, commutations and pardons, restore citizenship, and suspend and remit fines and forfeitures subject to procedures provided by law.

This section is derived from and similar to Article VII, section 9 of the 1889 Montana Constitution. Under the 1889 Constitution the governor's power to grant pardons was subject to the advice and approval of a Board of Pardons established by the legislature. The 1972 Constitution makes the governor's power to pardon more nearly absolute, although still subject to the procedures provided by law.

Executive power to grant pardons is a traditional provision found in most constitutions and intended to afford the chief executive officer the power to remedy mistakes in the criminal justice system that cannot be corrected otherwise. It is also a unique grant of power, permitting the exercise of institutional mercy as contrasted with the general requirements of institutional justice and equality. In the federal system, over the course of the last quarter century, executive pardons have mostly been granted to presidential political associates. Logically, there is no justification for an executive power to pardon, provided the criminal justice system affords a means to correct provable errors, regardless of when the errors are discovered.

The 1889 provision was technically more important because there was no other way to restore the full panoply of civil rights to any person who had been convicted of a felony. Under the 1972 Constitution there is far less justification or need for the provision since Article II, section 28 states that "[f]ull rights are restored by termination of state supervision for any offense against the state." It is difficult to justify the idea of pardons, commutations, or suspensions of fines or forfeitures by the executive branch in what is certain to be an erratic, discretionary, and arbitrary fashion. In one sense the provision informs the people that the criminal justice system is not to be completely trusted, but it is all that most people will be able to rely on. Some few may have the political acumen and financial and political power to go outside of the system and avoid punishment that others would suffer. However, in cases of capital punishment, given the severity of this sanction, it perhaps makes sense to allow the governor the right to determine if this ultimate penalty is warranted.

There are no cases interpreting the 1972 Montana constitutional provision on executive pardons. Under the 1889 Montana Constitution it was determined that the governor might impose conditions on executive pardons, so long as the conditions are not illegal, immoral, or impossible of performance (*In re Sutton*, 1914).

An Attorney General Opinion concluded that consecutive sentences may be commuted individually or in the aggregate and that the Board of Pardons may not postpone consideration of an application for executive clemency until the applicant has exhausted rights of appeal and sentence review (37 Op. Att'y Gen. 183 (1977)).

## SECTION 13

### Militia

1. The governor is commander-in-chief of the militia forces of the state, except when they are in the actual service of the United States. He may call out any part or all of the

forces to aid in the execution of the laws, suppress insurrection, repel invasion, or protect life and property in natural disasters.
2. The militia forces shall consist of all able bodied citizens of the state except those exempted by law.

Subsection (1) is derived from and similar to Article VII, section 6 of the 1889 Montana Constitution. The last phrase of subsection (1), "protect life and property in natural disasters," is new. Subsection (2) is derived from and similar to Article XIV, section 1 of the 1889 Montana Constitution. Subsection (2) removes sex and age qualifications for service in the militia.

This section grants the executive power over the military forces maintained by the state. It is necessary to identify the head of the state militia and the logical head of the state militia is the governor. Whether there is a continuing need for a state militia might be questioned, although the state militia does perform some useful functions that other parts of existing government organizations could not adequately do. Formerly, the state militia was an important part of the defense of every state and the nation. Over the years it has become increasingly less important in terms of repelling invasions and suppressing insurrections, and now is an adjunct to the national military operation in the first instance and a trained force to help in many non-military emergencies. Many of the Montana state guard troops were activated in 1990 and 1991, prior to and during the Gulf War. A second and perhaps more important function is the protection of life and property in the case of natural disasters. A third significant aspect of militia operation is to aid in the execution of the laws. This has occurred by calling on the state militia to operate the state prison during the course of labor disagreements and as a preventive force when there is a reasonable expectation of riots and civil disobedience; for example, in the wake of some trials that have been charged with racial overtones and urban riots and forced integration.

There are no significant case interpretations of the 1972 Montana constitutional provision, nor are there any significant case interpretations of the 1889 Montana constitutional provision regarding the state militia.

## SECTION 14

### Succession

1. If the governor-elect is disqualified or dies, the lieutenant governorelect upon qualifying for the office shall become governor for the full term. If the governor-elect fails to assume office for any other reason, the lieutenant governor-elect upon qualifying as such shall serve as acting governor until the governor-elect is able to assume office, or until the office becomes vacant.
2. The lieutenant governor shall serve as acting governor when so requested in writing by the governor. After the governor has been absent from the state for more than 45 consecutive days, the lieutenant governor shall serve as acting governor.

3. He shall serve as acting governor when the governor is so disabled as to be unable to communicate to the lieutenant governor the fact of his inability to perform the duties of his office. The lieutenant governor shall continue to serve as acting governor until the governor is able to resume the duties of his office.
4. Whenever, at any other time, the lieutenant governor and attorney general transmit to the Legislature their written declaration that the governor is unable to discharge the powers and duties of his office, the Legislature shall convene to determine whether he is able to do so.
5. If the Legislature, within 21 days after convening, determines by two-thirds vote of its members that the governor is unable to discharge the powers and duties of his office, the lieutenant governor shall serve as acting governor. Thereafter, when the governor transmits to the Legislature his written declaration that no inability exists, he shall resume the powers and duties of his office within 15 days, unless the Legislature determines otherwise by two-thirds vote of its members. If the Legislature so determines, the lieutenant governor shall continue to serve as acting governor.
6. If the office of governor becomes vacant by reason of death, resignation, or disqualification, the lieutenant governor shall become governor for the remainder of the term, except as provided in this constitution.
7. Additional succession to fill vacancies shall be provided by law.
8. When there is a vacancy in the office of governor, the successor shall be the governor. The acting governor shall have the powers and duties of the office of governor only for the period during which he serves.

This provision is new, although derived from and based on the Twenty-fifth Amendment to the U.S. Constitution. Article VII, sections 14, 15, and 16 of the 1889 Montana Constitution provided for executive succession. The arrangement under the 1889 Montana Constitution was more detailed in that it provided for succession beyond the lieutenant governor, whereas the 1972 Montana constitutional provision leaves the order of executive succession beyond lieutenant governor to subsequent determination by the legislature. In other regards the 1972 Montana constitutional provision on executive succession is more detailed than its 1889 predecessor. Under both constitutional provisions the lieutenant governor assumes the powers and duties of the governor if the governor is unable to serve. The 1972 Constitution is more specific about what creates a vacancy in the office of governor. For example, if the governor is gone from the state more than 45 days or is temporarily disabled, the lieutenant governor becomes acting governor. If the lieutenant governor and the attorney general think the governor is unable to perform his duties, they may so inform the legislature, and by a two-thirds vote the legislature can decide that the lieutenant governor shall serve as acting governor because the governor is unable to act.

The provision is a systematic method of insuring the continued exercise of the duties of the chief executive in a variety of circumstances in which the office might otherwise remain vacant in effect or in fact. It is an important, if rarely used, constitutional arrangement for the transfer of executive power in case of emergency. The more specific the arrangement for the transfer of executive power in case of emergency, the more expeditiously and effectively the transfer can be accomplished.

There are no cases interpreting the 1972 constitutional provision on executive succession, and the two cases interpreting the parallel provision in the 1889 Montana Constitution have little significance and no relevance to the 1972 Montana Constitution. The case of *State ex rel. homey v. Mitchell* (1934), decided under the 1889 Montana Constitution, did state that the powers and duties of the office of governor when transferred to the lieutenant governor are transferred immediately and there is no measurable vacancy in the office of governor.

## SECTION 15

### Information for Governor

1. The governor may require information in writing, under oath when required, from the officers of the executive branch upon any subject relating to the duties of their respective offices.
2. He may require information in writing, under oath, from all officers and managers of state institutions.
3. He may appoint a committee to investigate and report to him upon the condition of any executive office or state institution.

This section is derived from and similar to a portion of Article VII, section 10 of the 1889 Montana Constitution. There is no substantive change from the parallel provision in the 1889 Montana Constitution.

The provision authorizes the executive to obtain necessary information to carry out the functions of the office. There is probably an implied executive power to obtain all information from agents and officers of government that would be "necessary and proper" to carry out the obligations of the office. To expressly authorize the power eliminates the possibility of challenge by government officers who hold offices that are created by the constitution, and who are not subject to appointment or removal by the governor; such officers as identified in Article VI, section 2(1), including the "lieutenant governor, secretary of state, attorney general, superintendent of public instruction, and auditor" who are elected.

There are no cases interpreting this section of the 1972 Montana Constitution nor interpreting the parallel section in the 1889 Montana Constitution.

# Article VII

## *The Judiciary*

### SECTION 1

**Judicial Power.** The judicial power of the state is vested in one supreme court, district courts, justice courts, and such other courts as may be provided by law.

This section is derived from Article VIII, section 1 of the 1889 Montana Constitution. The parallel provision in the 1889 Constitution authorized the Legislative Assembly to establish inferior courts in incorporated cities or towns, whereas this section authorizes the legislature to establish "other courts." Presumptively, such other courts might include small claims courts, municipal courts, or intermediate courts of appeal. The former provision vested exclusive jurisdiction over impeachments in the Senate whereas Article V, section 13(2) of the 1972 Constitution gives the legislature the authority to designate the causes for impeachment, the tribunal to hear cases of impeachment, and the power to provide the procedure for impeachment.

The provision establishes the locus of judicial power in the state of Montana and outlines the basic court structure for the exercise of judicial power. In a tripartite scheme of representational democracy, and assuming the third branch to be the judicial branch with the power to decide disputes between and among a variety of parties, and possessed of the ultimate power to interpret laws, rules, and regulations including the constitution, the provision is extremely important. Subsections (2), (4), and (5) of Article VII describe the jurisdiction of the various courts in more detail and are more often relied upon when questions of judicial authority or separation of powers arise. The change in this section, from its predecessor provision in the 1889 Montana Constitution, authorizing the legislature to create "other courts," could be significant, but to date has not been.

The few cases that interpret this provision are significant to the extent they describe the scope of authority created in the judiciary. In *State ex rel. District Court v. Whitaker* (1984), the court held that a district court may issue orders for the payment of expenditures that are reasonable and necessary even though the expenditures exceed the approved budget. The Board of County Commissioners may not deny such expenditures on the basis that they are outside the budget if the court has duly ordered them paid. In *Kaiser v. Whitehall* (1986), the court held that supreme court decisions are binding authority even if the majority opinion is supported by three justices, plus a special concurrence with three justices dissenting. In State v. Abrams (1984), the court noted that Article VII, section 1 of the Montana Constitution authorizes a court to exercise the power of contempt to enforce its own judgments and maintain decorum in its proceedings. Under the parallel provision in the 1889 Montana Constitution the court stated that "judicial power" was the power of a court to decide and pronounce a judgment and carry it into effect (*Shea v. North-Butte Min. Co.* 1919). There is no reservation of judicial power to the people to be exercised by initiative or referendum (*Town of Whitehall v. Preece* 1998).

## SECTION 2

### Supreme Court Jurisdiction

1. The supreme court has appellate jurisdiction and may issue, hear, and determine writs appropriate thereto. It has original jurisdiction to issue, hear, and determine writs of habeas corpus and such other writs as may be provided by law.
2. It has general supervisory control over all other courts.
3. It may make rules governing appellate procedure, practice and procedure for all other courts, admission to the bar and the conduct of its members. Rules of procedure shall be subject to disapproval by the Legislature in either of the two sessions following promulgation.
4. Supreme court process shall extend to all parts of the state.

This provision is derived from and similar to Article VIII, sections 2 and 3 of the 1889 Montana Constitution. Most of the changes are as to form and grammar and not substance. The parallel provision in the 1889 Constitution is much more detailed relative to the use, nature, and type of writs. Subsection (3) authorizing the supreme court to make rules of practice and procedure and to regulate attorneys, subject to legislative veto, is new.

The provision establishes the basic geographic and subject matter jurisdiction of the Montana Supreme Court as well as the supreme court's original and appellate jurisdiction. The provision is an essential part of the tripartite system of constitutional representational democracy in which the courts are given the authority to interpret legislation, with the supreme court as the final arbiter of the meaning of the state constitution and the various state laws. It establishes the hierarchy of the various courts, giving the supreme court supervisory control over all other courts in the state. It also authorizes the supreme court to promulgate rules governing appellate procedure and practice and procedure for all courts of the state. This is an enormous legislative-like power, subject only to legislative veto. It also authorizes the supreme court to regulate attorneys.

Delegate Ben Berg, a member of the Montana Constitutional Convention Judiciary Committee, said that the rules promulgated under the supreme court rulemaking power were not intended to include rules of evidence (MCC Tr. 1037). Delegate John Schiltz, also on the Judiciary Committee, said that the objective of allowing for legislative disapproval of these rules was to prevent the supreme court from promulgating rules other than rules of practice and procedure (MCC Tr. 1072). However, the supreme court in 1977 did promulgate rules of evidence. One could perhaps argue that rules of practice and procedure do cover evidentiary rules.

Based on the authority granted in subsection (3), the Montana Supreme Court has adopted a plethora of rules on practice and procedure and on the regulation of the legal profession. Many of the cases cited in interpretation of this provision concern the application of the rules adopted by the supreme court. Another large group of cases addresses the problem of extraordinary writs and the supreme court's supervisory control. The legal interpretation of the use of extraordinary writs remains fairly traditional.

Rulemaking power of the supreme court extends to the promulgation of rules of practice and procedure for all courts (*McLaughlin v. Hart*, 1984). The court has also held that while rules of appellate and civil procedure are subject to disapproval by the legislature, rules promulgated by the court relative to admission to the bar and to regulate the practice of law are not subject to legislative disapproval (*Petitions of McCabe & Zeman*, 1975). Although the legislature is empowered to veto any court rule of practice and procedure, once a legislative veto is exercised, the legislature is not empowered to fill the vacuum by enacting its own legislation governing appellate procedure or court procedure; that is a sphere reserved expressly to the supreme court (*Coate v. Omholt*, 1983).

The parallel provision in the 1889 Montana Constitution was held to vest in the courts the exclusive power to construe and interpret legislative acts as well as provisions of the constitution (Cottingham v. State Bd. of Examiners, 1958). Earlier, Helena v. Helena Waterworks Co. (1911) held that the very purpose of a state constitution was to establish an exclusive court of review with all the auxiliary powers necessary to the exercise of this jurisdiction, except insofar as the constitution expressly declared otherwise.

## SECTION 3

**Supreme Court Organization**

1. The supreme court consists of one chief justice and four justices, but the Legislature may increase the number of justices from four to six. A majority shall join in and pronounce decisions, which must be in writing.
2. A district judge shall be substituted for the chief justice or a justice in the event of disqualification or disability, and the opinion of the district judge sitting with the supreme court shall have the same effect as an opinion of a justice.

This section is derived from and similar to Article VIII, section 5 of the 1889 Montana Constitution. The section authorizes the legislature to increase the number of justices from four to six (which did in fact occur in 1980) and designates one of the members of the court as chief justice. Article VIII, section 8 of the 1889 Montana Constitution used the language "chief justice" and "associate justices." The principal change is in syntax.

The provision establishes the number of persons who shall sit as members of the Montana Supreme Court, the requirement of a majority vote for all decisions, and the further requirement that all decisions must be written. It also provides that district court judges may serve as substitute justices on the Montana Supreme Court. The number of justices on the supreme court is necessarily arbitrary, but the work load and the known delay encouraged the drafters to provide for the possible expansion of the number of justices. The requirement that all decisions must be written seems significant, in fairness to litigants before the court, as a means of informing and advising district court judges who must apply the law, for lawyers who are charged with advising clients, and for the general public.

That all decisions must be in writing does not mean that all decisions are widely available. Although all decisions are written, they are not all published in the standard court reports for Montana Supreme Court decisions (*Montana Reports, Montana State Reporter, Pacific Reporter,* 2d Series), but beginning in 1998 are available in the two major legal databases (Westlaw and Lexis-Nexis) and are on the Internet. This is because Montana Supreme Court Internal Operating Rule I.3(c) permits non-citable abbreviated opinions which are not published. During the decade of the 1990s the Montana Supreme Court rendered between 350 and 400 opinions each year and approximately 25 percent were non-citable.[19]

---

[19] In 1994 there were 575 opinions handed down, of which 130 were abbreviated, non-citable opinions. In 1995 there were 406 opinions, of which 128 were non-citable; in 1996 there were 335 total, of which

In interpreting the requirement that a majority shall join in and pronounce all decisions the court held that a majority opinion signed by only three justices, with one justice specially concurring and three justices dissenting, is binding authority (*Kaiser v. Whitehall*, 1986). Under the 1889 constitutional provision the court held that it was immaterial that the majority failed to agree on the particular error justifying reversal, as long as the majority agreed that the court committed error resulting in denial of a fair trial (*State v. LeDuc*, 1931).

## SECTION 4

### District Court Jurisdiction

1. The district court has original jurisdiction in all criminal cases amounting to felony and all civil matters and cases at law and in equity. It may issue all writs appropriate to its jurisdiction. It shall have the power of naturalization and such additional jurisdiction as may be delegated by the laws of the United States or the state of Montana. Its process shall extend to all parts of the state.
2. The district court shall hear appeals from inferior courts as trials anew unless otherwise provided by law. The Legislature may provide for direct review by the district court of decisions of administrative agencies.
3. Other courts may have jurisdiction of criminal cases not amounting to felony and such jurisdiction concurrent with that of the district court as may be provided by law.

Subsections (1) and (2) are derived in part from and are similar to Article VIII, section 11 of the 1889 Montana Constitution, although the syntax has been changed. The provision in the 1889 Constitution is much more detailed. Under the 1889 Constitution the district court had jurisdiction over felonies and misdemeanors not otherwise provided for, whereas under subsection (1) of this section, criminal jurisdiction is limited to felonies. Article VIII, section 11 of the 1889 Montana Constitution granted district courts appellate jurisdiction from inferior courts as might be prescribed by law. The provision in this section [subsection(2)], requiring appeals from inferior courts to be tried de novo, is new. Jurisdiction to hear direct appeals from state agencies, if authorized by the legislature, is also new. Subsection (3) is a new provision allowing the legislature to endow "other courts" beyond the district courts, with limited criminal jurisdiction and civil jurisdiction concurrent with the district court (e.g., small claims courts, municipal courts, family courts, and probate courts) (MCC Tr. 1020, 1076).

---

61 were non-citable; in 1997 there were 384, of which 94 were non-citable; and in 1998 there were 344, of which 88 were non-citable.

This section establishes the basic trial and appellate jurisdiction for district courts, outlining, in part, the hierarchy of judicial power. The outline adheres to the historical pattern of trial court jurisdiction. The suggestion that "other" courts could be granted nearly concurrent jurisdiction with district courts opens the door to significant judicial change if the legislature were so inclined.

A number of cases have raised the issue of district court jurisdiction in a variety of contexts. In conflicts with federal jurisdiction the Montana Supreme Court held that a default judgment in U.S. District Court in New York that was attempted to be executed on property being probated in Montana was within the jurisdiction of the Montana state court and that the real property was subject to family protection allowances and exempt from execution (*In re Estate of Wil-helm*, 1988). In conflicts with tribal jurisdiction, the court held that there was no state jurisdiction over a civil debt action arising out of a commercial transaction on an Indian reservation and brought by a non-Indian creditor against an enrolled tribal member debtor, both of whom resided on the reservation. State jurisdiction was pre-empted by tribal jurisdiction (*Geiger v. Pierce*, 1988). In contrast, an attorney licensed to practice in Montana cannot make a contract to be performed both on and off the reservation and subsequently defeat state jurisdiction by claiming status as a tribal member (*Crawford v. Roy*, 1978).

Several cases have addressed the issue of standing necessary to invoke the jurisdiction of the district courts. The standing language is traditional. (See, e.g., *O'Donnell Fire Serv. & Equip. Co. v. Billings, 1985; and Stewart v. Board of County Comm'rs, 1977.) State v. Davis* (1984) noted that the issue of subject matter jurisdiction cannot be waived or conferred by consent of a party and the issue may be raised at any stage of a judicial proceeding. Because there was no published local court rule on disqualification and substitution of judges, the supreme court's rule was applicable (*State v. Dougherty*, 1979).

The district court has jurisdictional authority to order payment for reasonable and necessary expenditures in excess of fiscal year budget (*State ex rel. District Court v. Whitaker*, 1984).

A number of cases have addressed the issue of youth court jurisdiction, which is a district court with a different title and responsibility. The court has noted that on termination of youth court jurisdiction there is no bar to the exercise of jurisdiction by the district court under Article VII, section 4(1) (see Mont. Code Ann., Sections 3-5-302 and 46-2-201) over felony proceedings against a defendant. Exclusive original jurisdiction of the youth court does not divest a district court of jurisdiction over crimes committed by a juvenile defendant (*State v. Beach*, 1985). And further, the supreme court held that: (1) the term "original jurisdiction," as used in this section, does not mean exclusive jurisdiction; and (2) felonies may be prosecuted in the youth court because when it acts in jurisdiction the youth court is acting as a district court (*In re T.L.G. & M.E.H.*, 1984). Finally, the district court has jurisdiction to try an individual charged at age 22 for felonies allegedly committed at age 15, as provided in the court's constitutional grant of jurisdiction over all felonies (*State ex rel. Elliot v. District Court*, 1984).

As to appellate jurisdiction, the principal litigation concern has been review of administrative action. The Montana Supreme Court has emphasized the legislative role in providing for administrative review. Only the legislature may provide for judicial review of administrative actions (*Nye v. Department of Livestock*, 1982), and the legislature may deny or restrict the right of review from administrative decisions to a particular court. Failure of the legislature to provide for court appeal from the decision of a particular administrative action, in this case a school board, made it proper to review the decision pursuant to a general administrative appeal statute (*School Dist. v. Hughes*, 1976). The possibility of prosecution under a criminal statute is sufficient to bring a declaratory judgment action before the Montana Supreme Court (*Gryczan v. State*, 1997).

There are many cases interpreting the 1889 Montana Constitution. Most do not seem relevant to the current Montana Constitution. Most of the cases tended to deal with narrow issues; equity jurisdiction and the development of extraordinary writs were prominent. The cases reflect the narrow, detailed grants of jurisdiction characteristic of the 1889 Constitution.

## SECTION 5

### Justices of the Peace

1. There shall be elected in each county at least one justice of the peace with qualifications, training, and monthly compensation provided by law. There shall be provided such facilities that they may perform their duties in dignified surroundings.
2. Justice courts shall have such original jurisdiction as may be provided by law. They shall not have trial jurisdiction in any criminal case designated a felony except as examining courts.
3. The Legislature may provide for additional justices of the peace in each county.

This section is derived from Article VIII, sections 20 and 21 of the 1889 Montana Constitution. There have been a number of changes in substance and form. Subsection (1) revises the 1889 Constitution by requiring one justice of the peace in each county instead of two in each township and directs the legislature to set qualifications, training standards, and salaries. Provision for "dignified surroundings" is new. Subsection (2) establishes jurisdiction as provided by the legislature. The only limitation is as to felonies and then justice courts are limited to acting as examining courts. The 1889 Montana Constitution limited justice court jurisdiction by listing, in both a specific and general way, cases justice courts could not hear and writs they could not issue. Subsection (3) authorizes the legislature to provide for additional justices of the peace, whereas the 1889

Constitution implied that there could be more than two justices of the peace in each township.

Montana is geographically large, with a small population. District judges do not reside in every county. This insures that there will be a constitutional judicial officer in every county. There was a concerted effort to eliminate the justice of the peace as a constitutional officer and create a system of inferior court judges under the direct supervision of the district court judges, and to require that they be lawyers. The small rural communities lobbied vigorously and successfully for a continuation of the justice of the peace as a constitutional officer and for a justice of the peace in every county. The only concession that was made by this rural, grassroots effort was allowing the legislature to provide for qualifications, training, and monthly compensation and to include a requirement that each county provide dignified surroundings. By the end of the century justices of the peace received approximately $45,000 per annum.

The justice of the peace system may be as good as any for a state like Montana. As currently arranged, a justice is available in every county, and although many of the justices of the peace are not qualified to practice law, even in populous counties where they handle a large number of complicated cases, there has been a conscientious effort to provide professional training. Justice courts were also intended to act as small claims courts (MCC Tr. 1014).

The principal case dealt with the problem of funding justice courts and providing dignified surroundings. This section of the constitution was held to create a duty on the part of county commissioners to approve actual and necessary expenses of justice of the peace courts, even though the expense was unforeseen and not budgeted (*State ex rel. Browman v. Wood*, 1975). The cases interpreting the 1889 Montana Constitution were forced to struggle with the jurisdiction issues that arose from the detailed listing of the constitutional prohibitions to justice court jurisdiction juxtaposed against the grant of jurisdiction made by the legislature.

## SECTION 6

### Judicial Districts

1. The Legislature shall divide the state into judicial districts and provide for the number of judges in each district. Each district shall be formed of compact territory and be bounded by county lines.
2. The Legislature may change the number and boundaries of judicial districts and the number of judges in each district, but no change in boundaries or the number of districts or judges therein shall work a removal of any judge from office during the term for which he was elected or appointed.
3. The chief justice may, upon request of the district judge, assign district judges and other judges for temporary service from one district to another, and from one county to another.

Subsections (1) and (2) of this section are derived from and similar to Article VIII, sections 12, 13, and 14 of the 1889 Montana Constitution. Subsections (1) and (2) represent no substantive change. The syntax has been revised. Subsection (3) is a new provision allowing the chief justice to assign judges, for temporary service, in districts or counties other than where they were appointed or elected.

The section provides an organizational and locational scheme for district court operation. The organizational scheme provides trial court judges located in all parts of the state, although smaller communities are often without a sitting trial court judge. There is an attempt to increase flexibility and maximize resource allocation by allowing the chief justice to assign district court judges to districts most in need of their service. The language "upon request" in subsection (3) is intended to prevent the chief justice from assigning judges for improper reasons (MCC Tr. 1081). The request is to be from the judge asking for assistance (MCC Tr. 1083).

The principal problem that has erupted in the interpretation of this provision is the temporary utilization of retired judges and judges who have been voted out of office. In *State ex rel. Wilcox v. District Court* (1984), the supreme court held the term "other judges" in subsection (3) of this section to include retired judges empowering the chief justice of the supreme court, upon request of a district judge, to assign a retired judge for temporary service to any judicial district or county in Montana. Further, a retired district judge called into judicial duty has complete district court jurisdiction (*In re Marriage of Manus*, 1987). This judicial authority extends to judges who have been voted out of office and are subsequently given temporary judicial assignments by the chief justice (*State ex rel. Welch v. District Court*, 1984).

Finally, the court has held that statutory provisions providing for substitution of a disqualified district judge are not in conflict with subsection (3) of this section empowering the chief justice to temporarily assign a district judge for duty in another district (*State ex rel. Lane v. District Court*, 1975).

None of the cases decided under the 1889 Montana Constitution conflict with the above case interpretations or are otherwise significant.

## SECTION 7

### Terms and Pay

1. All justices and judges shall be paid as provided by law, but salaries shall not be diminished during terms of office.
2. Terms of office shall be eight years for supreme court justices, six years for district court judges, four years for justices of the peace, and as provided by law for other judges.

Subsection (1) of this section is derived from and similar to Article VIII, section 29 of the 1889 Montana Constitution, as amended in 1963. As originally enacted, the subsection provided annual pay of $4,000 for justices of the supreme court and $3,500 for district court judges to be paid quarterly, and further stipulated that judicial pay could be neither increased nor diminished during the term of office.[20] There was no provision about payment for justices of the peace. Subsection (2) of this section is derived from and similar to Article VIII, sections 7, 12, and 20 of the 1889 Montana Constitution. Subsection (2) increases supreme court justice terms from six to eight years, district court judges from four to six, and justices of the peace from two to four years.

The section authorizes the legislature to determine judicial salaries, limiting the legislative power to diminish pay during any given term of office. By the end of the millennium, supreme court justices received approximately $90,000 per annum and district judges received approximately $80,000 per annum. The section establishes terms of office. The length is necessarily arbitrary. The increase in length of terms reflects a concern about the time and expense associated with elections and the assumption that better qualified candidates will seek judicial office if the terms are longer.

Charging the legislature with the task of determining pay scales for the judiciary is important as a reflection of what the public is willing to pay, and allows the legislature to respond to changing economic conditions. The increased term is generally conceded to be favorable. Appointment for life on good behavior comparable to the federal system was considered but defeated. Arguments about democratic accountability coupled with a failure to perceive or accept the importance of an independent judiciary defeated the proposal for an appointed judiciary.

The prohibition against diminution of compensation during term of office was held to interdict a statute authorizing the judiciary to impose a sanction of one month's salary forfeiture for inordinate delay in reaching decisions or writing opinions. The court seemed to accept the argument that the constitutional prohibition against diminution of salary was intended to prevent legislative control of the judiciary, and in this case legislative control was at most indirect because the judiciary was imposing the sanction. The court held the statutes were, nonetheless, unconstitutional, because they impaired the obligation of contract (*Coate v. Omholt* , 1983). In another case the court held that judicial officers are entitled to actual and necessary expenses for travel. Any statutorily limited travel expenses are unconstitutional as applied to district judges and supreme court justices (*In re Actual Necessary Expense of Judges*, 1975).

[20] As of 1996 the salary for justices of the supreme court was $68,874 and $67,513 for district court judges.

## SECTION 8

### Selection

1. Supreme court justices and district court judges shall be elected by the qualified electors as provided by law.
2. For any vacancy in the office of supreme court justice or district court judge, the governor shall appoint a replacement from nominees selected in the manner provided by law. If the governor fails to appoint within thirty days after receipt of nominees, the chief justice or acting chief justice shall make the appointment from the same nominees within thirty days of the governor's failure to appoint. Appointments made under this subsection shall be subject to confirmation by the senate, as provided by law. If the appointee is not confirmed, the office shall be vacant and a replacement shall be made under the procedures provided for in this section. The appointee shall serve until the election for the office as provided by law and until a successor is elected and qualified. The person elected or retained at the election shall serve until the expiration of the term for which his predecessor was elected. No appointee, whether confirmed or unconfirmed, shall serve past the term of his predecessor without standing for election.
3. If an incumbent files for election and there is no election contest for the office, the name of the incumbent shall nevertheless be placed on the general election ballot to allow the voters of the state or district to approve or reject him. If an incumbent is rejected, the vacancy in the office for which the election was held shall be filled as provided in subsection (2).

This section is derived from Article VIII, sections 6, 12, and 34 of the 1889 Montana Constitution. Article VIII, sections 6 and 12 of the 1889 Montana Constitution required direct election of supreme court justices and district court judges. Article VIII, section 34 of the 1889 Montana Constitution provided that vacancies were to be filled by gubernatorial appointment. The 1972 Montana Constitution mandates direct election of supreme court justices and district court judges; prescribes how new justices and judges will acquire judicial office, how they will retain judicial office, and how judicial vacancies are to be filled.

The section provides for the election of justices of the supreme court and judges of the district court, and for their replacement. Rather than life tenure or good behavior, as in the federal judicial system, judicial selection and retention is popular democratic control with a vengeance. A sitting judge, at the conclusion of his/her term, must not only run against whomever files to run for the office but if no one files the incumbent must run against his/her record.

In making judicial appointments the governor is restricted to the extent that he must appoint from a list of three nominees selected by a judicial nominating committee and all appointments must be confirmed by the Senate. In 1992 this section was amended (CI-22) to insure that any judicial appointment not only be confirmed by the Senate but the appointee must also stand for election as soon as possible after appointment. This modification of the language was intended to eliminate the perceived problem of an appointed judge holding office and not being required to run for election until after Senate confirmation which, under optimum circumstances, could delay an appointed judge from standing for election for up to three years: one and one-half years before confirmation or rejection and if confirmed an additional one and one-half years before a scheduled general election. The original language was based on the expectation of annual legislative sessions; however, Amendment CI-1, passed in 1974, replaced annual sessions with biennial sessions. Subsequent to the reinstatement of annual legislative sessions, the Montana Supreme Court held that when the Senate had not had an opportunity to confirm a nominee, the nominee need not stand for election at the next election following appointment but must stand for election at the next election following Senate confirmation (*State ex rel. Racicot v. District Court*, 1990). Such delay prior to standing for election is no longer possible.

The approach taken does little to insure independence of the judiciary, nor does it encourage the most qualified persons to seek judicial office. It does guarantee maximum control over the judiciary by the voting public. Some Montana judicial elections have been vitriolic, and legitimate qualifications of the candidates have been obscured. The observance of the ethical demands prevents the candidates from addressing substantive issues for fear of discussing cases that are before the court or likely to come before the court. Ethical concerns also shield the candidate from revealing information about his or her judicial positions. Judicial races are more about available dollars, special interest concerns, and charisma than why the person would be a good judge. That is not to say that similar problems may not be facing federal judges via U.S. Senate confirmation proceedings. During most of the twentieth century the quality of the federal judiciary was perceived to be superior to the Montana state judiciary. That superiority may be related to lifetime tenure, to higher salaries, or to the enhanced prestige of the federal judiciary. Also, that superiority may be waning.

Few relevant or significant cases interpret the section. The court has defined an "incumbent" judge as one who is in office and who seeks to remain a district court judge (*Yunker v. Murray*, 1976). The supreme court held the procedures established by the legislature for filling judicial vacancies in Montana constitutionally acceptable (*Jones v. Judge*, 1978). Decisions interpreting parallel provisions found in the 1889 Montana Constitution are not relevant to an interpretation of the 1972 Constitution.

## SECTION 9

### Qualifications

1. A citizen of the United States who has resided in the state two years immediately before taking office is eligible to the office of supreme court justice or district court

judge if admitted to the practice of law in Montana for at least five years prior to the date of appointment of election. Qualifications and methods of selection of judges of other courts shall be provided by law.

2. No supreme court justice or district court judge shall solicit or receive compensation in any form whatever on account of his office, except salary and actual necessary travel expense.

3. Except as otherwise provided in this constitution, no supreme court justice or district court judge shall practice law during his term of office, engage in any other employment for which salary or fee is paid, or hold office in a political party.

4. Supreme court justices shall reside within the state. During his term of office, a district court judge shall reside in the district and a justice of the peace shall reside in the county in which he is elected or appointed. The residency requirement for every other judge must be provided by law.

Subsection (1) of this section revises the 1889 Montana Constitution by making residency requirements for candidates for district court judgeships the same as for the supreme court and by deleting age requirements to become a judge or justice. The requirement of five years of law practice is new. Subsection (2) revises the 1889 Constitution by specifically allowing travel expenses. The only change in subsection (3) is to specifically prohibit a judge from holding office in a political party. There is no change in subsection (4) except in grammar.

Constitutional Amendment Number 19, approved by the voters in 1988 and effective in 1989, substituted the second sentence of subsection (4), concerning residency of district court judges and justices of the peace, for the former second sentence that read: "Every other judge shall reside during his term of office in the district, county, township, precinct, city or town in which he is elected or appointed."

Subsection (1) of section 9 revises Article VIII, sections 10 and 16 of the 1889 Constitution; subsection (2) revises Article VIII, section 30; subsections (3) and (4) are similar to Article VIE, sections 33 and 35.

The Judiciary Committee of the Montana constitutional convention felt that the age of a judge is not as important as knowledge and experience (MCC Rep. 498), hence, no age requirement. Given the requirement of five years of the practice of law in Montana, it is not quite clear why there is the additional requirement of residing in the state two years immediately before taking office. Presumably, this would exclude the attorney who had practiced law in Montana for at least five years, moved out of state, and within two years after returning to Montana sought either a judicial appointment or to run for a judicial position.

The only supreme court case under the 1972 Constitution dealt with the travel expenses of the district court and supreme court judges. The case held that statutory travel expenses were unconstitutional if they were so low that judges had to, in part, pay their own travel expenses for necessary work-related travel (*In re Actual Necessary Expenses of Judges*, 1975).

Under the 1889 Constitution, a case held that judges on active duty could not serve as delegates to the constitutional convention (*Legislative Assembly v. Lennon*, 1971).

## SECTION 10

**Forfeiture of Judicial Position.** Any holder of a judicial position forfeits that position by either filing for an elective public office other than a judicial position or absenting himself from the state for more than 60 consecutive days.

This is a new provision: a judge may not run for any other public office (except judicial office) or be out of state for more than 60 days. This section is similar to Article VIII, section 37 of the 1889 Constitution.

Statutes requiring that a judge resign before running for another judicial office are in conflict with Article VII, section 10, and are therefore unconstitutional (*Committee for an Effective Judiciary v. State*, 1984). Under the 1889 Constitution, supreme court justices and the district court judges could not serve as delegates to the state constitutional convention since a delegate would hold public office (*Legislative Assembly v. Lennon*, 1971).

Section 10 was designed to prevent judgeships from being used as stepping stones for the fulfillment of political ambition. Section 10 applies to *all* judges in the state (*Committee for an Effective Judiciary v. State*, 1984). State law defines "judicial officers" as "justices of the supreme court, judges of the district courts, justices of the peace, municipal judges, and city judges" (Mont. Code Ann., Section 1-1-202(2)). Given the broad language of section 10 and in view of the supreme court's holding that it applies to *all* judges, the attorney general concluded that section 10 includes city judges, notwithstanding the lack of parallel statutory language (44 Op. Att'y Gen. 96 (1991)). In the same opinion the attorney general also noted that while serving in a judicial office might be compatible with serving in an elective non-judicial office, compatibility is not a factor under the language of the constitution.

## SECTION 11

**Removal and Discipline**

1. The Legislature shall create a judicial standards commission consisting of five persons and provide for the appointment thereto of two district judges, one attorney, and two citizens who are neither judges nor attorneys.
2. The commission shall investigate complaints, and make rules implementing this section. It may subpoena witnesses and documents.
3. Upon recommendation of the commission, the supreme court may: (a) Retire any justice or judge for disability that seriously interferes with the performance of his

duties and is or may become permanent; or (b) Censure, suspend, or remove any justice or judge for willful misconduct in office, willful and persistent failure to perform his duties, violation of canons of judicial ethics adopted by the supreme court of the state of Montana, or habitual intemperance.

4. The proceedings of the commission are confidential except as provided by statute.

This is a new provision. A judicial standards commission may investigate whenever a judge, because of disability or bad habits, performs his or her duties improperly. The commission can recommend to the supreme court that the judge be retired, censured, suspended, or removed. This procedure is intended to be less cumbersome than impeachment and less embarrassing to the individuals and the system (MCC Tr. 1123). It is intended to apply to such cases as illness, advanced age, and addiction (MCC Tr. 1125).

Constitutional Amendment Number 9, which the voters passed in 1980, deleted "and keep its proceedings confidential" at the end of the first sentence of subsection (2) and added subsection (4). Constitutional Amendment Number 13, which the voters passed in 1984, inserted "violation of canons of judicial ethics adopted in the supreme court of the state of Montana" after "duties" in subsection (3)(b).

Statutory provisions for the disqualification of district judges are not unconstitutional as being in conflict with section 11 (*State ex rel. Lane v. District Court*, 1975). Despite the constitutional status of the Judicial Standards Commission, the supreme court has power to issue a writ of prohibition to enjoin the Commission when acting in excess of its authority (*State ex rel Shea v. Judicial Standards Comm'n*, 1982). The Montana legislature has broad powers relating to removal of public officers and there can be no inhibition of the legislative power, irrespective of rulemaking authority granted to the Judicial Standards Commission, to make suitable provisions not in conflict with the constitutionally granted powers of the Commission, including the requirement that the Commission may act only upon a verified complaint (ibid.). Misconduct in office means conduct in or arising out of the duties of office and does not apply to alleged misconduct outside of office (ibid.). Unless a judge uses profane, vulgar, or insulting language that offends good morals in writing a judicial opinion, there is no judicial misconduct (ibid.).

The vast majority of complaints received by the Judicial Standards Commission concern dissatisfaction with a judge's ruling or final decision. However, the Commission cannot act upon or change judicial decisions and, consequently, these kinds of complaints are dismissed as requiring no further action. Court decisions in Montana are all subject to appeal or re-hearing.

# Article VIII

## *Revenue and Finance*

### SECTION 1

**Tax Purposes.** Taxes shall be levied by general laws for public purposes.

This section is derived from and similar to Article XII, section 11 of the 1889 Montana Constitution. The syntax has been changed and the requirement of uniformity by class of taxable subjects has been eliminated.

The section is intended to insure that money shall not be raised by special levies nor shall any money raised be expended to the special benefit of private persons as distinguished from public purpose. This requirement is at least partially redundant. Article V, section 12 prohibits the legislature from passing special or local acts when a general act is, or can be made, applicable. The language of this section, although specific to taxes, is otherwise broader in scope than the prohibition against special or local acts in Article V, section 12, and permits no deviation from the public purpose requirement.

A number of decisions have addressed the issue of what is a public purpose. Legislative authorization to use in-state investment fund money derived from taxation to guarantee loans or bonds of private entities was held to be unconstitutional in violation of the public purpose requirement (*Hollow v. State*, 1986). By contrast, the court previously determined that neither lending bond money to private individuals (*Douglas v. Judge*, 1977) nor providing low-income housing with public funds (*Huber v. Groff*, 1976) was violative of the"public purpose" requirement. It seems that the decision in *Hollow* casts substantial doubt on the continuing validity of the *Huber v. Groff* decision. In *Hollow* the court found the statutory scheme designed to guarantee private loans to be unconstitutional because: (1) it proposed to use coal tax monies for private purposes, as opposed to public purposes; (2) it gave private individuals appropriations for industrial and benevolent purposes; and (3) it violated the unified investment program by allowing guarantees of private obligations. The sweeping nature of the holding seems to overrule existing law, challenging both *Huber* and *Grossman v. State* (1984). In *Hollow* it was more difficult to perceive a direct benefit to the state from the loan guarantee, whereas in *Huber* the loan generated money for the state and was no more than an investment. Further, a low family housing subsidy might be construed much as welfare, benefitting a large group of persons and not named individuals. Even more understandable is the court determination that legislation authorizing issuance of state revenue bonds for loans to local governments for water systems did not violate this section. In reaching its decision the court emphasized that it would indulge every reasonable presumption in favor of the constitutionality of the legislative decision. In the *Grossman* case the use of the loan proceeds affected the inhabitants of the particular areas as communities and not merely as individuals and posited a clear public purpose beyond the income (investment) return for the risk taken.

Under the public purpose language of the 1889 Montana Constitution the supreme court defined a public purpose as one that affects the inhabitants as a community and not merely as individuals (*Stanley v. Jeffries*, 1929). In *State ex rel. Mills v. Dixon* (1923), the court noted that the words "public purpose" are synonymous with "governmental purpose."

There are a number of cases discussing a variety of individual taxes and problems of uniformity under the 1889 Montana Constitution. Some of the cases might be relied upon in interpreting the language of the 1972 Constitution. However, this provision of the 1972 Constitution does not include the uniformity language of the 1889 Constitution. The equal protection clause of Article II, section 4 might be used to the same end.

## SECTION 2

**Tax Power Inalienable.** The power to tax shall never be surrendered, suspended, or contracted away.

The section is new. The power to tax was implied under the 1889 Montana Constitution, and Article XII, section 7 of the 1889 Constitution stated that "the power to tax corporations . . . shall never be relinquished or suspended."

The political concern at the time was the power of the copper companies (company) and the fear that the "company" would exercise its legislative muscle and take financial advantage of the people of the state.

The section impliedly secures the sovereignty of the state to tax and explicitly prohibits the removal of the state's power to tax. The power of government to tax is fundamental; raising revenue is essential to the nature of a modern state. Implied police power that authorizes a state to pass any law for health, safety, or general welfare may necessarily include the power to tax and spend. It is not intended to prohibit the state from delegating taxing authority to local government, local government being a subdivision of the state government, nor is it intended to prevent the state from exempting certain classes of property from taxation (MCC Tr. 1379).

In the spring of 1993, the legislature adopted Chapter 634 which would have increased tax revenue by increasing corporate and some individuals' income taxes (although decreasing other individuals' income taxes). In the summer of 1993, Referendum Number 112 was circulated to repeal Chapter 634, and on September 3, 1993, the secretary of state certified that the referendum had enough signatures to put it on the ballot. Chapter 634 was suspended from taking effect pending the vote on the referendum in November 1994. Nicholson filed suit, claiming that the suspension of Chapter 634 constituted a surrender of the legislative power of taxation. The Montana Supreme Court held that the suspension of an income tax increase is not the surrender of the taxing power by the legislature (*Nicholson v. Cooney,* 1994).

After the legislature passed legislation to tax retirement pension benefits that had previously been untaxed, the retirees sued, claiming that they had a contractual right to a continued exemption from taxation. The supreme court held: (1) the tax exemption was only a policy statement that could be changed by the legislature; and (2) the state was prohibited by Article VIII, section 2 from promising any group of taxpayers that it would never tax them (*Sheehy v. Public Employees Retirement Div.,* 1993).

There are no cases interpreting this section. Under section 7 of Article XII of the 1889 Constitution, several cases discussed the problem of legislative largesse in corporate taxing schemes—the very fear for which the original provision in the 1889 Constitution sought protection. For example, the Montana Supreme Court held that the purpose of the introductory clause of Article XII, section 7, that the power to tax corporations shall never be relinquished or suspended, is to prevent the creation of corporations under laws whereby the right to tax corporations is either extinguished during their existence or suspended for a definite period of time. The action of the legislature in failing to make corporations subject to the income tax law does not amount to a relinquishment or suspension of the right to tax them, within the meaning of this section (*Mills v. State Board of Equalization,* 1934).

## SECTION 3

**Property Tax Administration.** The state shall appraise, assess, and equalize the valuation of all property which is to be taxed in the manner provided by law.

Basically, this is a new provision. Article XII, section 15 of the 1889 Montana Constitution outlined, in substantial detail, the creation and duties of county boards of equalization and a state board of equalization.

This section and the following section, Article VIII, section 4, place all authority for appraising, assessing, and equalizing property valuations in the state; eliminate mention of county boards of equalization and the state board of equalization; and give the legislature complete authority to assess and equalize property valuations. The section allows the state legislature to fashion a statewide scheme for appraising, assessing, and equalizing property valuations. Throughout history, property taxation has been notable for its lack of consistency, and the appraisal and assessment of property has been notably inequitable. This section is a recognition of the difficulty of appraising, assessing, and equalizing property valuation, placing the ultimate power for designing property tax administration in the legislature. It would be inadvisable to attempt to outline in detail the scheme for appraising, assessing, and equalizing property taxes in a constitution. The need for periodic changes to deal with practical administrative problems requires that the details be left to the legislature. It was intended to equalize the mill levy on a statewide basis (MCC Tr. 1386).

Cases interpreting this section have given the legislature wide discretion for implementation; for example, *Fallon County v. State* (1988), *Hartley v. Department of Revenue* (1983), *Patterson v. Department of Revenue* (1976), *Montana Nat'l Bank of Roundup v. Department of Revenue* (1975). However, the legislature is required to follow established criteria in equalizing property assessments. Blanket reductions that do not follow established criteria will be set aside. To prove that property has been assessed inequitably it must be shown: (1) that there are several other comparable properties within a reasonable area; (2) how these properties are assessed; (3) what is the actual value of these comparable properties; (4) the actual value of the property at issue; (5) what is the assessment complained of; and (6) that by comparison the property at issue has been assessed at a higher proportion of its actual value than comparable properties (*Department of Revenue v. State Tax Appeal Bd.*, 1980). The constitutional framers did not intend for equalization to require the use of a single method to estimate market value. Rather, the framers intended that the Department of Revenue use different methods such as income and market data (*Albright v. State*, 1997).

## SECTION 4

**Equal Valuation.** All taxing jurisdictions shall use the assessed valuation of property established by the state.

The section is similar to Article XII, section 5 of the 1889 Montana Constitution. The syntax has been changed.

The section is intended to guarantee that the same assessed value will be used by all taxing authorities within the jurisdictional reach of the state, protecting property from discriminatory taxation. The equal protection and antidiscrimination clauses found in Article II, section 4 might not include property classifications. The equal protection commands of the Fourteenth Amendment of the federal constitution demand only that property classification and assessment be rationally related to a legitimate state purpose. The objective is to prevent local government from varying assessment levels to evade statutory mill levy limitations (MCC Tr. 1410).

While no cases have cited this section of the 1972 Montana Constitution, the provision from which it was derived has been cited and interpreted. The cases interpreting the parallel predecessor provision indicate that the government entity in charge of assessing, equalizing, and taxing property has broad discretion in designing classification schemes (*State ex rel. Reid v. District Court*, 1958; *Yellowstone Pipe Line Co. v. State Bd. of Equalization*, 1960). As long as property of similar nature and productivity is treated the same, the constitutional mandate of uniformity has been met (ibid.). The supreme court held that intentional discrimination in favor of one county against another or between the different classes of property in any county or in favor of one individual and against another is unconstitutional (*State ex rel. Schoonover v. Stewart*, 1931).

## SECTION 5

### Property Tax Exemptions

1. The Legislature may exempt from taxation: (a) Property of the United States, the state, counties, cities, towns, school districts, municipal corporations, and public libraries, but any private interest in such property may be taxed separately; (b) Institutions of purely public charity, hospitals and places of burial not used or held for private or corporate profit, places for actual religious worship, and property used exclusively for educational purposes; (c) Any other classes of property.
2. The Legislature may authorize creation of special improvement districts for capital improvements and the maintenance thereof. It may authorize the assessment of charges for such improvements and maintenance against tax exempt property directly benefitted thereby.

This section is derived from Article XII, section 2 of the 1889 Montana Constitution. The 1889 Constitution mandated certain exemptions, whereas this section authorizes the legislature to exempt from taxation any class of property but does not require that any property be exempted from taxation. The section permits taxation of private interests in government-owned property and assessment of special improvement district charges on tax-exempt property.

The provision suggests tax exemptions for various public and private property but does not exempt any property. The authorization to tax private equities in government-owned property and the power to assess exempt property benefitted by special improvement districts suggest how exempt property might be required to pay for benefits received.

The provision authorizes taxation exemptions and exceptions to the exemptions without mandating anything, and is probably meaningless. Constitutional prohibitions against exemptions and exceptions to exemptions would probably be based on equal protection, and any breach of equal protection would create a problem in any event. Since rational basis would guide equal protection analysis of property tax assessments, it is unlikely that any classifications of property for tax or tax exemption would be found unconstitutional (*Montana Stockgrowers Ass'n v. State*, 1989). In that case the Montana Supreme Court applied the rational basis test to determine that legislation taxing livestock while exempting business inventories was constitutional. The early cases decided under the 1889 Constitution are largely irrelevant to an interpretation of this section.

## SECTION 6

### Highway Revenue Non-Diversion

1. Revenue from gross vehicle weight fees and excise and license taxes (except general sales and use taxes) on gasoline, fuel, and other energy sources used to propel vehicles on public highways shall be used as authorized by the Legislature, after deduction of statutory refunds and adjustments, solely for: (a) Payment of obligations incurred for construction, reconstruction, repair, operation, and maintenance of public highways, streets, roads, and bridges; (b) Payment of county, city, and town obligations on streets, roads, and bridges; (c) Enforcement of highway safety, driver education, tourist promotion, and administrative collection costs.
2. Such revenue may be appropriated for other purposes by a three-fifths vote of the members of each house of the Legislature.

Article XII, section 1(b) of the 1889 Montana Constitution was an amendment ratified in 1955, limiting expenditure of highway user fees. This section is derived from and similar to Article XII, section 1(b) of the 1889 Constitution. The syntax of the section has been revised. A number of changes have been made, including removal of motor vehicle registration fees from earmarked revenues; adding local government road and street systems, highway safety programs, and driver education programs as permissible uses of earmarked funds; and allowing the designated earmarked funds to be diverted to other purposes by a three-fifths vote of the legislature.

The provision is intended to control the expenditure of the substantial revenue obtained from highway user fees, insuring that most of it is returned to road building and maintenance. There was intense pressure from the road-building industry to earmark highway user fees. After extended debate, delegates compromised, voting to permit diversion of highway user fees to other government purposes by three-fifths vote of the legislature. A proposal to change the three-fifths to three-fourths failed by a vote of 43 to 42. The provision guarantees that ample money will be available to build and repair Montana highways and roads. It also reduces the flexibility of the legislature in taxing, spending, and budgeting, and fails to direct these user taxes to pay for the collateral costs of the automotive industry such as air pollution. One intention of the language "enforcement of highway safety" in subsection (1)(c) is to allow the Highway Patrol to be paid from this fund (MCC Tr. 1428).

There are no cases interpreting the section. The two cases that analyzed the comparable section of the 1889 Constitution approved the constitutionality of minor expenditures for items that were not specifically earmarked (*Highway Comm'n v. Flood Control & Drainage District*, 1970; *Harvey v. Blewett*, 1968).

## SECTION 7

**Tax Appeals.** The Legislature shall provide independent appeal procedures for taxpayer grievances about appraisals, assessments, equalization, and taxes. The Legislature shall include a review procedure at the local government unit level.

There is no comparable provision in the 1889 Montana Constitution. Article XII, section 15 of the 1889 Constitution outlined the procedure to be followed in adjusting and equalizing taxable property valuations, but it did not provide an independent appeal procedure for taxpayer grievances.

The section is intended to respond to the continuing complaints of taxpayers by providing a regularized appeal process to review appraisals, assessments, equalization, and taxes. The provision should force some improvement in the overall fairness of tax levies. It has the further merit of providing a forum for expressing discontent with taxing authorities and tax law. Additionally, the forum is accessible at the local level. The State Board of Tax Appeal is in the Department of Administration. The State Board of Tax Appeal may be more impartial, independent, and objective since it is not in the Department of Revenue (MCC Tr. 1490).

The cases interpreting this section have emphasized the importance of equality in property tax assessment. Proof of discrimination in valuation is necessary to support a revision in tax assessment, not just an error in true value (*Department of Revenue v. State Tax Appeal Bd.*, 1980). Most of the cases have dealt with procedural problems. The cases have emphasized the importance of the local review process (*Butte Country Club v. Department of Revenue*, 1980), but the State Tax Appeal Board retains the power to hear appeals, to hear appeals de novo (*Department of Revenue v. Burlington N.*, Inc., 1976), and the power to review appraisal methods (*Department of Revenue v. State Tax Appeal Bd.*, 1980).

## SECTION 8

**State Debt.** No state debt shall be created unless authorized by a two-thirds vote of the members of each house of the Legislature or a majority of the electors voting thereon. No state debt shall be created to cover deficits incurred because appropriations exceeded anticipated revenue.

This section is derived from and similar to Article XIII, section 2 of the 1889 Montana Constitution (limiting debt) and Article XII, section 12 (balancing appropriations and taxes). The section permits the creation of debt by two-thirds vote of each house of the legislature or majority vote of the electors, but the central concern is insistence on a balanced budget (see Article VIII, section 9). The comparable provision in the 1889 Constitution limited debt liability to $100,000 except by majority vote of the electors, and emphasized the necessity of being responsible for debts, requiring legislation to specify a tax levy to pay any debt incurred.

This section seeks to limit long-term state debt by requiring either a super majority of the legislature or the affirmative vote of the general public to create debt. More significantly, the legislature is prohibited from creating any debt to cover shortfalls in anticipated revenue. The provision supports the concept of a balanced budget, which is stated more specifically in Article VIII, section 9. It also encourages the legislature to maintain a financially conservative posture. An election to approve taking on debt could be a vote referred to the electorate by the legislature or a vote called by citizen initiative (MCC Tr. 1501). The intended definition of state debt is the definition the courts have declared, namely, only that debt which pledges the credit of the state. Revenue bonds are not intended to fall under that definition (MCC Tr. 1503).

State revenue bonds were issued to develop state water resources. The bonds were financed by coal severance taxes. The court held that the legislature could authorize long-term borrowing by issuing bonds and could designate the coal severance tax trust fund as the source for servicing such indebtedness. The court did not find this to be an invalid continuing appropriation in violation of Article VIII, section 8, nor was the coal severance tax trust fund held to be immune from use as a source of funding for long-term state bonds, although Article IX, section 5 states: "[t]he principal of the trust (coal tax) shall forever remain inviolate unless appropriated by vote of three-fourths (3/4) of the members of each house." This is to be contrasted with the requirement in Article VIII, section 8, that long-term indebtedness can be approved by a two-thirds vote of the legislature. The court noted that "[t]he state must live within its means as to its general expenditures, and must pay for new programs as it goes." (p. 1332).

But since the constitution provides for use of borrowed funds, and two-thirds of each house of the legislature can authorize debt, it follows that the state can borrow money and can create indebtedness (*Grossman v. State,* 1984).

## SECTION 9

**Balanced Budget**. Appropriations by the Legislature shall not exceed anticipated revenue.

This section is derived from and similar to Article XII, section 12 of the 1889 Montana Constitution. The language is different and there is no exception to pay for insurrections.

The provision reiterates the proposition that deficits shall not be incurred because legislative appropriations are made in excess of anticipated revenue. As stated in Article VIII, section 8: "No state debt shall be created to cover deficits incurred because appropriations exceeded anticipated revenue." The drafters of Montana's 1972 Constitution were serious about maintaining a balanced budget. The language of the constitution seems to demand conservative financial policy; nonetheless, substantial long-term indebtedness has been accumulated and the Montana Supreme Court has not found the indebtedness to violate the constitution.

In the only important interpretation rendered by the Montana Supreme Court involving the question of a balanced budget, the court in *Grossman v. State* (1984) stated:

> The state must live within its means as to its general expenditures, and must pay for new programs as it goes, without incurring debt. But if a project or new program will require the incurrence of debt, two-thirds of the members of each house can authorize it. Since the constitution provides for the use of borrowed funds, it undoubtedly follows that the state could in fact borrow money or create indebtedness. Incurrence of long-term debt through the issuance of bonds or similar instruments is a time-honored method of governmental financing at all levels. We hold it eminently clear that the Legislature can authorize borrowing long-term by issuing and selling bonds, and can provide for the servicing for such indebtedness by repayment or refunding, (p. 1332)

## SECTION 10

**Local Government Debt**. The Legislature shall by law limit debts of counties, cities, towns, and all other local governmental entities.

The provision is new. Article XIII, sections 5 and 6 of the 1889 Montana Constitution limited county, city, municipality, and school district debt.

Local government debt limits are now left to the discretion of the legislature. This section is intended to override any borrowing power the local government might acquire by charter government (MCC Tr. 1512).

The delegates sought to maximize local government autonomy but were not prepared to eliminate local government debt limits. Permitting the legislature to establish local government debt limits concedes to local units of government greater financial flexibility than rigid constitutional limitations. In general, the constitution maximizes local government autonomy, flexibility, and innovation. For example, Article XI encourages local government autonomy. Fixed limits on debt are not compatible with that purpose. Placing unlimited discretion as to local government debt in the control of the legislature is marginally more responsive to local government needs than fixed constitutional limitations.

No cases have been decided that rely on this section of the 1972 Montana Constitution. Under the parallel provision in the 1889 Constitution there was a plethora of cases involving everything from the definition of indebtedness to election requirements in approving indebtedness. None of the cases are relevant to an interpretation of this section.

## SECTION 11

**Use of Loan Proceeds**. All money borrowed by or on behalf of the state or any county, city, town, or other local governmental entity shall be used only for purposes specified in the authorizing law.

This section is derived from and substantively identical to Article XIII, section 3 of the 1889 Montana Constitution. Word usage and grammar have been changed.

The section is intended to limit administrative discretion in expenditure of borrowed money. Changed conditions might sometimes require or at least suggest that borrowed funds as approved by the electorate or the appropriate governing body should be expended in a way or for a purpose not clearly included in the authorizing legislation. Such administrative changes are prohibited. This section supports majoritarian control and conservative administration of public funds. The specificity of authorizing legislation for expenditure of borrowed funds leaves little discretion to the administrative agency in charge of spending the borrowed funds. An objective of this section is to guarantee proper management of borrowed funds and to prevent misuse or diversion of those funds (MCC Tr. 1516).

There are no cases interpreting this provision under the 1972 Montana Constitution. The identical provision found in the 1889 Constitution was clearly held to mean what it says. Funds provided by the sale of bonds to construct bridges could not be expended for other purposes (*State ex rel. Furnish v. Mullendore,* 1916). In the particular case the consent of the electors had been required and obtained prior to the sale of the bonds.

## SECTION 12

**Strict Accountability.** The Legislature shall by law insure strict accountability of all revenue received and money spent by the state and counties, cities, towns, and all other local governmental entities.

The section is derived from Article XII, section 13, of the 1889 Montana Constitution. The 1889 provision was more detailed and made the state treasurer and his sureties responsible for all government funds.

The provision is intended to insure accountability for all revenue received and money spent by every unit of government, but leaves the procedural details for accomplishing this purpose to the legislature. To require that all revenue received and money spent be accounted for is an essential part of financial integrity; it protects against embezzlement, corrupt use of funds, and other misappropriation. It is an essential part of maintaining public confidence in government operation.

There are no significant case interpretations relevant to this section.

## SECTION 13

**Investment of Public Funds and Public Retirement System Assets**

1. The Legislature shall provide for a unified investment program for public funds and public retirement system assets and provide rules therefor, including supervision of investment of surplus funds of all counties, cities, towns, and other local governmental entities. Each fund forming a part of the unified investment program shall be separately identified. Except as provided in subsection (3), no public funds shall be invested in private corporate capital stock. The investment program shall be audited at least annually and a report thereof submitted to the governor and Legislature.
2. The public school fund and the permanent funds of the Montana university system and all other state institutions of learning shall be safely and conservatively invested in: (a) Public securities of the state, its subdivisions, local government units and districts within the state, or (b) Bonds of the United States or other securities fully guaranteed as to principal and interest by the United States, or (c) Such other safe investments bearing a fixed rate of interest as may be provided by law.
3. Investment of public retirement system assets shall be managed in a fiduciary capacity in the same manner that a prudent expert acting in a fiduciary capacity and

familiar with the circumstances would use in the conduct of an enterprise of a similar character with similar aims. Public retirement system assets may be invested in private corporate capital stock.

This section is derived from but substantially different from Article XXI of the 1889 Constitution. The section provides for a unified investment program for all state funds.[21] It allows retirement funds to be invested in private corporate stock but provides that the public school fund and university system funds be invested only in interest-bearing securities. The prohibition in the 1889 Constitution on investment in corporate common stock for all but state retirement trust funds was retained.

The language in subsection (1) of sentence one regarding the legislature supervising local government funds is intended to insure careful treatment of local funds by local entities. Sentence two is intended to insure the proper distribution of interest to the individual funds when the funds are pooled and invested as a unit (MCC Tr. 1518). Sentence three is intended to prevent risky investment of public funds. Also, it is intended to prevent any conflict of interest for the legislature when they regulate businesses in which they might otherwise have invested state funds (MCC Tr. 1519).

Subsection (2) is intended to insure that the educational funds remain inviolate by preventing risky investment of those funds. Insofar as possible, it is intended to avoid replacing lost funds as required by law since the funds are guaranteed by the state. "Public securities of the state" is not intended to mean only state, city, or town bonds, but is intended to encompass all state governmental entities which issue public securities (MCC Tr. 1539).

Constitutional Amendment No. 25, approved by the voters in 1994 and effective in 1995, inserted in subsection (1) "and public retirement system assets" after "public funds" in the first sentence, and substituted "Except as provided in subsection (3)" for "Except for monies contributed to retirement funds" at the beginning of the third sentence. The amendment also inserted the new subsection (3) concerning retirement system assets. This section is similar to Article XXI of the 1889 Constitution, but represents a substantial change.

The use of in-state investment funds to guarantee private loans or bonds is unconstitutional (*Hollow v. State*, 1986). The provisions of section 13 for the unified investment fund do not require that all agencies participate regardless of the nature of the agency (*Huber v. Groff*, 1976)

[21] "[A] lmost fifteen percent of the General Fund budget for the state each year . . . comes from the unified investment system established under Article VIII, section 13." Thomas E. Towe, "Revenue and Finance Under Montana's 1972 constitution," *Montana Law Review*, 51 (1990): 404.

## SECTION 14

**Prohibited Payments.** Except for interest on the public debt, no money shall be paid out of the treasury unless upon an appropriation made by law and a warrant drawn by the proper officer in pursuance thereof.

Derived from and substantively identical to Article XII, section 10, and Article V, section 34 of the 1889 Montana Constitution, the provision is intended to protect public funds from misappropriation. The requirements to be followed have proven to be generally adequate to protect public funds and to provide an effective paper trail of expenditures of public funds for auditing purposes.

Although this section does not seem to limit its effect to revenue derived from taxation, the court held that money derived under the Housing Act of 1975, since it is not derived by taxation, need not be handled in the manner prescribed by this section (*Huber v. Groff*, 1976). The provisions for the unified investment fund do not require that all agencies participate regardless of the nature of the agency (ibid.; followed in *Grossman v. State*, 1984) (coal severance tax water bonds).

The court has held that state money is exempt from execution (*First Nat'l Bank v. Sourdough Land & Cattle Co.*, 1976). The court also in *Grossman v. State* (1984) held that an authorization contingent on legislative approval of a detailed project plan that made it impossible to predict bond revenue interest and to determine the exact cost of a project did not render unconstitutional the appropriation. When the bonds are issued and sold, the interest rate to be paid by the state would become certain and the amounts necessary to service and repay the indebtedness will be definite. The court relied on *State ex rel. Toomey v. State Bd. of Examiners* (1925), which held "that is certain which can be made certain" to uphold the authorization for the project.

## SECTION 15

**Public Retirement System Assets**

1. Public retirement systems shall be funded on an actuarially sound basis. Public retirement system assets, including income and actuarially required contributions, shall not be encumbered, diverted, reduced, or terminated and shall be held in trust to provide benefits to participants and their beneficiaries and to defray administrative expenses.
2. The governing boards of public retirement systems shall administer the system including actuarial determinations, as fiduciaries of system participants and their beneficiaries.

This section was enacted by Constitutional Amendment Number 25, which the voters approved in 1994 and which took effect in 1995. The section is meant to protect public retirement system assets. In *Peters v. State* (1997), the only case interpreting this section, the Montana Supreme Court held that there was nothing in a district court's order requiring a state board to deplete the pension trust assets.

## SECTION 16

**Limitation on Sales Tax or Use Tax Rates.** The rate of a general statewide sales tax or use tax may not exceed 4%.

This section was enacted by Constitutional Amendment Number 27, which the voters approved in 1994 and which took effect in 1995. In fact, as of 2000, Montana had no sales or use tax. This section would limit such a tax to 4 percent should the Montana legislature ever pass such a tax.

There have been no cases interpreting this section through the end of 1999.

# Article IX

## *Environment and Natural Resources*

### SECTION 1

**Protection and Improvement**

1. The state and each person shall maintain and improve a clean and healthful environment in Montana for present and future generations.
2. The Legislature shall provide for the administration and enforcement of this duty.
3. The Legislature shall provide adequate remedies for the protection of the environmental life support system from degradation and provide adequate remedies to prevent unreasonable depletion and degradation of natural resources.

This is a new provision without any counterpart in the 1889 Montana Constitution.

The section is intended to guarantee the preservation of the Montana environment. The preamble and Article II, section 3 address "[the desire] to improve the quality of life" and the right to "a clean and healthful environment." This article addresses the problem more specifically. At the time it was written, Montana's Constitution contained the strongest statement of conservation philosophy of any state constitution. Constitutional provisions of other states were considered inadequate for Montana's unique environment and so were not relied upon as a basis for Article IX (MCC Tr. 1200).

The section states an objective: "[t]he state and each person shall maintain and improve a clean and healthful environment." It charges the legislature with the responsibility to accomplish the objective. The section does not provide specific guidelines or establish pollution limits. Since traditionally such hortatory statements have not been self-executing,[22] any real environmental protection must come from the legislature or other provisions in the constitution. The language "each person" in subsection (1) is intended to include corporations and legal entities (MCC Tr. 1200). The language in subsection (3), "environmental life-support systems" is intended to be all-encompassing, including, but not limited to, air, water, and land. It would seem that since the word "unreasonable," used in the last clause of subsection (3), modifies "depletion and "degradation," the section presupposes some depletion and degradation of natural resources. By the same logic, since the word "degradation" as used in the first clause of subsection (3) has no modifying adjective, it must be absolute; that is, the legislature shall provide adequate remedies for the protection of the environmental life support system from *any* degradation. The delegates included no definitions to avoid having the section interpreted in a restrictive manner (MCC Tr. 1201).

The first consequential court decision justified the apparent intentions of the delegates. In *Montana Environmental Information Center et al. v. Dept of Environmental Quality and Seven-Up Pete Joint Venture* (1999), the court held that to the extent Montana Code Annotated, Section 75-5-317(2)(j) excludes mining activities from nondegradation review, it violates environmental rights guaranteed by the Montana Constitution. In so holding the court analyzed the following two provisions of the constitution.

> [Inalienable rights] . . . include the right to a clean and healthful environment. [Section 3 of Article II]
>
> The state and each person shall maintain and improve a clean and healthful environment in Montana for present and future generations. [Subdivision (1) of Section 1 of Article XI]

The court found the two provisions so interrelated, complimentary, and interdependent that they must be considered together and "applied in tandem." The court then concluded that state action or private action which implicates either

---

[22] "A self-executing constitutional provision is one that is immediately effective without the necessity of ancillary legislation; that is, it supplies a sufficient rule by which a right given may be enjoyed or a duty imposed may be enforced." Carl W. Tobias & Daniel N. McLean, "Of Crabbed Interpretations and Frustrated Mandates: The Effect of Environmental Policy Acts on Pre-existing Agency Authority," *Montana Law Review,* 41 (1980): 255.

provision must be scrutinized consistently and that scrutiny will be strict. Strict scrutiny was defined in the strongest terms possible.

> [To survive] strict scrutiny . . . [the] state [must first establish] a compelling state interest for the action taken. [Second the state must prove that the action taken] is closely tailored to effectuate affectuate . . . [the identified] interest. And [third the state must show that the means chosen] is the least onerous [means] . . . that can be taken to achieve the State's objective. (pp. 1245–1246)

In prior cases the court limited "strict scrutiny" or "compelling interest" analysis to government action that infringed fundamental rights or that established a suspect classification. Fundamental rights were rights protected by the declaration of rights in Article II, or rights without which other constitutional guaranteed rights would have little meaning (*In re* C.H., 1984). The court concluded that:

> [The constitution provides] language and protections which are both anticipatory and preventative. The delegates did not intend to merely prohibit that degree of environmental degradation which can be conclusively linked to ill health or physical endangerment. Our constitution does not require that dead fish float on the surface of our state's rivers and streams before its far sighted environmental protections can be invoked, (p. 1249)

However, somewhat curiously, the court omitted any discussion of subsection (2) of Section 1. A concurrence argued that the majority opinion should not have extended constitutional environmental protection to private action, at least not in this case. Assuming the issue of private action was not before the court, the majority opinion is nonetheless a significant dictum indicating how the court will analyze future private violations of constitutional environmental protections.

Two earlier cases, one holding that the Constitution does not mandate an environmental impact statement (*Kadillak v. The Anaconda Co.*, 1979), and a second, which exempted power companies from preconstruction review by the Environmental Protection Agency before granting a hard-rock mining permit (*Montana Power Co. v. E.P.A.*, 1977), have not been challenged but may be questionable precedent.

## SECTION 2

### Reclamation

1. All lands disturbed by the taking of natural resources shall be reclaimed. The Legislature shall provide effective requirements and standards for the reclamation of lands disturbed.

2. The Legislature shall provide for a fund, to be known as the resource indemnity trust of the state of Montana, to be funded by such taxes on the extraction of

natural resources as the Legislature may from time to time impose for that purpose.

3. The principal of the resource indemnity trust shall forever remain inviolate in an amount of one hundred million dollars ($100,000,000), guaranteed by the state against loss or diversion.

This is a new section. There was no comparable provision in the 1889 Montana Constitution. The constitutional convention committee report concerning subsection (1) said that the responsibility of protecting and restoring the surface conditions of Montana's lands for unborn generations should not be left to the legislature but should instead be protected by the fundamental law of the constitution (MCC Rep. 555–556). Constitutional Amendment Number 1, which the voters approved in 1974 and which became effective in 1975, added subsections

(2) and (3). The beginning of the decade of the 1970s brought a heightened sensitivity to environmental problems, and Montana, a prototypical colonial state, had been raped and pillaged by out-of-state economic interests for generations. A number of constitutional convention delegates were concerned about the environment while others were committed to private economic interests. Compromises were reached. Ultimately, section 1 was phrased to create a duty that the state and each person "shall maintain a clean and healthful environment" while leaving administrative detail and enforcement to the legislature and substantial interpretive latitude to the judiciary. The section instructs the legislature to protect the environment and seems to prohibit "unreasonable depletion and degradation of natural resources."

Section 2, Reclamation, requires restoration of land after removal of natural resources. Standards and enforcement are left to the legislature. If the legislature fails to act, enforcement could prove difficult. Presumptively, inadequate (ineffective) legislative standards could be challenged in court and the same would be true of ineffective administrative implementation of legislative standards. Amendments added in 1975 (subsections (2) and (3)), created the "resource indemnity trust," apparently to provide funding for the reclamation of lands disturbed by the taking of natural resources. The only case interpreting this section involved Butte-Silver Bow, a natural resources disaster area, that expected to be the focus of considerable state reclamation activity, with a large amount of money coming from the resource indemnity trust. The 1985 legislature used some of the interest income from the Resource Indemnity Trust Fund for general operating expenses and the court held that there is no limit on appropriation of principal or interest accumulated in the Resource Indemnity Trust Fund beyond the $100 million (*Butte-Silver Bow Local Gov't v. State,* 1989). A forceful dissent noted:

> the decision continues what has become a commonplace in the history of the state of Montana: the State gets the gold mine, Butte gets the shaft. . . . The close tailoring of

> the tax on the extraction of natural resources to the constitutional mandate that all lands disturbed by the taking of natural resources be reclaimed is ignored. Somehow the obvious connection between the tax and the purpose of the tax escapes the facile interpretation of the majority. . . . The Resource Indemnity Trust was never intended to fund the general operations of the State, (pp. 332–333)

In 1998 the Resource Indemnity Trust contained $96 million and is expected to reach the $100 million mark by 2002. The income generated by the trust, $7 to $8 million a year, has generally, and at least genetically, supported reclamation projects affecting Montana's air, soil, and water. The Conservation and Resource Development Division of the Department of Natural Resources and Conservation administers the trust.

## SECTION 3

### Water Rights

> 1. All existing rights to the use of any waters for any useful or beneficial purpose are hereby recognized and confirmed.
> 2. The use of all water that is now or may hereafter be appropriated for sale, rent, distribution, or other beneficial use, the right of way over the lands of others for all ditches, drains, flumes, canals, and aqueducts necessarily used in connection therewith, and the sites for reservoirs necessary for collecting and storing water shall be held to be a public use.
> 3. All surface, underground, flood, and atmospheric waters within the boundaries of the state are the property of the state for the use of its people and are subject to appropriation for beneficial uses as provided by law.
> 4. The Legislature shall provide for the administration, control, and regulation of water rights and shall establish a system of centralized records, in addition to the present system of local records.

This is a new provision except for subsection (2) that is derived from and substantively identical to Article III, section 15 of the 1889 Montana Constitution. Despite some legislative efforts before 1972 on both adjudicated and unadjudicated water sources, Montana water doctrine had progressed very little beyond the early self-help approach. Subsection (3) established ownership of all waters in the state subject to use by the people. Montana did not take strict control of its water rights until the people ratified the 1972 Constitution.

The provision guarantees existing water rights; restates that beneficial use of water is a public use; claims state ownership of water subject to private use and appropriation; and requires the creation of a centralized record system of all water rights. In effect, the section formed the legal foundation for future water right claims and placed administration, control, and regulation of water rights in the legislature. Records identifying water rights were to be located in both a centralized state depository and a local depository. The creation of a centralized record system has made verification of water rights much easier. Subsection (3) is not intended to allow access or trespass over private lands for the general public to get to streams, reservoirs, or other water (MCC Tr. 1303, 1306). The language "for the use of its people" is intended to imply that the state cannot sell the water without consent of the people (MCC Tr. 1308). An intent of subsection (3) is that, even though the state owns the water, the people may still appropriate it as they did before (MCC Tr. 1311). Many water users, particularly agricultural users, were opposed to the approach taken in this section. It was said that the voters of Gallatin County voted against the new constitution because of the inclusion of this section.

The Montana Supreme Court has held that all of this section, except subsection (4), is self-executing (*General Agriculture Corp. v. Moore*, 1975). This conclusion follows similar language found in the case of *Spratt v. Helena Power Transmission Co.* (1908). In *Spratt* the court reviewed Article III, section 15 of the 1889 Montana Constitution, the predecessor provision of subsection (2), and stated: "in the light of our history and natural conditions, in a region where the conservation and use of its waters are all-important to its development and progress" (p. 634), Article III, section 15 was not only self-executing but should receive a broad construction.

There is a continuing and often bitter struggle over the control of large portions of water that either originates or passes through the state of Montana. The struggle involves individual claimants who, under current legislation, will be contesting their rights well into the twenty-first century. Part of the struggle is between prior and subsequent appropriators; a second part of the struggle is between more general classifications of users such as recreational use of streams versus the rights of stream bank and stream bed owners (see *Montana Coalition for Stream Access v. Hildreth*, 1984; *Montana Coalition for Stream Access v. Curran*, 1984).

The struggle also involves the state of Montana and the various Indian tribes that are situated within the geographic boundaries of the state. Indian water rights arise when the federal government reserves land for particular purposes because it also reserves sufficient water, by implication, to accomplish those purposes. The rights carry a priority date, which is usually the date of the creation of the reservation, but in the case of Indian reservations the priority date may be immemorial. Reservation rights cannot be lost through lack of use. Montana has been trying to quantify how much water is embraced through such reserved rights by compacts, agreements, and litigation. In *State ex rel. Greely v. Confederated Salish and Kootenai Tribes* (1985), the Montana Supreme Court held that the state legislature's enactment of the Water Use Act (Title 85, chapter 2), pursuant to section 3 of this Article of the Montana Constitution, constitutes a valid and binding consent of the people of Montana to Congress's grant of state jurisdiction over Indian reserved water rights.

Subsection (1) of this section and of the Transition Schedule of the 1972 Constitution preserved all existing water rights, including those created by a petition for appropriation, that were filed before repeal of the former water law (*General Agriculture Corp. v. Moore*, 1975).

## SECTION 4

**Cultural Resources.** The Legislature shall provide for the identification, acquisition, restoration, enhancement, preservation, and administration of scenic, historic, archaeologic, scientific, cultural, and recreational areas, sites, records and objects, and for their use and enjoyment by the people.

This is a new section. There is no comparable provision in the 1889 Montana Constitution. The provision is intended to protect Montana's historical sites, a laudatory allusion to Montana's cultural and historical heritage. The directive that the legislature shall both locate and preserve Montana's culture and history is unequivocal and has been acted upon by the legislature. Thus, by statute, the legislature has mandated that Indian studies are required for teachers under certain circumstances; has established the Montana Arts Council, cultural and aesthetic projects, and art for state buildings; has set up historic preservation guidelines; and has established a natural resource information system.

There are no cases interpreting the section.

## SECTION 5

**Severance Tax on Coal—Trust Fund.** The Legislature shall dedicate not less than one-fourth (14) of the coal severance tax to a trust fund, the interest and income from which may be appropriated. The principal of the trust shall forever remain inviolate unless appropriated by vote of three-fourths (3/4) of the members of each house of the Legislature. After December 31, 1979, at least fifty percent (50%) of the severance tax shall be dedicated to the trust fund.

This new section was not a part of the original 1972 Constitution. The amendment emerged from the 1973 and 1974 legislative sessions, the only annual legislative sessions in Montana's history. The amendment was precipitated by an impending coal boom and agitation to prepare for the boom. Responding to the potential problem, a number of legislators, aware that Montana (a stereotypical colonial state used and abused by eastern financial and industrial powers) had periodically suffered a boom-and-bust economy, conceived the idea of a coal severance tax coupled with a "Coal Tax Trust Fund" as a means to blunt the problems associated with an expected economic downturn following any coal boom. To insure continuity for the trust fund the drafters formulated the proposal as a constitutional amendment. The proposed amendment was passed and became section 5 of Article IX in 1976.

Originally, the severance tax was 30 percent of the mine mouth value of the coal, the highest coal severance tax rate in the country. Governor Thomas Judge called the tax "the most significant piece of legislation enacted in Montana in this century."[23] The tax was vigorously opposed by coal mining interests and others. After passage, the law was immediately challenged in court as an unconstitutional violation of the interstate commerce clause of the U.S. Constitution. The U.S. Supreme Court upheld the constitutionality of the tax in *Commonwealth Edison Co. v. Montana* (1981). Losing the political battle to block passage of the tax and the permanent trust fund, as well as the legal battle to have the tax declared unconstitutional, opponents chipped away at the tax and the trust fund in other ways. First, there were attempts to reduce the rate of the tax. The principal argument justifying a reduction in the tax rate was that the tax delayed mining development in Montana, forcing coal purchasers to buy Wyoming coal where the tax was less. Opponents of a reduction in the tax rate argued that any reduction would only advantage wealthy out-of-state coal companies and eastern power users while leaving Montana with less money to recover from the aftermath of a coal boom.

In 1987 the tax rate on bituminous coal was reduced to 15 percent and to 10 percent on igneous coal. Second, there were ongoing attempts to exempt some coal production from taxation. The exemption covered the first 20,000 tons or less of production, which was subsequently increased to the first 50,000 tons. Third, opponents of the tax and trust fund sought to invade the corpus of the trust fund, but the requirement of a "three-fourths vote of the members of each house" stymied trust fund opponents. In 1992 the coal tax permanent trust fund was changed to include a sub-category identified as the Treasure State Endowment Trust Fund. The Treasure State Endowment was allocated 50 percent of the tax revenue previously placed in the Permanent Coal Tax Trust Fund. The fund, enacted by legislative referendum, was designed to provide money for local government infrastructure. The Treasure State Endowment Trust Fund not only generates interest income to be used to support local government improvements but acts as a guarantor for local government infrastructure bonding needs. Finally, in 1999, the legislature passed an ingenious law requiring coal producers to pay a license fee amounting to approximately 50 percent of the amount of the severance tax. The coal producers, pursuant to the law, were entitled to offset 101 percent of the license tax against coal severance tax liability. No portion of the coal producers' license fee revenue was to have been placed in any trust fund but would have been available to reduce taxes and fund the general operations of the state. This ploy effectively reduced, by 50 percent, the amount of the severance tax revenue constitutionally dedicated to the Permanent Coal Tax Trust fund. In *Montanans for the Coal Trust v. State* (2000), the Montana Supreme Court held that this law created an unconstitutional diversion from the Coal

[23] Malone et al., *Montana,* p. 397.

Tax Trust Fund without the required three-fourths vote of each house of the legislature.

The Coal Tax Trust Fund may be one of the more valuable and innovative dimensions of the constitution, although not included in the original document as passed in 1972. It has become an important hedge against the vicissitudes of an unstable economy and a largely fluctuating tax base.[24] Interest from the fund accounts for 10 percent of the state's general fund requirements. In 1978 the Permanent Coal Tax Trust Fund had a balance of $6,268,262. The balance increased slowly at first, but for the three-year period from 1983 to 1986 the fund balance increased by nearly $50 million each year, growing from $158,358,806 in 1983 to $309,384,000 in 1986. Because the tax rate was reduced and because the amount of coal being mined has decreased, the annual amount of coal tax revenue added to the trust fund has declined dramatically. For example, from 1993 to 1999 the trust fund increased less than $50 million. Part of the decrease is a result of the separate Treasure State Endowment Trust Fund. The Treasure State Endowment Trust Fund had a balance of over $70 million at the end of fiscal year 1999.

A recent U.S. Supreme Court decision has finally resolved a long-standing collateral challenge to the coal tax and Coal Tax Trust Fund. A case or series of cases brought against Montana and others by the Crow tribe, a tribe located within the boundaries of the state of Montana, have presented an interesting and difficult challenge to the coal tax and the Coal Tax Permanent Trust Fund. The cases and opinions started in the late 1970s with decisions and opinions by the Montana Federal District Court and the Ninth Circuit Court of Appeals being filed in 1979, 1985, 1987, and 1996. A U.S. Supreme Court opinion was handed down in 1998 (*Montana v. Crow Tribe of Indians*, 1998). The Supreme Court opinion outlines the facts, the legal issues, and the resolution of each.

Basically, in 1904, the Crow tribe ceded part of its Montana reservation to the United States for settlement by non-Indians. The United States holds rights to minerals underlying the ceded strip in trust for the tribe. Montana imposed a severance tax and a gross proceeds tax on all coal produced in the state, including coal underlying the reservation proper and the ceded strip. Mining companies paid royalties to the Crow tribe and taxes to Montana. The Crow tribe adopted its own severance tax, which was approved by the Department of the Interior as to coal underlying the reservation proper but not beneath the ceded strip. The Crow tribe brought a federal action for injunctive and declaratory relief against Montana and others based on pre-emption and tribal sovereignty, seeking termination of the Montana tax on minerals underlying the ceded strip

---

[24] As of 1999, the Coal Tax Trust Fund contained more than $618 million. The Treasure State Endowment Trust Fund is a derivative of the Coal Tax Trust Fund, that is, an additional fund derived from coal tax revenue used to back bonds sold for the development of local government infrastructure.

and the reservation. The Montana Federal District Court dismissed each case and the Ninth Circuit Court of Appeals regularly reversed the Montana Federal District Court. The end result was that Montana was ultimately denied the right to continue taxing the coal under the ceded strip and under reservation lands, but was not required to refund or disgorge the taxes previously collected.

In denying disgorgement of the taxes paid to Montana, the U.S. Supreme Court considered and dismissed the allegations: (1) that the Montana tax was not appropriate and infringed the sovereignty of the Crow tribe, (2) that the Montana tax was unconstitutional as pre-empted by federal law and tribal sovereignty, and (3) that Montana's severance tax was exorbitant, thereby reducing the amount of royalties to be collected by the tribe.

# Article X

## *Education and Public Lands*

### SECTION 1

**Educational Goals and Duties**

1. It is the goal of the people to establish a system of education which will develop the full educational potential of each person. Equality of educational opportunity is guaranteed to each person of the state.
2. The state recognizes the distinct and unique cultural heritage of the American Indians and is committed in its educational goals to the preservation of their cultural integrity.
3. The Legislature shall provide a basic system of free quality public elementary and secondary schools. The Legislature may provide such other educational institutions, public libraries, and educational programs as it deems desirable. It shall fund and distribute in an equitable manner to the school districts the state's share of the cost of the basic elementary and secondary school system.

This section is derived from sections 1, 6, and 7 of Article XI of the 1889 Constitution, but the educational philosophy announced by this section of the 1972 Constitution represents a substantial change. First, it demands that the state provide free, quality primary and secondary education (the former provision did not mention "quality" although it did use the term "thorough," and it required that the state maintain a public, free common school); second, equality of educational opportunity for all persons and equality of funding are guaranteed (the predecessor provision stated that the public schools are open to all children between the ages of 6 and 21); and third, it recognizes and promises to support Native American culture (this is a new provision and the only place in the Montana Constitution where Native Americans are separately recognized). The predecessor article was primarily concerned with financing schools, managing "school lands," and organizing the educational hierarchy. This section is not intended to mean that the state will aid private schools (MCC Tr. 1960). School districts may still have levies if they wish to enhance their local educational programs (MCC Tr. 1969).

The delegates indicated a high regard for basic education and a determination that the state provide not only a basic education but also equitable state funding for basic education. The section was intended to guarantee that all persons in the state be afforded a quality education with an emphasis on equality. There was to be no limitation based on age, sex, race, creed, religion, political beliefs, or national origin. (The full scope of anti-discrimination is detailed in section 7 of this article.) This was a mark of the time, giving voice to equality and to a sincere belief that most human problems could be resolved through education and equal protection under law. The delegates identified three concepts as essential to a healthy educational system: quality, equality, and flexibility (MCC Tr. 721–722, 724). The term "quality" in subsection (3) is intended to insure that the constitutional requirement of funding to the districts will not jeopardize the quality of education. "Quality" is intended to mean more than a minimum quality of education—it is to be an education capable of producing well-informed citizens (MCC Tr. 1960). A lengthy debate among the delegates centered on whether the constitution should mandate legislative funding. By a very close vote (46 to 43), the delegates elected to include the funding mandate (MCC Tr. 1973).

A second dimension of this section was the promise to preserve the cultural integrity of American Indians. This is altogether new. The Native American culture has been and continues to be at risk. Historical guilt, geography, and demography coalesce to place Montana in a position that requires a heightened responsibility in protecting the Native American culture; and within Montana, education is charged with the primary responsibility for the preservation of the cultural integrity of American Indians. The ideal is laudatory. The difficulty is in the details, and the legal and practical response has been minimal. Primary and secondary school teachers are required to be prepared to teach something about Native American culture, and even this minimal response has been challenged. There is an increasing sense of separation between the Montana tribes and the rest of the state. Struggles have focused on gambling and water rights, in particular.

A number of cases have referred to this section in discussing both a quality education and equality of educational opportunity. The primary problem has been equality of funding, although limitations on extracurricular activities based on grade averages was held to be permissible (*State ex rel. Bartmess v. Board of*

*Trustees,* 1986). An earlier Montana Federal District Court case, decided under the 1889 Montana Constitution, held that a school district rule prohibiting extracurricular activities to married students denied them the equal protection of the laws with respect to the right granted by Article XI, section 1 of the 1889 Montana Constitution, the predecessor to this provision (*Moron v. School Dist.,* 1972). However, private school students are not entitled to participate in public school extracurricular events (*Kaptein v. Conrad School District,* 1997). In other cases the courts have held that school authorities have a duty to place retarded and/or emotionally disturbed children in appropriate special education programs. Failure to do so may result in an award of damages against the school district (*B.M. v. State,* 1982). A wrongful placement may likewise result in damages (*In re the "A#X201D; Family,* 1979).

Spending disparities among school districts resulted in a denial of equality of educational opportunity in violation of this section (*School District v. State,* 1989). Federal funding may be considered in equalizing educational expenditure if the system meets the federal definition of an equalized program (ibid.).

According to an Attorney General Opinion, a school district may not charge deposit fees for any course or activity for which credit may be earned for graduation (36 Op. Att'y Gen. 483 (1976)).

## SECTION 2

**Public School Fund. The public school fund of the state shall consist of:**

1. Proceeds from the school lands which have been or may hereafter be granted by the United States,
2. Lands granted in lieu thereof,
3. Lands given or granted by any person or corporation under any law or grant of the United States,
4. All other grants of land or money made from the United States for general educational purposes or without special purpose,
5. All interests in estates that escheat to the state,
6. All unclaimed shares and dividends of any corporation incorporated in the state,
7. All other grants, gifts, devises or bequests made to the state for general educational purposes.

The section is derived from section 2 of Article XI of the 1889 Montana Constitution and is substantively identical. The grammar has been changed.

The section identifies funds that make up the public school fund. The public school fund is a trust fund for educational purposes and is composed primarily of school lands that were transferred to the state of Montana from the federal government. A second source of revenue included in the public school fund is property that escheats to the state plus all unclaimed shares and dividends for corporations incorporated under the laws of this state. The final source of revenue added to the public school fund is the gifts, grants, and transfers that are specifically designated as being for education. The creation of the public school fund is intended to provide a continuing source of money for public education in the state of Montana. It has provided a substantial amount of revenue for education over the course of the years, notwithstanding the fact that financing education has become an increasingly difficult task.

There have been no cases interpreting the section since 1972. Under the identical provision of the 1889 Montana Constitution two cases discussed what property might be considered left (escheated) to the state: *In re Nielsen's Estate* (1946) and *Bottomly v. Meagher County* (1943). In *Barnes-King Dev. Co. v. Corette* (1970), the court held that unclaimed corporate shares or dividends were in effect abandoned and could be taken by the state and placed in the public school fund.

## SECTION 3

**Public School Fund Inviolate.** The public school fund shall forever remain inviolate, guaranteed by the state against loss or diversion.

This section is derived from and identical to the first sentence of section 3, Article XI of the 1889 Montana Constitution. The intent of the provision is to protect forever the public school fund, which is the primary source of state revenue for education. The fund has been effectively preserved.

The only case that has considered the section approved payment of attorney fees and costs from state aid money (*Missoula High School Legal Defense Ass'n v. Superintendent of Pub. Instruction,* 1981). An earlier case under the parallel provision of the 1889 Montana Constitution held that the requirement that the public school fund shall forever remain inviolate refers to the permanent school fund and not to funds raised by tax levies (*School Dist. v. Helena,* 1930).

## SECTION 4

**Board of Land Commissioners.** The governor, superintendent of public instruction, auditor, secretary of state, and attorney general constitute the board of land commissioners. It has the authority to direct, control, lease, exchange, and sell school lands and lands which have been or may be granted for the support and benefit of the various state educational institutions, under such regulations and restrictions as may be provided by law.

The section is derived from and nearly identical to section 4 of Article XI of the 1889 Montana Constitution. The state auditor is added as a member of the Board of Land Commissioners. The section provides the structure and authority for the management of school lands. The policy choice of placing control of school lands in the hands of elected state officials has worked well. The Board can give wider scrutiny to management decisions than could a single elected official.

There are no cases interpreting the section.

## SECTION 5

### Public School Fund Revenue

1. Ninety-five percent of all the interest received on the public school fund and ninety-five percent of all rent received from the leasing of school lands and all other income from the public school fund shall be equitably apportioned annually to public elementary and secondary school districts as provided by law.
2. The remaining five percent of all interest received on the public school fund, and the remaining five percent of all rent received from the leasing of school lands and all other income from the public school fund shall annually be added to the public school fund and become and forever remain an inseparable and inviolable part thereof.

The section is derived from and similar to Article XI, section 5 of the 1889 Montana Constitution. The section requires that the bulk (95%) of the interest and income obtained from school lands be apportioned equitably among the various elementary and secondary schools. The parallel section in the 1889 Constitution detailed the apportionment method, whereas this section leaves the specific apportionment arrangements to the discretion of the legislature. This school financing standard is narrow enough to be consistent with the equal protection doctrine and broad enough to give the legislature flexibility to create and modify as conditions change.

There are no cases interpreting this section and no significant cases interpreting the parallel provision of the 1889 Montana Constitution.

## SECTION 6

### Aid Prohibited to Sectarian Schools

1. The Legislature, counties, cities, towns, school districts, and public corporations shall not make any direct or indirect appropriation or payment from any public fund or monies, or any grant of lands or other property for any sectarian purpose or to aid any church, school, academy, seminary, college, university, or other literary or scientific institution, controlled in whole or in part by any church, sect, or denomination.
2. This section shall not apply to funds from federal sources provided to the state for the express purpose of distribution to nonpublic education.

Subsection (1) of this section is derived from and substantively identical to Article XI, section 8 of the 1889 Montana Constitution. Grammatical changes have been made. Subsection (2) is new and is an attempt to protect substantial federal grants from being rejected by constitutional mandate.

The entire section represents a continuing concern about public financial support of religion. It is an absolute prohibition against public support of private religious schools. Article II, section 5 prohibits the state from the"establishment of religion" by the state. This section is an addendum to that provision, prohibiting the spending of public funds for religious purposes. Although included in the article on education, the language of this section reaches beyond the boundaries of education, stating that public funds shall not be spent for any religious purpose. This represents a clear and forceful commitment to separation of church and state. The exception for federal funds recognizes the inability of the state to control federal funding arrangements and expresses the policy choice that the state should accept federal money even if the money is available to religious organizations, an arrangement forbidden when the appropriated funds come from state sources.

There are no cases interpreting this provision. Under the parallel provision of the 1889 Constitution the court approved payment of public funds to an indigent mother for medical care, hospitalization, and foster home care, although the indigent mother had applied to a private adoption agency for counseling and adoptive services (*Montana State Welfare Board v. Lutheran Social Services of Montana*, 1971).

An Attorney General Opinion concluded that alternative renewable energy source grants may not be awarded to any church or to any school, academy, seminary, college, university, or other literary or scientific institution controlled in whole or in part by any church, sect, or denomination (37 Op. Att'y Gen. 683 (1971)). An earlier Attorney General Opinion held that religious groups may use public school property on an occasional and short-term basis upon securing the consent of the school district trustees. The trustees should charge a fair rental in order to preclude a"grant" of property under this section. The use may not interfere with the use of the school for school purposes (36 Op. Att'y Gen. 445 (1976)). This opinion is possibly in conflict with both this section of the constitution insofar as it grants something of value to a religious organization and the dictum of the opinion may be in conflict with *Lamb's Chapel v. Center Moriches Union Free Sch. Dist.* (1993), in which the U.S. Supreme Court held that while a school district may legally control property under its control and need not permit after hours use, it cannot deny access to a nonpublic forum based on subject matter or speaker identity only. Distinctions may be made so long as they are viewpoint neutral. Permitting school property to be used for the presentation of all views about family issues and child-rearing except those dealing with the subject from a religious standpoint is unconstitutional.

Finally, an interesting Attorney General Opinion interpreting this section in the context of an elementary school district composed entirely of property belonging to North Harlem Hutterite Colony (Harlem, Montana) held that the Hutterite school would be eligible to receive public money for school purposes provided the school remained under the authority, control, and operation of the public school system and open to all persons eligible to attend this public school (36 Op. Att'y Gen. 298 (1975)). However, compare *Board of Educ. v. Grumet* (1994), in which the U.S. Supreme Court held that a New York statute creating a special school district for the religious enclave of Satmar Hasidim, practitioners of a strict form of Judaism, violated the establishment clause of the First Amendment to the U.S. Constitution.

The only evidence available that indicates Montana might be more rigorous in prohibiting official support of established religions is an Attorney General Opinion stating that alternative renewable energy source grants may not be awarded to any church or to any school, academy, seminary, college, university, or other literary or scientific institution controlled in whole or in part by any church, sect, or denomination (37 Op. Att'y Gen. 683 (1978)).

Note that the language of Article X, section 6 suggests that there could be constitutionally acceptable federal grants to sectarian organizations that would not be acceptable if the money originated within the state.

## SECTION 7

**Non-Discrimination in Education.** No religious or partisan test or qualification shall be required of any teacher or student as a condition of admission into any public educational institution.

Attendance shall not be required at any religious service. No sectarian tenets shall be advocated in any public educational institution of the state. No person shall be refused admission to any public educational institution on account of sex, race, creed, religion, political beliefs, or national origin.

This section is derived from and similar to section 9 of Article XI of the 1889 Montana Constitution and is intended to prohibit discrimination in public education. The parallel 1889 constitutional provision prohibited the "teaching" of any sectarian tenets; the new section prohibits "advocating" sectarian tenets. Teaching about religion would not violate the section; for example, a study of comparative religion would not have been permissible under the language of the 1889 provision but would be permissible under this provision. In addition to permitting the teaching of sectarian tenets, this provision has expanded the prohibition against discrimination to encompass not only sex but race, creed, religion, political beliefs, and national origin.

There are no cases directly implicating this section.

## SECTION 8

**School District Trustees.** The supervision and control of schools in each school district shall be vested in a board of trustees to be elected as provided by law.

This section is basically new, although Article XI, section 10 requires that the legislature shall provide that elections for school district officers be separate from state and county elections. The section is intended to vest control of schools in local school boards, although it leaves the design to the state legislature. It is intended to assure that local school boards continue to be autonomous, although funding is centralized (MCC Tr. 2046). The convention delegates contemplated a preservation of the powers of the local boards of trustees, but not an expansion of those powers (MCC Tr. 6258–6259).

An Attorney General Opinion noted that school board trustees have only those powers expressed or implied by law and were not authorized to incorporate under the Montana Nonprofit Corporation Act (35 Op. Att'y Gen. 112 (1973)). A subsequent state supreme court case held that this article of the Montana Constitution does not grant control and supervision of the schools of each district solely to the boards of trustees, and statutes granting review powers over the dismissal of teachers under contract to county superintendents of schools were not unconstitutional (*School Dist. v. Hughes*, 1976).

Finally, the court declined to support existing spending disparities between school districts as a result of constitutionally mandated local control (*Helena Elementary School District v. State*, 1989).

## SECTION 9

**Boards of Education**

1. There is a state board of education composed of the board of regents of higher education and the board of public education. It is responsible for long range planning, and for coordinating and evaluating policies and programs for the state's educational systems. It shall submit unified budget requests. A tie vote at any meeting may be broken by the governor, who is an ex officio member of each component board.

2. (a) The government and control of the Montana university system is vested in a board of regents of higher education which shall have full power, responsibility, and authority to supervise, coordinate, manage and control the Montana university system and shall supervise and coordinate other public educational institutions assigned by law. (b) The board consists of seven members appointed by the governor, and confirmed by the senate, to overlapping terms, as provided by law. The governor and superintendent of public instruction are ex officio nonvoting members

of the board. (c) The board shall appoint a commissioner of higher education and prescribe his term and duties. (d) The funds and appropriations under the control of the board of regents are subject to the same audit provisions as are all other state funds.

3. (a) There is a board of public education to exercise general supervision over the public school system and such other public educational institutions as may be assigned by law. Other duties of the board shall be provided by law. (b) The board consists of seven members appointed by the governor, and confirmed by the senate, to overlapping terms as provided by law. The governor, commissioner of higher education and state superintendent of public instruction shall be ex officio nonvoting members of the board.

This section deals with the state administrative structure for education. Section 11 of Article XI (the Education Article) of the 1889 Constitution provided for the administrative structure that existed prior to the 1972 Constitutional Convention. This new section 9 provides a substantially revised framework for the operation of the educational system.

Under the 1889 Constitution a single state board of education exercised supervision and control over the state educational system: primary, secondary, and higher education institutions. The 1972 Constitutional Convention delegates changed to a two-board system for the following reasons: (1) the increasing complexity of school administration brought on in part by increased state and federal funding; (2) the difference in the roles between, on the one hand, primary and secondary education and, on the other hand, higher education; (3) the desire to keep as much power as possible at the local level with respect to primary and secondary education while at the same time granting to one body the control over all the higher education institutions of the state; and (4) the desire to insulate the governing board of higher education (the board of regents) from the politics of normal state administration and legislation, thereby preserving academic freedom. Under the 1972 Constitution, the board of regents was transformed from a purely legislative creation to a constitutional department.

While creating two distinct boards which focus on the two separate segments of the education system, the 1972 Constitution retained a single board for the purpose of bringing the two other boards together for coordinating policies and programs and budget requests. In should be noted that the Board of Regents was to have power and authority to act quickly and to respond to university problems (MCC Tr. 2128), and the Board of Public Education was not intended to usurp the powers of local school boards (MCC Tr. 2051).

Two boards with two functions address the problems and frustrations caused by board members trying to comprehend and address the distinct needs of the two broad realms of education. In the case of primary and secondary education, the Board of Public Education administers the increasingly complex funding mechanisms without unnecessarily usurping local power over schools.

In the case of higher education, each higher education institution is controlled by a statewide, independent corporate entity instead of being directly controlled by an executive agency. This mechanism hopefully protects academic freedom from direct political manipulation from the executive or the legislature. A source for constitutional academic freedom lies in the constitutional provision endowing state universities with the status of being constitutionally separate and a largely autonomous department of government.[25] The separation is not complete because the universities, since they are state funded, must still account for the use of their funds.

The Education and Public Lands Committee of the constitutional convention provided an example of why this mechanism would be valuable for higher education. Under the old system the legislature apparently would review specific higher education budget items. This resulted, on a number of occasions, in the legislature trying to eliminate salaries of individual professors who conducted studies that some legislators found to be threatening (MCC Tr. 2057). The Committee hoped that a separate board empowered to govern the higher education institutions would insure that the higher education system would have freedom from "political changes of fortune" (ibid.). The value of the third board, the joint board, is that it provides a forum for the two independent boards to address mutual concerns.

In 1996 the voters rejected a proposed constitutional amendment to replace the Board of Regents and Board of Public Education with a Commission of Higher Education within the Department of Education and a State Education Commission subject to the ultimate authority of the governor.

This provision and other supporting constitutional provisions (Article III, section 1; Article V, section 1; Article VIII, section 12) justify legislative power to appropriate money for education, but do not permit the legislature to exercise control over private money or to limit salaries of college presidents (*Board of Regents v. Judge*, 1975). A second supreme court decision addressing the constitutional authority of the State Board of Education held that legislation designating the State Board of Education as the State Board of Vocational Education was unconstitutional because it was in excess of designated constitutional authority (*Board of Pub. Educ. v. Judge*, 1975).

A number of cases interpreted the authority possessed by the State Board of Education under the predecessor provision. The earlier section was sufficiently different that those cases are only marginally useful in analyzing the meaning of the current section.

[25] J. Peter Byrne, "Academic Freedom: A 'Special Concern' of the First Amendment," *Yale Law Journal* 99, (1989): 327. Byrne cited to Article X, section 9 of the Montana Constitution.

## SECTION 10

**State University Funds.** The funds of the Montana university system and of all other state institutions of learning, from whatever source accruing, shall forever remain inviolate and sacred to the purpose for which they were dedicated. The various funds shall be respectively invested under such regulations as may be provided by law, and shall be guaranteed by the state against loss or diversion. The interest from such invested funds, together with the rent from leased lands or properties, shall be devoted to the maintenance and perpetuation of the respective institutions.

The section was derived from and is substantively identical to section 12 of Article XI of the 1889 Montana Constitution. It is intended to protect funds dedicated to institutions of learning from diversion to other purposes. Section 13 of Article VIII, Revenue and Finance, provides for the investment of the funds of all state institutions. The Constitutional Convention Education and Public Lands Committee proposed this section without change because "it has served real well" (MCC Tr. 2142).

There are no cases interpreting this section. The parallel and nearly identical provision of the 1889 Constitution was considered in a number of opinions. The cases considered various expenditures, investments, and pledges of the identified funds. Most of the cases support the constitutionality of pledging the identified state funds for educational purposes (see *State ex rel. Wilson v. State Bd. of Educ,* 1936; *State ex rel. Blume v. State Bd. of Education,* 1934). An Attorney General Opinion supports the constitutionality of a gift by the Board of Public Education to a private, non-profit corporation created and controlled by the Board (38 Op. Att'y Gen. 383 (1980)). The gift was of money donated for the benefit of the Montana School for the Deaf and the Blind. The non-profit corporation was created for the benefit of the School for the Deaf and Blind.

## SECTION 11

**Public Land Trust, Disposition**

1. All lands of the state that have been or may be granted by congress, or acquired by gift or grant or devise from any person or corporation, shall be public lands of the state. They shall be held in trust for the people, to be disposed of as hereafter provided, for the respective purposes for which they have been or may be granted, donated or devised.
2. No such land or any estate or interest therein shall ever be disposed of except in pursuance of general laws providing for such disposition, or until the full market value of the estate or interest disposed of, to be ascertained in such manner as may be provided by law, has been paid or safely secured to the state.

> 3. No land which the state holds by grant from the United States which prescribes the manner of disposal and minimum price shall be disposed of except in the manner and for at least the price prescribed without the consent of the United States.
> 4. All public land shall be classified by the board of land commissioners in a manner provided by law. Any public land may be exchanged for other land, public or private, which is equal in value and, as closely as possible, equal in area.

This section is derived from Article XVII of the 1889 Montana Constitution. Subsections (1), (2), and (3) are substantively identical to the first several sentences of Article XVII, section 1 of the 1889 Constitution. Subsection (4) is similar to the remainder of sections 1, 2, and 3 of Article XVII. Subsection (4) provides for the classification of state lands by the Board of Land Commissioners pursuant to defining legislation. It also provides for land exchanges, which is new.

The purpose of this section, in both the current constitution and its 1889 predecessor, is to take into account the mandate of the Enabling Act of 1889 through which the United States granted public land to the state of Montana. Some dispute exists as to exactly what the Enabling Act mandated. The Montana Supreme Court in *State ex rel. Thompson v. Babcock* (1966) interpreted the mandate as requiring management for the general public benefit. The Constitutional Convention Education and Public Lands Committee recognized the reality that exactly what this means is still open for debate. The Committee pointed out, however, that one portion of the Enabling Act clearly mandates that the lands deeded as school lands were "for the support of common schools" (MCC Rep. 750–751).

This section appears to incorporate the Enabling Act, without interpreting it, with language specifying that the lands shall be held in trust "for the respective purposes for which they have been or may be granted, donated or devised" (subsection (1) of section 11). Section 4 of this article (Article X) created the Board of Land Commissioners for managing the school lands. Subsections (2), (3), and (4) of section 11 mandate the disposition and classification of all state public lands.

Subsection (4) provides that public land shall be classified but defers to the legislature to make those classifications. Subsection (4) changes the 1889 Constitution by allowing for the exchange of public land for other land, public or private, if certain criteria are met.

One value of section 11 is that, as mentioned above, it embodies the Enabling Act without interpreting the ambiguous portions of it. With regard to subsection (4), the Committee felt that allowing the legislature to make the classifications provided more flexibility for accommodating changing public values regarding the use of public land.

The court has required that land sales must comply with statutory requirements. Failure to comply with statutory requirements voids a sale of state lands

(*Norman v. State,* 1979; *State ex rel. Olsen v. Armory Bd.,* 1954). Sales and leases of public land have been reviewed by the court in a number of cases that have considered mineral rights and appropriated water rights, concluding that both are incidents of land rights (*Texas Pac. Coal & Oil Co. v. State,* 1951; *Department of State Lands v. Pettibone,* 1985).

# Article XI

## *Local Government*

### SECTION 1

**Definition.** The term "local government units" includes, but is not limited to, counties and incorporated cities and towns. Other local government units may be established by law.

Section 1 is a new provision defining the term "local government unit" to include counties, cities, and towns. Although, in general, the 1889 Constitution was overly detailed, some of the greatest problems arose over constitutional silence concerning what powers cities and counties should have. An objective of Article XI is to address these issues (MCC Tr. 298).

There are no cases interpreting or referring to the section.

### SECTION 2

**Counties.** The counties of the state are those that exist on the date of ratification of this constitution. No county boundary may be changed or county seat transferred until approved by a majority of those voting on the question in each county affected.

This section is derived from Article XVI, sections 1, 2, and 3 of the 1889 Montana Constitution. It reaffirms and continues existing county boundaries and county seats as they existed at the time the constitution was ratified. It also protects from change or removal of existing county boundaries and county seats unless approved by a majority vote within the county affected. This is a change from the 1889 Constitution which required a majority vote of all eligible electors of the county before a county seat could be changed. While the section implies the possibility of changing a county boundary, unlike the predecessor provision it does not provide for the creation of new counties nor the manner of adjusting liabilities or equities if such a new county were created.

There are no significant case interpretations of the section. Under the predecessor provision the court noted that denying power to the legislature to remove a county seat was a self executing provision (*State ex rel. Stringfellow v. Board of Comm'rs*, 1910). This might not be equally applicable to this section since the former parallel provision explicitly referred to the legislative assembly and denied that body the power to remove county seats, whereas this section implies the same by giving exclusive power to the voters of the county affected.

## SECTION 3

**Forms of Government**

1. The Legislature shall provide methods for governing local government units and procedures for incorporating, classifying, merging, consolidating, and dissolving such units, and altering their boundaries. The Legislature shall provide such optional or alternative forms of government that each unit or combination of units may adopt, amend, or abandon an optional or alternative form by a majority of those voting on the question.
2. One optional form of county government includes, but is not limited to, the election of three county commissioners, a clerk and recorder, a clerk of district court, a county attorney, a sheriff, a treasurer, a surveyor, a county superintendent of schools, an assessor, a coroner, and a public administrator. The terms, qualifications, duties, and compensation of those offices shall be provided by law. The Board of county commissioners may consolidate two or more such offices. The Boards of two or more counties may provide for a joint office and for the election of one official to perform the duties of any such office in those counties.

This section is derived from Article XVI, sections 4, 5, 6, 7, and 8 of the 1889 Montana Constitution. The substance of the provision directs (rather than permits) the legislature to provide alternative forms of city, county, or city-county governments. The substantive change is less dramatic than might at first appear, since the legislature is directed to provide, as one alternative, the existing and traditional form of local government, including a list of elected officials, comparable in name and authority to elected officials then in place.

There was an intent to encourage the legislature to make available the widest possible range of government forms while leaving the choice of local government up to the discretion of the local electorate. In fact, very few communities have taken advantage of the possibilities to make changes in the structure of local government.

The few cases that have interpreted this section are not significant.

## SECTION 4

### General Powers

1. A local government unit without self-government powers has the following general powers:
   a. An incorporated city or town has the powers of a municipal corporation and legislative, administrative, and other powers provided or implied by law.
   b. A county has legislative, administrative, and others powers provided or implied by law.
   c. Other local government units have powers provided by law.
2. The powers of incorporated cities and towns and counties shall be liberally construed.

The section is new. It authorizes the legislature to provide for the powers of local governments that have not chosen to adopt a self-government charter as provided in section 5 of this article. An important part of this section is the direction that the powers of incorporated local units of government be liberally construed, that there are implied powers beyond the powers specifically provided by legislation, and that the legislature may delegate certain legislative powers to counties (MCC Tr. 7699–7700).

A number of cases have challenged the exercise of various powers by local governments. In each case the power exercised by the local government has been upheld. In several cases the court has made specific reference to the constitutional requirement that the powers of local government be liberally construed. The most significant cases relate to the power of local government to acquire property by prescription in one case (*Granite County v. Komberec,* 1990), and by eminent domain in another (*Lake v. Lake County,* 1988).

## SECTION 5

### Self-Government Charters

1. The Legislature shall provide procedures permitting a local government unit or combination of units to frame, adopt, amend, revise, or abandon a self-government

charter with the approval of a majority of those voting on the question. The procedures shall not require approval of a charter by a legislative body.
2. If the Legislature does not provide such procedures by My 1, 1975, they may be established by election either:
   a. Initiated by petition in the local government unit or combination of units; or
   b. called by the governing body of the local government unit or combination of units.
4. Charter provisions establishing executive, legislative, and administrative structure and organization are superior to statutory provisions.

This is a new provision. It is intended to guarantee self-government for local units. The legislature is directed to act, and local units are given the constitutional power to initiate action to create self-government charters if the legislature has failed to act. Finally, if local self-government charter provisions conflict with statutory provisions, the self-government provisions are superior.

The section was intended to maximize home rule or the power of the local government to make independent decisions on all matters that are local in nature. It is doubtful that self-government charters have increased the independent power of local governments that have chosen to adopt them.

The court held that a self-governing charter did not permit the city of Billings to supersede state law relating to municipal fire departments. Self-governing charters are superior to statutory provisions only insofar as the charter provision establishes executive, legislative, or administrative structure and organization (*Billings Firefighters Local 521 v. Billings*, 1985). A city with self-government charter powers can prohibit uninvited door-to-door solicitation notwithstanding the existence of a state licensing statute for itinerant vendors (*Tipco Corp. v. City of Billings*, 1982). A county charter may provide that the legislative body or commission will perform the executive functions in addition to its legislative duties (46 Op. Att'y Gen. No. 14 (1996)).

## SECTION 6

**Self-Government Powers.** A local government unit adopting a self-government charter may exercise any power not prohibited by this constitution, law, or charter. This grant of self-government powers may be extended to other local government units through optional forms of government provided for in section 3.

This is a new provision designed to maximize the independent, autonomous power of local governments. Under the 1889 Montana Constitution, legislative control over units of local government was supreme. This is no longer true. This section grants charter governments increased autonomous power. There remain considerable limits on the power of local governments, even those that have adopted charters. Constitutional prohibitions and legislative prohibitions can limit the power of charter governments. However, under this section local government units have all powers not specifically denied, not only powers specifically granted. It is called the shared-powers concept (MCC Rep. 797).

The supreme court has held that before state legislation pre-empts the self-government powers of a charter municipality, there must be an express statutory prohibition specifically forbidding the local government from the challenged action. There is no doctrine of implied pre-emption applicable to local governments that possess self-government powers (*State ex rel. Swart v. Molitor*, 1981; *Tipco Corp. v. City of Billings*, 1982). The exception, in which charter provisions are superior to state legislation, is provisions establishing executive, legislative, or administrative structure and organization. The one relevant case has interpreted the phrase "executive, legislative, or administrative structure and organization," in a somewhat restrictive fashion (*Billings Firefighters Local 521 v. Billings*, 1985).

Illustrative of the increased power of local governments are the several cases interpreting this provision that have upheld municipal charter powers as diverse as regulating nude dancing (*Billings v. Laedeke*, 1991) and imposing a surcharge on developers (*Diefenderfer v. Billings*, 1986), but not an annual tax on lawyers (*Brueggemann v. Billings*, 1986). There is also the somewhat anomalous opinion in *United States Mfg. & Distrib. Corp. v. Great Falls* (1976) denying a local government the authority to have a more restrictive law on obscenity.

## SECTION 7

**Intergovernmental Cooperation**

1. (1) Unless prohibited by law or charter, a local government unit may
    a. cooperate in the exercise of any function, power, or responsibility with,
    b. share the services of any officer or facilities with,
    c. transfer or delegate any function, power, responsibility, or duty of any officer to one or more other local government units, school districts, the state, or the United States.
2. (2) The qualified electors of a local government unit may, by initiative or referendum, require it to do so.

This is a new provision, permitting local governments to share power with other governments and to delegate powers to officers of other units of government. The delegates intended to maximize the flexibility of government operations and to create opportunities for new approaches to providing government services. Local residents, through the initiative, may force their local governments to cooperate and to stop senseless duplication of services (MCC Rep. 798).[26]

[26] One expert on Montana local government has commented: "Montana's record conserving total local government consolidation since 1972 is amazing, to say the least." James J. Lopach, "Local Government under the 1972 Montana Constitution," *Montana Law Review*, 51 (1990): 465.

There are no cases interpreting this section. An Attorney General Opinion states that counties may enter into joint self-insurance programs (38 Op. Att'y Gen. 261 (1980)).

## SECTION 8

**Initiative and Referendum.** The Legislature shall extend the initiative and referendum powers reserved to the people by the constitution to the qualified electors of each local government unit.

This is a new provision requiring the legislature to extend the powers of initiative and referendum to qualified electors within the context of local government. It is the intent of this section to keep government within reach of the people, not only in regard to government activities at the state level but also at the local level. Residents have the power to initiate local ordinances by petition or to petition to vote on ordinances passed by local governments.

Three significant cases have narrowed the utility of the section. The cases have held that administrative actions are not subject to either the initiative or the referendum. In *Shelby v. Sandholm* (1984), the court concluded that a resolution creating a municipal special improvement district encompassing less than the entire city was an administrative procedure and not subject to referendum; and in *Dieruf v. Bozeman* (1977), the court concluded that a proposed ordinance and resolution for a parking lot facility was not subject to either initiative or referendum, because it was administrative rather than legislative. In *Town of Whitehall v. Preece* (1998), the court noted the distinction between legislative acts (whether the act created a new law) and administrative acts (executing an already existing law) in relation to the powers of initiative and referendum. To permit referenda on administrative actions would hamper the efficient administration of local justice. Under Montana's Constitution, the court said that the people have retained the powers of initiative and referendum as to legislative acts only, and gave guidelines as to which actions are administrative.

In addition, the court has noted that re-zoning ordinances are subject to referendum and there is no distinction between zoning and re-zoning for referendum purposes (*Greens at Fort Missoula, L.L.C. v. City of Missoula,* 1995).

## SECTION 9

**Voter Review of Local Government**

1. The Legislature shall, within four years of the ratification of this constitution, provide procedures requiring each local government unit or combination of units to review its structure and submit one alternative form of government to the qualified electors at the next general or special election.

2. The Legislature shall require an election in each local government to determine whether a local government will undertake a review procedure once every ten years after the first election. Approval by a majority of those voting in the decennial general election on the question of undertaking a local government review is necessary to mandate the election of a local government study commission. Study commission members shall be elected during any regularly scheduled election in local governments mandating their election.

This is a new provision. It required the legislature to provide for the electorate of each local unit of government to vote on an alternative form of government by 1976. It further obligated the legislature to require periodic local elections on the issue of whether to create a study commission to review local government. Residents of each local government unit must have an opportunity to vote on whether to adopt an alternative form of local government (MCC Rep. 800).

In 1974, during the first cycle of voter review, more than 700 persons filed for the 642 study commissioner positions on the 182 study commissions. Seventy-one percent of the county proposals and 53 percent of the municipal proposals contained major reforms. In 1976 voters adopted 4 county and 27 reorganization proposals.[27]

After the first round of voter review of local government in 1976, many considered the review process unnecessary and argued that its observance every 10 years should be optional. In 1978 the voters passed Constitutional Amendment Number 6 which provided that, in 1984 and every 10 years thereafter, residents of each Montana county and municipality would vote on whether to have a study commission. Fifty-four percent of the state's local governments voted in 1984 to have a study commission. Seventeen adoptions were approved in 1986.[28] In 1994, 62 percent of local governments voted to have study commissions; this included 33 out of 56 counties and 79 out of 126 municipalities. "One assessment of city-county consolidation . . . attributed the state's high rate of merger success to the 'facilitative advantage' of the voter review process."[29]

The section is based on a policy determination that local governments should be regularly reconsidered and that the electorate should be involved in the process of reconsideration. The perceived problem of entrenched local politicians

---

[27] One expert on Montana local government has commented: "Montana's record conserving total local government consolidation since 1972 is amazing, to say the least." James J. Lopach, "Local Government under the 1972 Montana Constitution," *Montana Law Review,* 51 (1990): at 463.

[28] One expert on Montana local government has commented: "Montana's record conserving total local government consolidation since 1972 is amazing, to say the least." James J. Lopach, "Local Government under the 1972 Montana Constitution," *Montana Law Review,* 51 (1990): at 463.

[29] One expert on Montana local government has commented: "Montana's record conserving total local government consolidation since 1972 is amazing, to say the least." James J. Lopach, "Local Government under the 1972 Montana Constitution," *Montana Law Review,* 51 (1990): at 465.

and employees diligently opposing structural or organizational change as a threat to personal power, and to job security, is probably true.

In one case the supreme court found that the findings of fact and conclusions of law of the district court upholding the validity of city and county alternative form of government elections, and proceedings leading thereto, were supported by substantial evidence (*Schuman v. Study Comm'n of Yellowstone County*, 1978).

# Article XII

## *Departments and Institutions*

### SECTION 1

**Agriculture**

1. The Legislature shall provide for a Department of Agriculture and enact laws and provide appropriations to protect, enhance, and develop all agriculture.
2. Special levies may be made on livestock and on agricultural commodities for disease control and indemnification, predator control, and livestock and commodity inspection, protection, research, and promotion. Revenue derived shall be used solely for the purposes of the levies.

The two subsections were originally introduced as individual sections of a separate article dedicated to agriculture. Subsection (1) was intended to replace the reference to "agriculture" found in Article XVIII of the 1889 Montana Constitution (MCC Rep. 530). Subsection (2) was intended to replace authority for special levies on livestock previously provided in Article XII, section 9 of the 1889 Constitution (ibid.). The Natural Resources and Agriculture Committee delegates wanted to insure that "the largest and most important industry in the state" be recognized by retaining a constitutional provision for a Department of Agriculture (MCC Tr. 1363.) Committee comments indicate that retention of this language was necessary to insure that the legislature protect, enhance, and develop agriculture (ibid.). The second subsection, extending the use of special levies on livestock to other agricultural activities and earmarking those levies for the benefit of agriculture, was in response to an old Montana Supreme Court case holding that special livestock levies would not be allowed if not specifically authorized in the constitution (MCC Tr. 1367).

Because of agriculture's importance to the state, the delegates thought it should be afforded some form of constitutional recognition. This subsection insures that the Department of Agriculture be continued and has symbolic value (MCC Tr. 1364), if nothing more. The importance of the second subsection was in authorizing the agricultural industry to both tax itself and protect revenue so generated from being diverted to purposes other than agriculture. As used in this section, the term "agriculture" includes the livestock industry.

There are no significant cases interpreting this section. The one case that makes reference to this section supported a tax exemption for business inventories and not for inventories of livestock. The issue was basically one of equal protection for the livestock industry, but the court held that it was constitutionally acceptable, under the rational basis test, to classify livestock differently than business inventories (*Montana Stockgrowers Ass'n v. State*, 1989).

## SECTION 2

### Labor

1. The Legislature shall provide for a Department of Labor and Industry, headed by a Commissioner appointed by the governor and confirmed by the senate.
2. A maximum period of 8 hours is a regular day's work in all industries and employment except agriculture and stock raising. The Legislature may change this maximum period to promote the general welfare.

Subsection (1) is derived from Article XVIII, section 1 of the 1889 Constitution. The subsection retains a constitutional department of labor but deletes the requirement that it be located at the Capitol (MCC Rep. 672). It also retains the office of commissioner but deletes reference to a specific term (ibid.). Subsection (2) is derived from and similar to Article XVIII, section 4 of the 1889 Constitution, but affords greater flexibility by permitting the legislature to change the maximum number of hours as needed. The 1889 Constitution prohibited the legislature from increasing the number of hours.

Subsection (1) gives complete assurance that the Department of Labor and Industry will continue to exist and that a commissioner will be appointed as head of the Department. Just as agriculture is important to the state, labor pervades all industries and thus should be afforded the same constitutional recognition as the agricultural industry (MCC Tr. 2308–2315). Unlike the parallel subsection mandating a Department of Agriculture, this subsection does not require that the Department be funded. During the constitutional debates a handful of delegates argued that specific departments should not be carved out by the constitution. The executive branch should retain the flexibility to create departments as necessary, especially in light of the previous statewide vote on executive re-organization. This same argument was made in the debate on the Department of Agriculture, Article XVII, section 1 (MCC Tr. 2308–2315).

Subsection (2) was created by independent motion. It was intended to protect workers from being compelled to work longer than eight hours. Opponents noted the limit on flexibility of alternate work patterns such as the four days of ten hours (MCC Tr. 2316–2328). Interestingly, a 40-hour-work week was not discussed. Legislative prerogative to vary working hours allows alternatives and flexibility. It also eliminates protection from majoritarian determinations.

There are no cases interpreting this section of the 1972 Montana Constitution. Earlier cases and recent Attorney General Opinions primarily discuss problems of overtime work, what constitutes a work week, and pay for holidays (*Weston v. Montana Highway Comm'n*, 1980; *Glick v. State*, 1973; 43 Op. Att'y Gen. 42 (1989); 37 Op. Att'y Gen. 62 (1977)).

## SECTION 3

### Institutions and Assistance

1. The state shall establish and support institutions and facilities as the public good may require, including homes which may be necessary and desirable for the care of veterans.
2. Persons committed to any such institutions shall retain all rights except those necessarily suspended as a condition of commitment. Suspended rights are restored upon termination of the state's responsibility.
3. The Legislature may provide such economic assistance and social and rehabilitative services for those who, by reason of age, infirmities, or misfortune are determined by the Legislature to be in need.
4. The Legislature may set eligibility criteria for programs and services, as well as for the duration and level of benefits and services.

Subsection (1) is derived from and similar to Article X, section 1 of the 1889 Constitution. Subsection (2) is a new provision. Subsection (3) is derived from Article X, section 5 of the 1889 Constitution, although this subsection is substantially changed from the parallel provision in the 1889 Constitution. Subsection (4) was added as part of a constitutional amendment approved by the electorate in 1988 and is new.

Subsection (1) carries forward the constitutional assignment of responsibility to create and support public institutions and facilities. Pursuant to this subsection the state must establish and support institutions and facilities "as the public good may require." The subsection deletes reference to specific facilities and institutions other than reference to veterans' homes (MCC Tr. 2370–2378).

Specific reference to veterans' homes was to indicate that veterans' homes are not institutions and that veterans residing at veterans' homes are voluntary residents and not "committed" residents (MCC Tr. 2270–2271).

Subsection (2) addresses the loss of rights of mentally ill people who have been committed to state-operated institutions. Prior to commitment a person must be judged incompetent. This provision automatically restores a person's rights upon release from a state institution without a separate legal proceeding (MCC Tr. 2304–2308). This is an important advantage for poor persons who cannot afford private care and who must be judged incompetent before they can receive public assistance. One commentator notes that although subsection (2) is probably intended to apply specifically to civil competency (contractual, testamentary, and testimonial), there is no reason for it to be construed in such a narrow fashion.[30]

Subsection (3), as originally passed, mandated that the state should provide for the welfare of the least fortunate members of the society. However, "[t]he intent . . . is not to create a substantive right for all the necessities of life to be provided by the public treasury" (MCC Rep. 627). The delegates determined that the constitution was the proper mechanism for empowering the legislature to provide for the indigent; and further, that the legislature should have the power to spread the financial burden of welfare programs evenly across the state instead of concentrating the burden on the taxpayers of the larger counties. Empowering the legislature to determine whether welfare funding will be statewide or county wide (MCC Tr. 2287) was a fundamental change from the 1889 Constitution, which provided county welfare funding. This gives the legislature more flexibility in deciding how to apportion the cost of welfare programs. In 1988, subsection (3) was amended and the mandatory language was revised, permitting but not requiring the Legislature to provide for needy persons. This was buttressed by subsection (4), part of the 1988 amendment, authorizing the legislature to set eligibility criteria, levels of benefits, and duration of help for needy persons without limits or constitutional guidelines. This gives the legislature absolute discretion to establish if welfare shall be provided and, if provided, to whom it shall be provided, of what it shall consist, and for how long it will be given.

As originally ratified in 1972, this section on public assistance or welfare was mandatory. Nonetheless, the Montana Supreme Court determined that welfare is not a fundamental right. In order to be fundamental, a right must be found within the Declaration of Rights in the Montana Constitution or be a right "without which other constitutionally guaranteed rights would have little meaning" (p. 940) (*In re C.H.*, 1984). Article XII, section 3 is not part of the

---

[30] Alan Meisel, "The Rights of the Mentally I11 Under State Constitutions," *Law and Contemporary Problems*, 45, no. 3 (1982): 33.

Declaration of Rights, and the right to welfare is not a right upon which constitutionally guaranteed rights depend (*Butte Community Union v. Lewis*, 1986). Although not a fundamental constitutional right, the state must demonstrate a substantial government interest/3-middle-tier analysis/3-to justify a welfare classification. In the case before the court two factors had to be satisfied: (1) that its classification of welfare recipients on the basis of age was reasonable; and (2) that state interest in such classification was more important than the people's interest in obtaining welfare benefits. The state failed to meet the test and the statutory classification based on age was held to be unconstitutional (ibid.). The decision was not well received by the Montana legislature and a constitutional amendment was proposed and ratified. The amendment changed the mandatory language of subsection (3) and added subsection (4) specifically authorizing the legislature to establish eligibility criteria. An interesting aside that relates more to the referendum process than to public assistance was the challenge to the sufficiency of the title of the amendment. The title of the referendum said it would "[allow] the Legislature greater discretion to determine the eligibility, duration, and level of economic assistance and social services to those in need." In fact, the most dramatic change was to change public assistance from mandatory to permissive. The referendum title was found to be legally sufficient (*Harper v. Greely*, 1988).

# Article XIII

## *General Provisions*

### SECTION 1

**Non-Municipal Corporations**

1. Corporate charters shall be granted, modified, or dissolved only pursuant to general law.
2. The Legislature shall provide protection and education for the people against harmful and unfair practices by either foreign or domestic corporations, individuals, or associations.
3. The Legislature shall pass no law retrospective in its operations which imposes on the people a new liability in respect to transactions or considerations already passed.

The 1972 Constitution has had a significant impact on the corporation laws of Montana The Montana Constitution of 1889 contained numerous restrictions on the activities of certain types of corporations, such as prohibiting competing railway corporations from consolidating with each other. More importantly, the old constitution required cumulative voting in all corporate director elections, while the [1972 Constitution] . . . makes no such provision.[31]

[31] Hugh V. Schaefer, "The Status of the Adoption of the Model Business Corporation Act in Montana—A Commentary," *Montana Law Review*, 36 (1975): 30.

Subsection (1) is derived from Article XV, sections 2 and 3; Article XVIII, section 1; and Article X, section 1 of the 1889 Constitution. The subsection provides no substantive change except that it deletes a portion of the old Article XV, which had abolished all corporate bodies that existed only on paper prior to 1889. The only danger of the deletion is that pre-1889 corporations would once again commence business. However, Revised Code of Montana, Section 15-808, although repealed in 1966, probably annulled any pre-1889 corporations. Subsection (2) is a new provision requiring the legislature to pass consumer protection laws. Subsection (3) is derived from Article XV, section 13 of the old constitution. Except for the deletion of "county and municipal subdivisions of the state," the language and intent of the section is the same.

Subsection (1) grants the legislature the general power to grant, modify, or dissolve corporate charters. Subsection (1) subjects corporate bodies to dissolution in the event their principal activity is contrary to the promotion of the general welfare. It also prohibits chartering corporations by special law.

Subsection (2) was intended to encompass and prohibit various business practices by foreign corporations which are deemed harmful and injurious to the people. An example is the practice of foreign corporations in real estate soliciting through the mail for questionable investments. Subsection (2) authorizes the legislature to prohibit: (a) arbitrary discrimination in rate and service for transportation; (b) the receipt of greater rights and privileges by foreign corporations than are granted to domestic corporations; (c) price-fixing and regulation of production on an intrastate basis which is harmful to the state economy; and (d) any act which is generally not conducive to efficiently allocating scarce resources.

Subsection (3) was meant to preserve the sanctity of contractual obligations by prohibiting the exercise of state police power to burden existing contracts. Subsection (3) extends protection beyond the Declaration of Rights, Article 2, section 31 on ex post facto laws, which provides that there shall be no law made which impairs the obligation of contract. It is broader than the Declaration of Rights provision in that it extends protection to retroactive taxation. The legislature could not impose a tax or liability on a prior transaction.

The court has applied the section to legislation that changed the method of loss carry over calculations and found the law to be retroactive and unconstitutional (*First Fed. Sav. & Loan Ass'n v. Department of Revenue*, 1982).

## SECTION 2

**Consumer Counsel.** The Legislature shall provide for an office of consumer counsel which shall have the duty of representing consumer interests in hearings before the public service commission or any other successor agency. The Legislature shall provide for the funding of the office of consumer counsel by a special tax on the net income or gross revenues of regulated companies.

This is a new provision. Prior to the passage of this section, there existed ad hoc consumer organizations to oppose rate increases by power companies. The ad hoc organizations were able to raise small amounts of money to oppose the great expenditures by the power companies to support their rate increases. In one contested case, the existing Montana consumer organizations raised $15,000 against $300,000 by the power company (MCC Tr. 2400–2401).

The object of this section is to mandate the legislature to provide an Office of Consumer Counsel to represent consumer interests in hearings before the Public Service Commission and provide for its funding through a special tax on the net income or gross revenues of regulated companies (utilities) (MCC Tr. 2400).

This provision provides for public protection against powerful utility companies. Rate cases before the Public Service Commission are extremely difficult and complicated. With built-in funding and a constitutional mandate, the Consumer Counsel should adequately prepare and effectively represent the consumers for these cases before the Public Service Commission.

There are no significant cases interpreting the section.

During the convention the possibility of creating the office of Ombudsman or People's Advocate was considered. Nebraska, Hawaii, and Oregon have ombudsman or ombudsman-like offices, but they have been created by the state legislatures and are not of constitutional stature. The idea was rejected by a vote of 48 to 43. The issue of cost was raised and many delegates thought that if such office was desired it should be the prerogative of the legislature.

## SECTION 3

**Repealed.** Section 3 was repealed by section 1 of Constitutional Amendment No. 16, 1986. Section 3 had created a salary commission to recommend compensation for the judiciary and elected members of the legislative and executive branches. These salaries are now covered by statute, using the average salaries of similar offices in four neighboring states as a basis.

## SECTION 4

**Code of Ethics.** The Legislature shall provide a code of ethics prohibiting conflict between public duty and private interest for members of the Legislature and all state and local officers and employees.

This is a new provision addressing the problem of state officials and employees using government position to individual or private advantage. The need for conflict of interest laws to establish a policy and standard of honesty and fair dealing on the part of officers and employees of state and local government was addressed by a similar section in the new constitutions in Florida and North Dakota (MCC Tr. 796).

This section mandates the legislature to pass conflict of interest laws that would be difficult to spell out in the constitution. By requiring the legislature to pass laws on ethics in government, the section has dealt with an important problem but one that would be inappropriate to detail in a constitution.

There are no significant cases interpreting the section.

## SECTION 5

**Exemption Laws.** The Legislature shall enact liberal homestead and exemption laws.

The language is identical to Article XIX, section 4 of the 1889 Montana Constitution. The section is intended to insure liberal homestead and exemption laws and mandates the legislature to establish liberal laws in the legislative arrangement of insolvency, debt seizure, and attachments. This is a humanitarian section which recognizes that human beings have certain basic necessities to preserve and maintain their human dignity, and that these necessities should be protected from creditors.

There are no cases interpreting the section. Under the parallel provision in the 1889 Constitution, the supreme court held that exemption laws were to be liberally construed and that a waiver clause in an executory contract was against public policy (*Anaconda Fed. Credit Union v. West,* 1971).

## SECTION 6

**Perpetuities.** No perpetuities shall be allowed except for charitable purposes.

This section is derived from and is identical to Article XIX, section 5 of the 1889 Montana Constitution. It prohibits perpetuities while acknowledging the public policy of encouraging charitable contributions.

The rule against perpetuities requires "the vesting of future estates within a limited time period after their creation and to bar the creation of future interests depending on remote contingencies."[32] The fundamental purpose of the rule against perpetuities is the public policy opposing restrictions on marketability of property over long periods of time by indirect restraints upon its alienation.[33]

There are no cases interpreting this section.

---

[32] "Perpetuities and Restraints on Alienation," *American Jurisprudence* (2nd ed.), vol. 61 (1981): section 7, pp. 13–14.

[33] "Perpetuities and Restraints on Alienation," *American Jurisprudence* (2nd ed.), vol. 61 (1981): section 7, p. 14.

# Article XIV

*Constitutional Revision*

## SECTION 1

**Constitutional Convention.** The Legislature, by an affirmative vote of two-thirds of all the members, whether one or more bodies, may at any time submit to the qualified electors the question of whether there shall be an unlimited convention to revise, alter, or amend this constitution.

The language is similar to the first part of Article XIX, section 8 of the 1889 Constitution, although the language of the 1972 Constitution adds the word"unlimited" to the 1889 provision, making it clear that the legislature cannot call a constitutional convention for a limited purpose (Montana Constitutional Convention Explanation). This section makes it possible, although politically difficult, for the legislature to place before the state electors the issue of holding an unlimited constitutional convention. By requiring two-thirds of the entire legislature, this section both covers the possibility of a unicameral legislature and makes it more difficult for one legislative body to block or approve a call for a constitutional convention.

There are no cases interpreting the section and no significant cases interpreting the parallel provision in the 1889 Montana Constitution.

## SECTION 2

**Initiative for Constitutional Convention**

1. The people may by initiative petition direct the secretary of state to submit to the qualified electors the question of whether there shall be an unlimited convention to revise, alter, or amend this constitution. The petition shall be signed by at least ten percent of the qualified electors of the state. That number shall include at least ten percent of the qualified electors in each of two-fifths of the legislative districts.
2. The secretary of state shall certify the filing of the petition in his office and cause the question to be submitted at the next general election.

This section is a revised version of Article XIX, section 9 of the 1889 Montana Constitution. Before this provision was drafted, the people of Montana did not have the power to call a constitutional convention by initiative. The constitutional delegates believed that the power to call a constitutional convention belonged to the people and this section allows the people, independent of a Legislative Assembly, to call a constitutional convention. Obtaining the "ten percent of voter signatures in each of two-fifths of the legislative districts" is an arduous task. It prevents frivolous attempts at constitutional change, while allowing the people to initiate a constitutional convention.

There are no cases interpreting this section.

## SECTION 3

**Periodic Submission.** If the question of holding a convention is not otherwise submitted during any period of 20 years, it shall be submitted as provided by law at the general election in the twentieth year following the last submission.

This section is new, providing for automatic referral to the electorate every 20 years the question of whether to hold another constitutional convention. It is intended to implement the policy judgment that a state constitution should be reconsidered periodically and not subject to years of piecemeal amendment without serious reconsideration of the entire document. Periodic reconsideration of the state constitution recognizes the need to meet changing conditions without sacrificing traditional constitutional stability. The convention committee felt that periodic consideration strengthens, rather than weakens, a constitution and government, as it builds into the constitution a recognition of, and a remedy, if need be, of changing conditions (MCC Rep. 358). In 1990 on the question of calling a constitutional convention, 245,009 voted against and 53,630 voted for.

There are no cases interpreting this section.

## SECTION 4

**Call of Convention.** If a majority of those voting on the question answer in the affirmative, the Legislature shall provide for the calling thereof at its next session.

The number of delegates to the convention shall be the same as that of the larger body of the Legislature. The qualifications of delegates shall be the same as the highest qualifications required for election to the Legislature. The Legislature shall determine whether the delegates may be nominated on a partisan or a nonpartisan basis. They shall be elected at the same places and in the same districts as are the members of the legislative body determining the number of delegates.

This section is derived from Article XIX, section 8 of the 1889 Montana Constitution, that outlined the details for calling a constitutional convention. The parallel provision in the 1889 Constitution did not require partisan elections, but a 1971 Montana Supreme Court decision determined constitutional convention delegates must run as partisan candidates (*Legislative Assembly v. Lennon*, 1971). The 1889 Constitution left unclear whether constitutional delegates were to be elected on a partisan or non-partisan basis. The determination of whether to have partisan elections or not is probably best left to the legislature.

There are no cases interpreting this section.

## SECTION 5

**Convention Expenses**. The Legislature shall, in the act of calling the convention, designate the day, hour, and place of its meeting, and fix and provide for the pay of its members and officers and the necessary expenses of the convention.

The section is derived from Article XIX, section 8 of the 1889 Montana Constitution and is designed to insure appropriate arrangements and funding if a constitutional convention is called. The provision is an outline of details necessary to conduct a constitutional convention and of minimal substantive significance. This provision is intended to preclude a legislative attempt to thwart a constitutional convention by withholding funds (MCC Tr. 485). However, the legislature could effectively frustrate a convention by limiting the appropriation (MCC Tr. 485–489).

There are no cases interpreting this section.

## SECTION 6

**Oath, Vacancies**. Before proceeding, the delegates shall take the oath provided in this constitution. Vacancies occurring shall be filled in the manner provided for filling vacancies in the Legislature if not otherwise provided by law.

This section is similar to Article XIX, section 8 of the 1889 Montana Constitution. The oath of office referred to is in Article III, section 3 of the 1972 Constitution. This section will"assist future conventions in their tasks" (MCC Tr. 490).

There are no cases interpreting this section.

## SECTION 7

**Convention Duties.** The convention shall meet after the election of the delegates and prepare such revisions, alterations, or amendments to the constitution as may be deemed necessary. They shall be submitted to the qualified electors for ratification or rejection as a whole or in separate articles or amendments as determined by the convention at an election appointed by the convention for that purpose not less than two months after adjournment. Unless so submitted and approved by a majority of the electors voting thereon, no such revision, alteration, or amendment shall take effect.

The 1889 Constitution required that the convention meet within three months after the election of the delegates and that the election on the proposed constitution be held within six months. Otherwise, section 7 is similar to Article XIX, section 8 of the 1889 Constitution. In the last sentence of the section, the word "thereon" is used to avoid the potential dilemma of what majority is intended by clarifying that it is not the majority of those voting, (which could include people voting on matters other than the question of amending the constitution), but rather the majority of those voting specifically on the amendment question (MCC Tr. 491). This section also sets a structure for future constitutional conventions and clarifies the delegates' intent with regard to certain fundamental due process logistics.

There are no cases interpreting the section.

## SECTION 8

**Amendment by Legislative Referendum.** Amendments to this constitution may be proposed by any member of the Legislature. If adopted by an affirmative roll call vote of two-thirds of all the members thereof, whether one or more bodies, the proposed amendment shall be submitted to the qualified electors at the next general election. If approved by a majority of the electors voting thereon, the amendment shall become a part of this constitution on the first day of July after certification of the election returns unless the amendment provides otherwise.

This section is derived from and similar to Article XIX, section 9 of the 1889 Constitution. It changes the amendment process by allowing the legislature to propose constitutional amendments by a two-thirds vote of the total membership (rather than two-thirds of each house) and by providing for a July 1 effective date for amendments. By requiring a two-thirds vote of the entire legislature, this section makes it more difficult for one legislative body to block a proposed constitutional amendment. As passed, this section preserved the notion that the people voting would have the final say.

In the last sentence of the section, the word "thereon" is used to avoid the potential dilemma of what majority is intended by specifying that it is not the majority of those voting (which could include people voting on matters other than the question of amending the constitution), but rather the majority of those voting on the amendment question (MCC Tr. 496).

"State constitutions are easier to amend and are amended more often than the United States Constitution."[34] In Montana, Article XIV, section 8 (legislative resolution) and section 9 (citizen initiative) make this possible. From 1972 to 1998 there were 34 proposed amendments by legislative referendum, of which the voters approved 19. Perhaps the most notable was Constitutional Amendment Number 3 in 1976, which created the Coal Tax Trust Fund that has generated over $600 million to date. Twice the legislature has passed an amendment that would allow annual sessions, but the voters rejected both proposals, although much more narrowly in 1988 than in 1981. One other noteworthy rejection was in 1978 when a proposed amendment would have allowed a legislative member to run for public office during his or her term. This presumably would have allowed sitting legislators to run for election to a constitutional convention. The voters rejected this proposal by a two-to-one margin.

The Montana Supreme Court threw out one proposed legislative amendment. In *Cobb v. State* (1996) the court rejected the proposal (Senate Bill 37) to abolish the constitutional office of secretary of state because the bill left one duty assigned to that office with no provision of who would assume that duty.

However, in *Harper v. Greely* (1988), the court refused to intervene to remove a referendum from the ballot prior to a vote of the people to avoid violating the constitutional rights of popular sovereignty and self-government. The court noted a strong presumption in favor of the constitutionality of legislative enactments and said the ballot language was not purposely misleading and would result in an informed vote.

## SECTION 9

### Amendment by Initiative

1. The people may also propose constitutional amendments by initiative. Petitions including the full text of the proposed amendment shall be signed by at least ten percent of the qualified electors of the state. That number shall include at least ten percent of the qualified electors in each of two-fifths of the legislative districts.
2. The petitions shall be filed with the secretary of state. If the petitions are found to have been signed by the required number of electors, the secretary of state shall cause the amendment to be published as provided by law twice each month for two months previous to the next regular statewide election.
3. At that election, the proposed amendment shall be submitted to the qualified electors for approval or rejection. If approved by a majority voting thereon, it shall

[34] James J. Lopach, "The Montana Supreme Court in Politics," *Montana Law Review*, 48 (1987): 294.

become a part of the constitution effective the first day of July following its approval, unless the amendment provides otherwise.

This is a new section. Ten percent of the voters may propose constitutional amendments by petition in each of two-fifths of the legislative districts: a number high enough to prevent frivolous attempts at change, yet low enough to insure citizen control of the constitution (MCC Tr. 506–508). The delegates felt it should be more difficult to amend the constitution than to initiate changes in the statutes; therefore, a higher percentage of signatures is required to change the constitution (10 percent) than to change or propose statutes per Article III, section 4 (5 percent). The original committee proposal called for 15 percent of the voters to sign the petition to amend the constitution.

Between 1972 and 1998 there were 79 attempts to amend the constitution by initiative. Five of the proposed amendments were withdrawn before signatures were solicited. Sixty-two of the proposed amendments failed to obtain sufficient signatures, demonstrating how difficult it is to obtain the required number of signatures. The Montana Supreme Court enjoined the secretary of state from placing one of the proposed initiatives, CI-23, on the ballot. The 11 remaining initiatives to amend the constitution were submitted to the voters. Voters approved four and rejected seven. Of the four approved, two were subsequently voided by the court.

Proposed amendments failing to obtain sufficient signatures included those making school attendance non-mandatory, authorizing local option gambling, abolishing the property tax, reducing the size of the legislature, reducing the number of supreme court justices, making lawyers ineligible for executive or legislative office, requiring paper ballots only, and making hunting a constitutional right.

The court rarely intercedes to enjoin placing an initiative to amend the constitution on the ballot. In *State ex rel. Mont. Citizens for the Preservation of Citizens' Rights v. Waltermire* (1986), the court declined to assert pre-election jurisdiction where the initiative was not unconstitutional on its face and where it was not improperly submitted. Likewise, in *State ex rel. Mont. School Board v. Waltermire* (1986), a proposal to abolish all property taxes and to require a referendum or initiative to levy a sales tax or to increase either a sales tax or an income tax, the court refused to enjoin submission of the initiative to a vote absent extraordinary causes. The court maintained that to hold otherwise would infringe the people's constitutional right to amend the constitution by initiative. In *State ex rel. Harper v. Waltermire* (1984), the court enjoined the secretary of state from certifying a ballot and delivering a voter pamphlet containing initiative CI-23 directing the legislature to apply to Congress to call a convention to consider a federal balanced budget amendment. It could be argued that this court decision did not enjoin an initiative to amend the Montana Constitution but rather enjoined an initiative purporting to amend the constitution, but in fact calling for a legislative resolution to amend the U.S. Constitution. The court said that the initiative power conferred by the constitution does not include the power to enact a legislative resolution: the electorate cannot circumvent the constitution by doing indirectly that which cannot be done directly.

Twice the Montana Supreme Court has voided initiatives after they have been passed. Initiative CI-30 (1986) authorized the legislature to determine the rights and remedies for injury to persons, property, or character. After a favorable vote, the Montana Supreme Court voided the initiative, principally because the text of the amendment in the voter information pamphlet contradicted what CI-30's supporters intended and conflicted with the language of CI-30 as filed and certified by the secretary of state. The error was critical in substantive content and, in this case, the voter information pamphlet was the only source of information for voters as to the full text of the proposed amendment (*State ex rel. Mont. Citizens for the Preservation of Citizens' Rights v. Waltermire*, 1987). After approval by the voters, constitutional initiative CI-75 (1998), mandating voter approval of all new taxes, was declared unconstitutional in an opinion supported by a unanimous court.[35] The opinion stated that CI-75 amended three parts of Montana's constitution and failed to allow a separate vote for each amendment thereby violating Article XIV, section 11 of Montana's Constitution (*Marshall v. State ex rel. Cooney*, 1999). Article XIV, section 11 states: "If more than one amendment is submitted at the same election, each shall be so prepared and distinguished that it can be voted upon separately."

## SECTION 10

**Petition Signers.** The number of qualified electors required for the filing of any petition provided for in this Article shall be determined by the number of votes cast for the office of governor in the preceding general election.

This is a new provision and is self-explanatory. This provision is intended to guard against technical circumvention of the initiative and referendum process (MCC Tr. 514).

There have been no cases interpreting this section, but an Attorney General Opinion said that a petition for a proposed constitutional amendment must be signed by 10 percent of the qualified electors (voters) of the state, and that number must include at least 10 percent of the qualified electors in each of two-fifths of the House districts throughout the state (35 Op. Att'y Gen. 200 (1974)).

[35] All of the justices supported the opinion. A concurring opinion by Justice Nelson found CI-75 unconstitutional on the grounds outlined in the principal opinion and for additional reasons also.

## SECTION 11

**Submission.** If more than one amendment is submitted at the same election, each shall be so prepared and distinguished that it can be voted upon separately.

This section is similar to Article XIX, section 9 of the 1889 Montana Constitution. However, the 1889 provision dealt only with constitutional amendments proposed by the Montana Senate or House of Representatives. Under the 1889 Constitution it was not possible to amend the constitution by citizen initiative. This only became possible under the 1972 Constitution. The new section 11 provision is intended to guard against grouping of several issues under one innocuous title (MCC Tr. 514). Also, there is no longer an intent to limit the number of proposed amendments (MCC Tr. 516), but each must be voted on separately. Before 1972, competition for the limited number of amendments resulted in legislators who proposed amendments, lobbying against other amendments, regardless of merit, to obtain a place for their proposed amendment. As a consequence many worthwhile amendments never made it to the voters.

In *Marshall v. State ex rel. Cooney* (1999), an original proceeding was brought for a declaratory judgment that a constitutional amendment by initiative (CI-75), approved by the voters, violated the section 11 separate-vote provision. The court held that this provision has a substantively different meaning from that of Article V, section 11(3), which says that each bill shall contain only one subject. Bills and proposed constitutional amendments under the 1889 Constitution allowed debate and deliberation by legislators. "For present-day constitutional initiatives, however, there is no guarantee that Montana voters will have similar deliberative opportunities" (p. 330). The court said that the CI-75 initiative explicitly amended three parts of the constitution and thus violated section 11.

The court also declined to accept the unity-of-subject or single-subject rule, saying it was "so elastic it could swallow Montana's entire constitution" (p. 331). The court said that the section 11 separate-vote requirement is a different and narrower requirement than a single-subject requirement.

# ■ BIBLIOGRAPHIC ESSAY

## BACKGROUND READING

Several excellent works cover Montana's history. See Merrill G. Burlingame, *The Montana Frontier* (Helena, MT: State Publishing Co., 1942); J. M. Hamilton, *History of Montana: From Wilderness to Statehood* (Portland, OR: Binfords and Mort, 1957); Joseph Kinsey Howard, *Montana: High, Wide, and Handsome* (1943; reprint, Lincoln: University of Nebraska Press, 1988); K. Ross Toole, *Montana: An Uncommon Land* (Norman: University of Oklahoma Press, 1957); K. Ross Toole, *History of Montana*, 3 vols. (New York: Lewis Publishing Co., 1957); Michael P. Malone, *Montana: A Contemporary Profile* (Helena, MT: American and World Geographic Publishing, 1996).

There are two more recent books which pay particular attention to the forces which led to the 1972 Montana Constitution. K. Ross Toole's *Twentieth-Century Montana: A State of Extremes* (Norman: University of Oklahoma Press, 1972) is a portrait of cyclical twentieth-century patterns in Montana. It covers the setting, the periods of boom-and- bust, the university system, and the press. Michael P. Malone, Richard B. Roeder, and William L. Lang's *Montana: A History of Two Centuries*, rev. ed. (Seattle: University of Washington Press, 1991) develops further the traditionally neglected years since the 1920s. Its final chapter deals with politics and government between 1945 and 1990. The authors note that Montana is a state where open and direct democracy thrives and that this culture produced "one of America's most highly regarded constitutions" in 1972.

Two periodical articles focused on the 1972 Montana Constitutional Convention: Charles S. Johnson, "The Press and the Constitutional Convention," *Montana Journalism Review*, no. 17 (1974): 53–58; "Montana: Fresh Chance Gulch," *Time*, 99, no. 18 (April 10, 1972): 18.

## GENERAL BACKGROUND SOURCES FOR THE 1972 CONSTITUTION


Eastman, Elizabeth. "The 1971–1972 Montana Constitutional Convention." *Montana Public Affairs Report*, no. 9 (January 1972): 1–4.

Graybill, Leo, Jr. "The New Montana Constitution." *State Government* Spring 1973): 89–94. (Graybill was the President of the Constitutional Convention.)

Harris, Leo, Jr. "Constitutional Revision: The Montana Opportunity." *Montana Business Quarterly* (Summer 1970): 12–21.

League of Women Voters of Montana. *A Constitutional Convention for Montana*. Billings, January 1971.

"The Montana Constitution." *Montana Law Review* (Winter 1972): 1–186.

Montana Constitutional Revision Commission. *Montana Constitutional Revision*. Bozeman: Cooperative Extension Service, Montana State University, 1970.

Montana Constitutional Revision Commission. *1889–1970: The Montana Constitution: Resource or Burden*? Missoula, 1970.

Montana Legislative Council. *The Montana Constitution*. Helena, 1968.

"Montana's Proposed Constitution of 1972." *Montana Public Affairs Report*, no. 11 (April 1972): 1–16.

Payne, Thomas & Elizabeth Eastman. "The Montana Voter and the 1972 Constitutional Election." *Montana Public Affairs Report*, no. 13 (December 1972): 1–4.

Waldron, Ellis. "Constitutional Issues in Montana." *Montana Public Affairs Report*, no. 4 (October 1968): 1–8.

Waldron, Ellis. "The Montana Constitution of 1972." *National Civic Review* (November 1972): 494–500.

Waldron, Ellis. "Thinking About a New Constitution for Montana." *Montana Business Quarterly* (Autumn 1971): 5–12.

## MONTANA CONSTITUTIONAL CONVENTION COMMISSION SOURCES

### *Occasional Papers*

Occasional Paper Number 1: *Montana Constitution of 1884*.

Occasional Paper Number 2: *Enabling Act for the Montana Constitutional Convention of 1889*.

Occasional Paper Number 3: *Montana Territory Organic Act*.

Occasional Paper Number 5: *Comparison of the Montana Constitution with the Constitutions of Selected Other States*.

Occasional Paper Number 6: *Legislative Council Report on the Montana Constitution*.

Occasional Paper Number 7: *Constitutional Provisions Proposed by Constitutional Revision Commission Subcommittees*.

### *Studies*

Study Number 1: *Constitutional Convention Enabling Act*.

Study Number 3: *The Constitution of Montana and the Constitutions of the United States*.

Study Number 4: *A Collection of Readings on State Constitutions, Their Nature and Purpose*.

Study Number 6: *New State Constitutions*.

Study Number 10: *Bill of Rights*.

Study Number 11: *Suffrage and Elections*.

Study Number 12: *The Legislature*.

Study Number 13: *The Executive*.

Study Number 14: *The Judiciary*.

Study Number 15: *Taxation and Finance*.

Study Number 16: *Local Governments*.

Study Number 17: *Education*.

Montana Constitutional Convention. *Transcript of Proceedings*. 12 vols. and index. Helena, 1972.

The *Proceedings* are noted in the Preface of this book (*The Montana State Constitution: A Reference Guide*) and are referred to frequently throughout this book: the committee reports in volumes I and II with the citation "MCC Rep. [page]," and delegate comments in volumes III through VII with the citation "MCC Tr. [page]." No volume number is given because of the consecutive pagination. The "Proposed 1972 Constitution for the State of Montana: Official Text with Explanation," submitted by the Montana Constitutional Convention, was distributed to the voters and was intended to explain the various articles and sections to the voters.

## SOURCES INTERPRETING THE 1972 CONSTITUTION AFTER ITS PASSAGE

Ellis Waldron, "The Constitutional Tradition and Political Culture of Montana," in James J. Lopach (ed.), *We the People of Montana: The Workings of a Popular Government* (Missoula, MT: Mountain Press Publishing Co., 1983), pays particular attention to the pre-1972 movement for constitutional revision and gives a useful overview of the 1972 Constitution. Waldron also explores the political culture of Montana which led to the constitution. James Lopach's chapter, "Local Government in Montana," notes the important constitutional provisions for local government. Lauren S. McKinsey's chapter, "Natural Resource Policy in Montana," notes that three types of natural resource policy problems persist because of the constitution: (1) widely accepted standards of environmental quality do not exist, (2) obligations of state agencies for guaranteeing environmental quality are not clear, and (3) procedures for citizen assertion of rights to a clean and healthful environment are uncertain.

James H. Goetz, "Interpretations of the Montana Constitution: Sometimes Socratic, Sometimes Erratic," *Montana Law Review*, 51 (1990): 289–355, focuses on the unique features of the constitution, unique because they have no counterpart in the federal constitution or because the Montana courts have chosen to interpret certain provisions of Montana's Constitution independently. The article first discusses the proper role of a state constitution in the federal system. The article, by examining Montana Supreme Court cases, discusses two general categories: the protection of individual rights (found largely in Article II of the constitution) and the state government role in the furtherance of education and the protection of public lands, the environment, and water rights.

Commentators have paid a good deal of attention to Article II, "Declaration of Rights," of the constitution. This is Montana's equivalent to the Bill of Rights of the federal constitution. Tia Rikel Robbin, "Untouched Protection from Discrimination: Private Action in Montana's Individual Dignity Clause," *Montana Law Review*, 51 (1990): 553–570, argues that if the Montana Supreme Court were to apply a proper analysis of Article II, section 4 (the dignity clause), Montana would provide its citizens greater protection from discrimination than any other state. Individuals would be protected from private as well as public discrimination, and from unequal protection of the laws. Her article focuses on the intent of the constitutional convention delegates and the Montana Supreme Court's reluctance to give substance to that intent. John S. Kutzman,

"The King's Resurrection: Sovereign Immunity Returns to Montana," *Montana Law Review*, 51 (1990): 529–551, notes that with Article II, section 8 of the constitution, Montana became the first state to enact a constitutional provision to abrogate sovereign immunity and to require full governmental tort liability. However, the author argues that the Montana Supreme Court has eviscerated that provision by broadly construing a statute that purports to grant only legislative immunity to protect school districts and local governments for liability for purely administrative acts. Larry M. Elison & Dennis NettikSimmons, "Right of Privacy," *Montana Law Review*, 48 (1987): 1–52, articulate the historical underpinnings of the right of privacy (Article II, section 10), review the intention of the framers of the constitutional rights of privacy, and analyze how the Montana Supreme Court has interpreted this right. Matthew B. Hayhurst, "Parental Notification of Abortion and Minor's Rights under the Montana Constitution," *Montana Law Review*, 58 (1997): 565–598, notes that Article II, section 15 (Rights of Persons Not Adults), unlike its federal counterpart, guarantees minors all fundamental rights unless precluded by laws that clearly enhance their protection.

Other articles of the constitution have also received attention. Jean M. Bowman, "The Judicial Article: What Went Wrong," *Montana Law Review*, 51 (1990): 492–508, comments that the judicial article (Article VII) has been said to be the worst such article in the 50 state constitutions. The author addresses the question of how the judicial article came to be, shows that it really is not better and not much different from the judicial article of the 1889 Montana Constitution, and offers some suggestions for improvement. Thomas E. Towe, "Revenue and Finance Under Montana's 1972 Constitution," *Montana Law Review*, 51 (1990): 399/3-410, says that Article VIII brought about momentous changes in the area of revenue and finance. The statewide equalization of the values used for property taxes represented the most significant change brought about by the constitution in the area of taxation. Deborah Beaumont Schmidt & Robert J. Thompson, "The Montana Constitution and the Right to a Clean and Healthful Environment," *Montana Law Review*, 51 (1990): 411–448, discuss Article IX (Environment and Natural Resources). They analyze the constitutional convention debate of this article and also discuss later statutory and judicial developments. Hugh V. Schaefer, "The Legal Status of the Montana University System under the New Montana Constitution," *Montana Law Review*, 35 (1974): 189–226, discusses the impact of Article X (Education and Public Lands) on the legal status of higher education in Montana and analyzes the debate over the education article in the convention. James J. Lopach, "Local Government under the 1972 Montana Constitution," *Montana Law Review*, 51 (1990): 458/3-491, analyzes the local government article (Article XI). He notes particularly that convention delegates gave local residents wide discretion in designing and empowering their local governments, and also that the delegates believed that the new constitution should revitalize the critical political relationship between citizens and local government officials. In another article, "The Montana Supreme Court in Politics," *Montana Law Review*, 48 (1987): 267–296, Lopach says that, with respect to welfare policy, the Montana Supreme Court has ignored the constitutional intent of Article XII, section 3 (Institutions and Assistance).

## DETAILED BIBLIOGRAPHY OF THE 1972 MONTANA CONSTITUTION

### *Overall*

Collins, Ronald K.L. "Reliance on State Constitutions—The Montana Disaster." *Texas Law Review*, 63 (1985): 1095.

Goetz, James H. "Interpretations of the Montana Constitution: Sometimes Socratic, Sometimes Erratic." *Montana Law Review*, 51 (1990).

### *Article I (Compact with the United States)*

Beck, Monte. "State v. Stasso: Off-Reservation Hunting Rights." *Montana Law Review*, 39 (1978): 323.

Bellis, James R. "Crow Tribe v. Montana: New Limits on State Intrusion into Reservation Rights, New Lessons for State and Tribal Cooperation." *Montana Law Review*, 50 (1989): 133.

Elison, Larry M. & Dennis NettikSimmons. "Federalism and State Constitutions: The New Doctrine of Independent and Adequate State Grounds." *Montana Law Review*, 5 (1984): 177.

Fredericks, John, III. "State Regulation in Indian Country: The Supreme Court's Marketing xemptions Concept, A Judicial Sword Through the Heart of Tribal Self-Determination." *Montana Law Review*, 50 (1989): 49.

Lamb, Michael F. "Adjudication of Indian Water Rights: Implementation of the 1979 Amendments to the Water Use Act." *Montana Law Review*, 41 (1980): 73.

Mitchell, Carole H. "Oliphant v. Schlie: Tribal Criminal Jurisdiction of Non-Indians." *Montana Law Review*, 38 (1977): 339.

Morrison, Sharon M. "Comments on Indian Water Rights." *Montana Law Review*, 41 (1980): 39.

Simpson, Michael J. "Accommodating Indian Religions: The Proposed 1993 Amendment to the American Indian Religious Freedom Act." *Montana Law Review*, 54 (1993): 19.

Wilson, Scott W. "Criminal Jurisdiction in Montana Indian Country." *Montana Law Review*, 47 (1986): 513.

### *Preamble*

Himmelfarb, Dan. "The Preamble in Constitutional Interpretation." *Seton Hall Constitutional Law Journal*, 2 (1991): 127.

### *Article II (Declaration of Rights)*

#### ***Section 3 (Inalienable Rights)***

Tobias, Carl W. & Daniel N. McLean. "The Effect of the Environmental Policy Acts on Pre-Existing Agency Authority." *Montana Law Review*, 41 (1980): 177.

#### ***Section 4 (Individual Dignity)***

Hileman, William E. "In the Army Now: United States v. Reiser." *Montana Law Review*, 37 (1976): 191.

Koester, Jeanne M. "Equal Rights." *Montana Law Review*, 39 (1978): 238.

Murphy, Daniel C. "Noll v. Bozeman: Notice of Claim Provisions in Montana." *Montana Law Review*, 37 (1976): 206.

Paxinos, Dennis. "Montana Green River Ordinances." *Montana Law Review*, 44 (1983): 297.

Ramlow, Jim. "Montana Outfitters v. Fish and Game Commission: Of Elk and Equal Protection." *Montana Law Review*, 38 (1977): 387.

Robbin, Tia Rikel. "Untouched Protection from Discrimination: Private Action in Montana's Individual Dignity Clause." *Montana Law Review*, 51 (1990): 553.

Runnette, Deirdre Lardin. "Judicial Discretion and the Homosexual Parent: How Montana Courts Are and Should Be Considering a Parent's Sexual Orientation in Contested Custody Cases." *Montana Law Review*, 57 (1996): 177.

Uda, Joan. "Equality for Men and Women, Three Approaches: Frontiero, The Equal Rights Amendment, and the Montana Equal Dignities Provision." *Montana Law Review*, 35 (1974): 325.

***Section 5 (Freedom of Religion)***

Conkle, Daniel O. "The Religious Freedom Restoration Act: The Constitutional Significance of an Unconstitutional Statute." *Montana Law Review*, 56 (1995): 39.

Cooper, Abbott. "Dam the RFRA at the Prison Gate: The Religious Freedom Restoration Act's Impact on Correctional Litigation." *Montana Law Review*, 56 (1995): 325.

Gedicks, Frederick Mark. "RFRA and the Possibility of Justice." *Montana Law Review*, 56 (1995): 95.

Gregory, David L. "Religious Harassment in the Workplace: An Analysis of the EEOC's Proposed Guidelines." *Montana Law Review*, 56 (1995): 119.

Laycock, Douglas. "RFRA. Congress and the Ratchet." Montana Law Review, 56 (1995): 145.

Lupu, Ira C. "Of Time and the RFRA: A Lawyer's Guide to the Religious Freedom Restoration Act." *Montana Law Review*, 56 (1995): 171.

Marshall, William P. "The Religious Freedom Restoration Act: Establishment, Equal Protection and Free Speech Concerns." *Montana Law Review*, 56 (1995): 227.

O'Brien, Sharon L. "Freedom of Religion in Indian Country." *Montana Law Review*, 56 (1995): 451.

Paulsen, Michael Stokes. "A RFRA Runs Through It: Religious Freedom and the U.S. Code." *Montana Law Review*, 56 (1995): 249.

Rhodes, John. "An American Tradition: The Religious Persecution of Native Americans." *Montana Law Review*, 52 (1991): 13.

Simpson, Michael J. "Accommodating Indian Religions: The Proposed 1993 Amendment of the American Indian Religious Freedom Act." *Montana Law Review*, 54 (1993): 19.

Smith, Rodney K. "Sovereignty and the Sacred: The Establishment Clause in Indian Country." *Montana Law Review*, 56 (1995): 295.

***Section 6 (Freedom of Assembly)***

Hall, Kernit L. *American Legal History: Cases and Materials*. New York: Oxford University Press, 1991.

***Section 7 (Freedom of Speech, Expression, and Press)***

Carey, Steve. "Fair Trial and Free Press: The Courtroom Door Swings Open." *Montana Law Review*, 45 (1984): 323.

Finkelman, Paul (ed.). *A Brief History of the Case and Tryal of John Peter Zenger*. Union, NJ: Lawbook Exchange, 2000.
Parish, Richard. "First Amendment Rights of Non-Tenured Teachers." *Montana Law Review*, 37 (1976): 217.
Reger, Lawrence F. "Montana's Criminal Syndicalism Statute: An Affront to the First Amendment." *Montana Law Review*, 58 (1997): 287.
Rotering, Diane. "Political Patronage and the First Amendment: To the Victor Go Fewer Spoils." *Montana Law Review*, 38 (1977): 365.

***Section 9 (Right to Know)***

Elison, Larry M. & Deborah E. Elison. "Comments on Government Censorship and Secrecy." *Montana Law Review*, 55 (1994): 175.
Gorman, David. "Rights in Collision: The Individual Right of Privacy and the Public Right to Know." *Montana Law Review*, 39 (1978): 249.
Work, Clemens P. "Whose Privacy?" *Montana Law Review*, 55 (1994): 175.

***Section 10 (Right of Privacy)***

Elison, Larry M. & Deborah E. Elison. "Comments on Government Censorship and Secrecy." *Montana Law Review*, 55 (1994): 175.
Elison, Larry M. & Dennis NettikSimmons. "Right of Privacy." *Montana Law Review*, 48 (1987): 1.
Even, Jeffrey T. "The Fourth Amendment and Drug-Detecting Dogs." *Montana Law Review*, 48 (1987): 101.
Gorman, David. "Rights in Collision: The Individual Right of Privacy and the Public Right to Know." *Montana Law Review*, 39 (1978): 249.
Hayhurst, Matthew B. "Parental Notification of Abortion and Minors' Rights under the Montana Constitution." *Montana Law Review*, 58 (1997): 565.
Johnson, W. Bjarne. "State v. Brecht: Evolution or Offshoot of the Fourth Amendment Exclusionary Rule?" *Montana Law Review*, 34 (1973): 187.
Lovas, Sol. "Criminal Procedure: The Exclusionary Rule." *Montana Law Review*, 40 (1979): 132.
Rava, William C. "Toward a Historical Understanding of Montana's Privacy Provision." *Albany Law Review*, 61 (1998): 1681.
Reep, Richard A. "Intrusion, Exclusion, and Confusion." *Montana Law Review*, 41 (1980): 281.
Towe, Thomas E. "A Growing Awareness of Privacy in America." *Montana Law Review*, 37 (1976): 39.
Uda, Joan. "Abortion: Roe v. Wade and the Montana Dilemma." *Montana Law Review*, 35 (1974): 103.
Uda, Joan. "Privacy, Law Enforcement, and Public Interest: Computerized Criminal Records." *Montana Law Review*, 36 (1975): 60.
Warren, Samuel & Louis Brandeis. "The Right to Privacy." *Harvard Law Review*, 4 (1890): 193.
Work, Clemens P. "Whose Privacy?" *Montana Law Review*, 55 (1994): 209.

***Section 11 (Searches and Seizures)***

Elison, Larry M. "Criminal Procedure—Montana Law and the Federal Impact." *Montana Law Review*, 38 (1977): 27.
Elison, Larry M. & Dennis NettikSimmons. "Right of Privacy." *Montana Law Review*, 48 (1987): 1.

Even, Jeffrey T. "The Fourth Amendment and Drug-Detecting Dogs." *Montana Law Review,* 48 (1987): 101.

Johnson, W. Bjarne. "State v. Brecht: Evolution or Offshoot of the Fourth Amendment Exclusionary Rule?" *Montana Law Review,* 34 (1973): 187.

Lovas, Sol. "Criminal Procedure: The Exclusionary Rule." *Montana Law Review,* 40 (1979): 132.

Parish, Richard L. "Consent Searches in Montana: Basic Elements of the Test for Voluntariness." *Montana Law Review,* 38 (1977): 327.

Reep, Richard A. "Intrusion, Exclusion, and Confusion." *Montana Law Review,* 41 (1980): 281.

***Section 12 (Right to Bear Arms)***

Becker, Edward R. "The Second Amendment and Other Federal Constitutional Rights of the Private Militia." *Montana Law Review,* 58 (1997): 7.

Dowd, Donald W. "The Relevance of the Second Amendment to Gun Control Legislation." *Montana Law Review,* 58 (1997): 79.

McAffee, Thomas B. "Constitutional Limits on Regulating Private Militia Groups." *Montana Law Review,* 58 (1997): 45.

Morriss, Andrew P. "Private Actors & Structural Balance: Militia & the Free Rider Problem of Law." *Montana Law Review,* 58 (1997): 115.

Neiwert, David. "Ash on the Sills: The Significance of the Patriot Movement in America." *Montana Law Review,* 58 (1997): 19.

***Section 15 (Rights of Persons Not Adults)***

Hayhurst, Matthew B. "Parental Notification of Abortion and Minors' Rights under the Montana Constitution." *Montana Law Review,* 58 (1997): 565.

***Section 16 (The Administration of Justice)***

Lopach, James J. "The Montana Supreme Court in Politics." *Montana Law Review,* 48 (1987): 266.

***Section 17 (Due Process of Law)***

Alke, John. "A Critical Analysis of Garrett Freight Lines, Inc. v. Montana Railroad Commission." *Montana Law Review,* 37 (1976): 175.

Carey, Steve. "Fair Trial and Free Press: The Courtroom Door Swings Open." *Montana Law Review,* 45 (1984): 323.

Cromwell, Gardner. "Federalism and Due Process: Some Ruminations." *Montana Law Review,* 42 (1981): 183.

Curtis, Gregory L. "In Defense of a Youth." *Montana Law Review,* 36 (1975): 225.

Horwich, John L. & Hertha L. Lund. "Montana Supreme Court Unnecessarily Misconstrues Takings Law." *Montana Law Review,* 55 (1994): 455.

Huff, Thomas P. "Protecting Due Process and Civic Friendship in the Administrative State." *Montana Law Review,* 42 (1981): 1.

McDermott, John T. "The Supreme Court's Changing Attitude Toward Consumer Protection and Its Impact on Montana Prejudgment Remedies." *Montana Law Review,* 36 (1975): 165.

McDermott, John T. "The Supreme Court's Still Changing Attitude Toward Consumer Protection and Its Impact on the Integrity of the Court." *Montana Law Review,* 37 (1976): 27.

McGuinness, J & L. Parlagreco. "The Reemergence of Substantive Due Process as a Constitutional Tort: Theory, Proof, and Damages." *New England Law Review*, 24 (1900): 1133.

Nevin, Jack F. "Montana's Real Property Forfeiture Statute: Will It Pass Constitutional Muster?" *Montana Law Review*, 54 (1993): 69.

Ramlow, Jim. "Montana Outfitters v. Fish and Game Commission: Of Elk and Equal Protection." *Montana Law Review*, 38 (1977): 387.

Rossbach, William A. "The Long Arm of Montana's Rule 4B: Due Process Limits to the Exercise of Jurisdiction over Foreign Defendants." *Montana Law Review*, 37 (1976): 420.

Swartley, Christopher B. "Recent Consumer Protection Developments in Montana." *Montana Law Review*, 37 (1976): 371.

Troland, Mary B. "Involuntary Commitment of the Mentally I11." *Montana Law Review*, 38 (1977): 307.

Trueb, Linda M. "The Expectancy of Parole in Montana: A Right Entitled to Some Due Process." *Montana Law Review*, 48 (1987): 379.

Zirkel, Perry A. "Over-Due Process Revisions for the Individuals with Disabilities Education Act." *Montana Law Review*, 55 (1994): 403.

***Section 18 (State Subject to Suit)***

Conwell, James E. "Limitations on Legislative Immunity: A New Era for Montana's Sovereign Immunity Doctrine." *Montana Law Review*, 54 (1993): 127.

Kutzman, John A. "The King's Resurrection: Sovereign Immunity Returns to Montana." *Montana Law Review*, 51 (1990): 529.

Lopach, James J. "The Montana Supreme Court in Politics." *Montana Law Review*, 48 (1987): 266.

***Section 19 (Habeas Corpus)***

Khandelwal, Sharad. "The Path to Habeas Corpus Narrows: Interpreting 28 U.S.C. § 2254(d)(l)." *Michigan Law Review*, 96 (1997): 434–439.

***Section 21 (Bail)***

Elison, Larry M. "Criminal Procedure—Montana Law and the Federal Impact." *Montana Law Review*, 38 (1977): 27.

Renz, Jeffrey T. "Post-Conviction Relief in Montana." *Montana Law Review*, 55 (1994): 331.

***Section 22 (Excessive Sanctions)***

Tweeten, Christian D. "Montana's Death Penalty after State v. McKenzie." *Montana Law Review*, 38 (1977): 209.

***Section 24 (Rights of the Accused)***

Carey, Steve. "Fair Trial and Free Press: The Courtroom Door Swings Open." *Montana Law Review*, 45 (1984): 323.

Elison, Larry M. "Criminal Procedure—Montana Law and the Federal Impact." *Montana Law Review*, 38 (1977): 27.

Fetscher, Candace C. "Argensinger v. Hamlin: A Demand for Change in Administration of Criminal Justice." *Montana Law Review*, 35 (1974): 151.

Kampfe, D. Frank. & Joan Dostal. "Discovery in the Federal Criminal System." *Montana Law Review*, 36 (1975): 189.

Kirscher, Ralph B. "Criminal Procedure: The Legal Mechanics after Arrest and Investigation." *Montana Law Review,* 40 (1979): 151.

Ostby, Carolyn. "The Right to Effective Trial Counsel: State v. McElveen." *Montana Law Review,* 37 (1976): 387.

***Section 25 (Self-Incrimination and Double Jeopardy)***

Elison, Larry M. "Criminal Procedure—Montana Law and the Federal Impact." *Montana Law Review,* 38 (1977): 27.

***Section 28 (Rights of the Convicted)***

Cooper, Abbott. "Dam the RFRA at the Prison Gate: The Religious Freedom Restoration Act's Impact on Correctional Litigation." *Montana Law Review,* 56 (1995): 325.

### *Article III (General Government)*

Brant, Joanne C. "Taking the Supreme Court at Its Work: The Implications for RFRA and Separation of Powers." *Montana Law Review,* 56 (1995): 5.

### *Article VII (The Judiciary)*

Bennett, Gordon R. "Advocacy and Responsibility: Conflicting Paradigms?" *Montana Law Review,* 51 (1990): 1.

Bowman, Jean M. "The Judicial Article: What Went Wrong?" *Montana Law Review,* 51 (1990): 492.

Jones, Kevin S. "Attornery Advertising in Montana: The Peel Decision and the Growing Need for a State Certification Program." *Montana Law Review,* 52 (1991): 177.

Lopach, James J. "The Montana Supreme Court in Politics." *Montana Law Review,* 48 (1987): 266.

Reynolds, Jim. "Compulsory Bar Dues in Montana: Two (and a Half) Challenges." *Montana Law Review,* 39 (1978): 268.

Rice, Clarke B. "Legal Specialization: A Proposal for More Accessible and Higher Quality Legal Services." *Montana Law Review,* 40 (1979): 287.

Strong, R. Keith. "The Model Rules of Professional Conduct: No Standard for Malpractice." *Montana Law Review,* 47 (1986): 363.

### *Article VIII (Revenue and Finance)*

Ellingson, Mae Nan & Jerry C. D. Mahoney. "Public Purpose and Economic Development: The Montana Perspective." *Montana Law Review,* 51 (1990): 356.

Even, Jeffrey T. "Of Castles and Kings: A Perspective for Property Tax Reform." *Montana Law Review,* 50 (1989): 243.

Fitzgerald, Wendy A. "Montana's Constitutionally Established Investment Program: A State Investing Against Itself." *Montana Law Review,* 51 (1990): 378.

Sullivan, John F. "Real Property Tax Assessment in Montana." *Montana Law Review,* 34 (1973): 300.

Towe, Thomas E. "Revenue and Finance under Montana's 1972 Constitution." *Montana Law Review,* 51 (1990): 399.

### *Article IX (Environment and Natural Resources)*

***Overall***

Cross, C. Louise. "The Battle for the Environmental Provisions in Montana's 1972 Constitution." *Montana Law Review,* 51 (1990): 449.

Kemrnis, Daniel. "Environmental Rights." *Montana Law Review,* 39 (1978): 224.

***Section 1 (Protection and Environment)***

Horwich, John. "Montana's Constitutional Environmental Quality Provisions: Self-Execution or Self-Delusion." *Montana Law Review*, 57 (1996): 323.

Huffman, James L. "Markets, Regulation, and Environmental Protection." *Montana Law Review*, 55 (1994): 425.

Schmidt, Deborah Beaumont & Robert J. Thompson. "The Montana Constitution and the Right to a Clean and Healthful Environment." *Montana Law Review*, 51 (1990): 411.

***Section 2 (Reclamation)***

Meissner, Thomas P. "A Constitutional Challenge to the Surface Mining Control and Reclamation Act." *Public Land Law Review*, 2 (1981): 138.

Shanahan, Ward A. "Hardrock Mining on the Public Lands." *Public Land Law Review*, 2 (1981): 57.

***Section 3 (Water Rights)***

Hightower, Elaine M. "A New Rule of Law for the Abandonment of Water Rights." *Montana Law Review*, 45 (1984): 167.

Ladd, David E. "Federal and Interstate Conflicts in Montana Water Law: Support for a State Water Plan." *Montana Law Review*, 42 (1981): 267.

Lamb, Michael F. "Adjudication of Indian Water Rights: Implementation of the 1979 Amendments to the Water Use Act." *Montana Law Review*, 41 (1980): 73.

Maclntyre, Donald D. "The Adjudication of Montana's Waters—A Blueprint for Improving the Judicial Structure." *Montana Law Review*, 49 (1988): 211.

Maclntyre, Donald D. "The Prior Appropriation Doctrine in Montana: Tooted in Mid-Nineteenth Century Goals—Responding to Twenty-First Century Needs." *Montana Law Review*, 55 (1994): 303.

Meshorer, Hank. "Once Released Irrigation Waters: Liability and Litigation." *Montana Law Review*, 36 (1975): 14.

Morrison, Sharon M. "Comments on Indian Water Rights." *Montana Law Review*, 41 (1980): 39.

Stone, Albert W. "Montana Water Rights—A New Opportunity." *Montana Law Review*, 34 (1973): 57.

Stone, Albert W. "Privatization of the Water Resource: Salvage, Leases and Changes." *Montana Law Review*, 54 (1993): 99.

Stone, Albert W. "Public Use of the Banks and Beds of Montana Streams." *Montana Law Review*, 52 (1991): 107.

*Article X (Education and Public Lands)*

Aronofsky, David. "Voters Wisely Reject Proposed Constitutional Amendment 30 to Eliminate the Montana Board of Regents." *Montana Law Review*, 58 (1997): 333.

Byrne, J. Peter. "Academic Freedom: A 'Special Concern' of the First Amendment." *Yale Law Journal*, 99 (1989): 251.

Harper, Lori Anne. "Classroom v. Courtroom: Is the Right to Education Fundamental?" *Montana Law Review*, 51 (1990): 509.

Monzie, Kathleen S. "The Right to a Special Education." *Montana Law Review*, 57 (1996): 151.

Schaefer, Hugh V. "The Legal Status of the Montana University System under the New Montana Constitution." *Montana Law Review*, 35 (1974): 189.

Woodgerd, David & Bernard F. McCarthy. "State School Trust Lands and Oil and Gas Royalty Rates." *Public Land Law Review*, 3 (1982): 119.

### *Article XI (Local Government)*

Lopach, James J. "Local Government under the 1973 Montana Constitution." *Montana Law Review,* 51 (1990): 458.

### *Article XII (Departments and Institutions)*

Meisel, Alan. "The Rights of the Mentally I11 under State Constitutions." *Law and Contemporary Problems,* 45, no. 3 (1982): 7.

Wurster, Scott C. "Butte Community Union v. Lewis: A New Constitutional Standard for Evaluating General Assistance Legislation." *Montana Law Review,* 48 (1987): 163.

### *Article XIV (Constitutional Revision)*

Dowling, Diana S. "Implementation and Amendment of the 1972 Constitution." *Montana Law Review,* 51 (1990): 282.

Waldron, Ellis. "The Role of the Montana Supreme Court in Constitutional Revision." *Montana Law Review,* 35 (1974): 227.

# ■ TABLE OF CASES

## A



## B

## C



## D



## E



## F

## G



## H

## I



## J



## K



## L



## M

## N



## O



## P

## R



## S

## T



## U



## V



## W

## Y



## Z

# INDEX

## About the Author

LARRY M. ELISON is Professor Emeritus of Constitutional Law at the University of Montana School of Law.

FRITZ SNYDER is Associate Professor of Law and Director of the Law Library at the University of Montana School of Law.

www.ingramcontent.com/pod-product-compliance
Ingram Content Group UK Ltd.
Pitfield, Milton Keynes, MK11 3LW, UK
UKHW020848150926
475595UK00003B/62

9 780199 778812